THE ANATOMY OF
SPEED

BILL PARISI
FOUNDER, PARISI SPEED SCHOOL INC.

HUMAN KINETICS

Library of Congress Cataloging-in-Publication Data

Names: Parisi, Bill, author.
Title: The anatomy of speed / Bill Parisi.
Description: Champaign, IL : Human Kinetics, 2022. | Includes
  bibliographical references and index.
Identifiers: LCCN 2021022645 (print) | LCCN 2021022646 (ebook) | ISBN
  9781492598992 (paperback) | ISBN 9781492599005 (epub) | ISBN
  9781492599029 (pdf)
Subjects: LCSH: Sports--Physiological aspects.
Classification: LCC RC1235 .P36 2022 (print) | LCC RC1235 (ebook) | DDC
  612/.044--dc23
LC record available at https://lccn.loc.gov/2021022645
LC ebook record available at https://lccn.loc.gov/2021022646

ISBN: 978-1-4925-9899-2 (print)

Acquisitions Editor: Michael Mejia; **Content Developer:** Johnathon Allen; **Developmental Editor:** Laura Pulliam; **Managing Editor:** Hannah Werner; **Copyeditor:** Amy Pavelich; **Indexer:** Nan N. Badgett; **Permissions Manager:** Martha Gullo; **Senior Graphic Designer:** Sean Roosevelt; **Cover Designer:** Keri Evans; **Cover Design Specialist:** Susan Rothermel Allen; **Photograph (cover):** James Jankiewicz for Human Kinetics; **Photographs (interior):** James Jankiewicz, unless otherwise noted; Photos on pp. x, 116, 141, 171, 235, and 237 by Bill Parisi; **Photo Production Manager:** Jason Allen; **Senior Art Manager:** Kelly Hendren; **Illustration (cover):** Human Kinetics / Illustrator: Heidi Richter; **Illustrations (interior):** © Human Kinetics, unless otherwise noted; Figures on pp. 121-122, 159, 209, and 234 by Jen Van Horn and James Jankiewicz; **Printer:** Versa Press

Printed in the United States of America   10   9   8   7   6   5   4   3   2   1

The paper in this book is certified under a sustainable forestry program.

Human Kinetics
1607 N. Market Street
Champaign, IL 61820
USA

United States and International
Website: **US.HumanKinetics.com**
Email: info@hkusa.com
Phone: 1-800-747-4457

Canada
Website: **Canada.HumanKinetics.com**
Email: info@hkcanada.com

E8104

Tell us what you think!
Human Kinetics would love to hear what we
can do to improve the customer experience.
Use this QR code to take our brief survey.

This book is dedicated to all the Parisi Speed School performance coaches who support our mission: to change the world one athlete at a time by improving speed of movement and strength of character. This book represents all your tireless work on the training floor.

CONTENTS

FOREWORD

"Hey, you can't teach speed," one of my coaches once said.

Those words rang in my ears like a bad pop song. As a competitive high school athlete who was not gifted with natural speed, I really hated hearing them. All I wanted was to play small college football, and the reality was that I just wasn't fast enough to make the cut. Luckily for me, I had very supportive parents, and my dad was a high school football coach (among other things) who disagreed with my coach's view of speed. Even back in the 1980s and 1990s, when it was still a nascent field, he believed in the concept of speed training and was convinced there were things we could do to make me faster.

So we focused on speed training together and set out on a mission to defy conventional thinking. As part of this mission, my father drove me down from our home in Connecticut one weekend to the Parisi Speed School in Fair Lawn, New Jersey, to have a one-on-one training session with Bill Parisi, who was just starting to make his mark as a successful speed-training coach. This was a key turning point in my life. Doing good, dedicated speed training in my teenage years opened a lot of doors for me, and the impact it had on my world was profound. I discovered that there are in fact targeted training strategies that will help you get faster. The truth is you *can* teach speed.

After a lot of hard work and focused training, I went on to realize my dream and became an All-Conference Division III running back at Swarthmore College. I then continued my journey into the science of speed by pursuing my PhD in applied physiology and biomechanics at Southern Methodist University, where I had the opportunity to study with Dr. Peter Weyand and Dr. Larry Ryan at the most advanced human locomotion lab in the country. Today, I teach biomechanics and motor learning—which is essentially coaching science—at West Chester University (WCU) and conduct research primarily focused on sprint mechanics. I have also helped coach track-and-field athletes and team sport athletes from WCU and other local colleges to help them get faster. It's fair to say that understanding the biomechanics of speed and applying those principles in the real world have become both my passion and my profession. I get a tremendous amount of joy out of blending the science and art of coaching to yield better results for athletes. What I find interesting about exercise science in general and speed training in particular is that there *is* a science to it. The foundation of science is that it always starts with asking good questions. One of the main philosophical questions I've long asked is: What makes fast people fast and slow people slow? And what I've discovered along the way is that when you do good scientific experiments to answer those questions, you can take the findings learned from doing the research and apply them to help athletes improve their speed, injury resilience, and other attributes in demonstrable ways.

One of the things I've always admired about Bill Parisi, from the very first time I met him as a high school senior, is that he is intensely driven to understand the scientific research surrounding speed at the deepest levels. And, perhaps more importantly, he has the natural ability to take what is often dense scientific information and communicate it to practitioners in clear, easily accessible ways. This book is a perfect example of that talent. Bill makes every effort to understand the implications of the latest research and explain it in ways that coaches and athletes of all kinds can apply, with real Monday morning impact. He has a gift for identifying valid, evidence-based knowledge about improving speed mechanics—whether that knowledge is acquired through research or experience—and making it fun, interesting, and practical for anyone who, like me, just wants to get faster or make their athletes faster. If you are interested in enhancing speed, I sincerely believe you will find this book both enjoyable to read and extremely useful as a training tool. And if anyone ever tells you that "you can't teach speed" . . . hand them this book.

Ken Clark, PhD, teaches biomechanics, kinetic anatomy, and motor learning at West Chester University of Pennsylvania. He is also the founder of Ken Clark Speed, a firm that provides independent consulting services to athletes, teams, and coaches to help them improve athletic performance and reduce injury.

PREFACE

Speed is the most mythical of human capabilities. From elementary school playground races to 40-yard dashes at the NFL Combine, speed has long been the gold standard for athletic performance. If I ask you who the fastest human in the world is, 99 percent of people will correctly answer Usain Bolt without even pausing to think about it. If I ask you who the best long jumper, weightlifter, or javelin thrower is, just as many people will have to whip out their smartphone. When it comes to competitive bipeds, speed is king. But speed is "mythical" because, while it's an essential trait in virtually all ground-based sports, it's also highly nuanced and misunderstood. Making someone faster is far more complex and mysterious than making them stronger. There are multiple factors involved. Also, there are many different *kinds* of speed—the maximum velocity of world-class sprinters, the explosive acceleration and agility of NFL wide receivers and cornerbacks, the faster-than-you-can-blink changes of direction that happen in professional soccer and basketball, and so on. Speed comes in many forms.

As a result, there's a lot of misinformation and confusion about what speed is and how to train it. Some people will even suggest that achieving truly competitive levels of speed is primarily a matter of genetics. And while it's true that some people are natural-born cheetahs, I can say with absolute certainty that speed is a physical skill anyone can develop and improve with targeted training and a solid understanding of the mechanics. This confidence comes from watching the Parisi Speed School produce first-round draft picks and Olympic medalists in every major sport over the past 25-plus years of applying the Parisi method at more than 100 locations worldwide. I assure you there is an evidence-based science to speed—a secret to the sauce. The trick is having a solid understanding of the key ingredients. Once you understand how to identify and blend the different ingredients for specific results, you can create highly successful speed-training programs for any athlete based on their individual sport, position, body type, movement preference, and training history.

The first thing to remember is that speed is the result of multiple anatomical systems working together in highly coordinated unison, including the cross-body co-contractions of deep myofascial tissues that create core stiffness; the pulsing contract-and-release cycle of the nervous system that efficiently generates rapid, powerful ground contact; and the hormonal reactions that produce adrenalin, cortisol, and lactic acid. This is what we mean when we refer to the "anatomy of speed." Each system plays an integral role in generating speed, and they all matter. The other important thing to keep in mind is that, as previously mentioned, there are different kinds of speed, which can lead to a lot of confusion. This means it's important to start any discussion on the subject by defining what the fundamental categories and terms are, just to make sure we're all on the same semantic page. My goal in *The Anatomy of Speed* is to clearly define these terms, provide you with a solid understanding of the biological systems that drive them, and give you scientifically proven drills and exercises for tuning them so you can create individualized training programs for the specific type of speed you want to develop.

Think of it as a recipe book for speed.

Of course, there's an abundance of options, techniques, and trademarked systems in the marketplace for training speed. But what many of them overlook is the fact that different athletes need different kinds of training, depending on their personal history and sport. There isn't a single way. There is no one size that fits all. It's common to see rapid improvements in athletes with a young training history (regardless of their age) because developing basic movement literacies and improving strength deficiencies is relatively easy. But eventually they will hit a performance plateau. This is where understanding the anatomy of speed comes into play. If you want to make a good athlete great, you need to understand how the neuromuscular, fascial, and lymphatic systems all factor into the speed equation. You need to recognize the importance of rest and recovery. You need to account for individual body type, diet, and injury history. And you need to assess where they are in their personal development. Are they just starting out? Are they recovering from an injury? Are they a solid performer who needs highly targeted training to get to the next level? Or are they an elite professional who just needs to focus on dialing in the right ingredients at just the right levels to unlock their maximum potential?

The other thing often missing from commercially popular programs is evidence-based research. You can debate the effectiveness of lunges versus squats and deadlifts until they kick you out of the juice bar, but you can't argue with data. That's why I've collaborated with some of the top researchers in the field to help explain and validate the science behind the techniques presented in this book—including biomechanist Ken Clark, PhD, who started out as a student of Parisi Speed School when he was a teenager and is now a human locomotion specialist and kinesiology professor at West Chester University of Pennsylvania, and Stu McGill, PhD, who is recognized as the world's leading expert on spinal mechanics and the author of more than 240 published research papers. I also worked with a team of professional photographers and illustrators to present the drills, exercises, and anatomical concepts in visually interesting ways that make it easy for you to understand and apply. In addition to designating the respective exercises and drills as basic, moderate, and advanced, I also organized them based on their speed-related categories—including active dynamic warm-up (ADW), acceleration, maximum velocity, change of direction (COD), deceleration, agility, maneuverability, and speed-specific strength. This structure will allow you to use the tables in the programming chapter at the end of this book to quickly create your own personalized, evidence-based training recipes for different athletes, disciplines, and outcomes. Ultimately, good coaching is like good cooking: It requires equal parts of science, art, and inspired improvisation.

And it all starts with having a solid understanding of the ingredients.

ACKNOWLEDGMENTS

There is a tremendous amount of collective knowledge presented in the pages of this book. This is not just one person's perspective on how to improve speed and athletic performance. It represents the combined real-world experience of the many outstanding performance coaches I've worked with over the past 30-plus years. Thank you to our team of Parisi Speed School master coaches, which includes Steve Leo, who is the longest-tenured coach in our network and has been fundamental in developing the Parisi Training System, along with John Cirilo—our longest-tenured master coach—Eric Mitchel, Chad Coy, Sullivan Parker, Casey Lee, and Liz Madden. They have all worked tirelessly to deliver the science of performance training in a way that all coaches and athletes can benefit from. Also, Martin Rooney, author and founder of Training for Warriors, who joined Parisi Speed School in 1999 and was a pillar of the organization for 10 years. Developing the Parisi Training System really has been a team effort. Additionally, Seth Forman recently joined the Parisi team and helped immensely with the development of the programming menus and other practical elements in this book, working in collaboration with Steve Leo and Danny Stickna.

Parisi Speed School flagship facility in Fair Lawn, New Jersey.

Special thanks to Rob Gilbert, PhD, who has inspired me since the age of 18 to always strive to be the best I can be through collaboration and keeping an open mind. Stuart McGill, PhD, is a true leader—not only in spine health but also in evaluating and helping the best athletes in the world to improve performance. You have always been so generous with your knowledge. Thank you to Joe Camisa, DPT, and Mike Holmgren, DPT, my local physical therapists, who I am constantly learning so much from. Thank you to world-renowned powerlifter Rich Sadiv, who is the facility owner of our Parisi Speed School flagship in Fair Lawn, New Jersey, and his entire staff. The Fair Lawn facility has been, and continues to be, the ultimate speed-training facility and laboratory for me, and it is unmatched anywhere in the world. Thank you to Todd Wright, assistant coach and vice president of performance for the Los Angeles Clippers, a true friend and one of the greatest coaches of all time. Jerry Palmieri, thank you for being a great friend and colleague who has helped me take the Professional Football Strength and Conditioning Coaches Association (PFSCCA) to new heights. Thank you to Mike Woicik, who I first saw speak when he was a coach at Syracuse University in 1986—that was the spark that lit my fire for this industry. Chris Poirier, CEO of Perform Better, thank you for all you do for our industry. Damion Martins, MD, of Atlantic Health, your support and insight into sports medicine have been invaluable. L.J. Mattraw, creating the vertical jump course with you was extremely informative. Frans Bosch, your education and forward thinking have been hugely enlightening. Khalil Harrison, creating the Olympic lifting course with you was a great benefit to me and our network. Dave Schmidt, founder of OHM, thank you for your support and for the cutting-edge equipment that has allowed me to experiment with and develop effective new training protocols. Lastly, I want to thank the two athlete models who worked with us to document the drills and exercises in this book: Angel Rowe and my son, Dan Parisi, who has been my tireless training subject and Parisi Speed School model for his entire life.

I also want to extend my endless gratitude, appreciation, and respect to the subject-matter experts who agreed to be interviewed for this book. Each one of them is recognized as a top-shelf specialist in their respective fields, and they all provided valuable insights, research, and perspectives. Their contributions raised the bar significantly.

- Ken Clark, PhD, who teaches biomechanics, kinetic anatomy, and motor learning at West Chester University of Pennsylvania. Ken was a Parisi Speed School athlete in his teens who went on to receive his PhD in applied physiology and biomechanics from SMU, where he worked with renowned speed expert Dr. Peter Weyand on groundbreaking research with some of the world's fastest humans.

- Michol Dalcourt, who is the founder of the Institute of Motion and developer of the ViPR PRO loaded-movement training tool. Michol is an internationally recognized expert on human movement and athletic performance who never ceases to amaze me with his depth of knowledge.

- Dan Pfaff, a legendary track-and-field coach with more than 40 years of success, who has helped athletes achieve more than 55 national records and served on the coaching staffs of five Olympic Games in five different countries. Dan is a longtime friend and mentor who contributed significantly to my understanding of how to train high-performance athletes.

- William Kraemer, PhD, who is one of the world's top researchers in resistance training and is currently head of the Neuroscience and Neuromuscular Laboratory at Ohio State University.

- Karrie L. Hamstra-Wright, PhD, who is a certified athletic trainer with doctoral and postdoctoral training in lower-extremity biomechanics and is currently a clinical professor in the Department of Kinesiology and Nutrition at University of Illinois Chicago.

- Dave Tate, who is an elite powerlifter, strength trainer, and the founder of EliteFTS. Dave has spent more than 40,000 hours training and consulting with athletes and coaches of all skill levels over the past three decades.

- Evan Chait, who is a physical therapist, acupuncturist, and creator of the Chait neuropathic release technique (CNRT). Evan is also the founder and owner of Kinetic PT in Ramsey, New Jersey, where he focuses on bridging the gap between physical therapy and athletic training.

- Paul Robbins, who is EVP of Sports Performance for Kinexon, owner of Cardio2Tech LLC, and an internationally recognized expert on metabolic testing, workload tracking, and training optimization. In addition to overseeing the load management program for the NBA, Paul is head of the STATS wearable tech division for Kinexon and has served as a consultant for Intel, Google, and Adidas, among others.

I have learned so much from all of you. Thank you for your contributions to this book. May the journey never end.

THE MANY FORMS OF SPEED

Why is speed the gold standard for athletic performance and human endeavor—as opposed to the ability to jump high, lift heavy objects, or throw things long distances? Why is Jamaican-born 100-meter dash world-record holder Usain Bolt a global phenomenon and household name when you've probably never heard of Javier Sotomayor, the Cuban-born world-record holder in the high jump since 1993; Lasha Talakhadze, the Georgian world-record holder for both the snatch and the clean and jerk; or Jan Železný, the Czech world-record holder in the javelin throw? Achieving elite-level speed gives you competitive superiority in virtually any ground sport, but I believe its mythical status is rooted in a deeper, more primal part of the human psyche. The thing with high-speed running is that, in addition to allowing you to excel as an athlete, it represents the front line in humanity's eternal battle against the most powerful force in the universe: gravity! But here's the rub: This is a battle we can never win. Not to get all Dr. Doom on you at the beginning of the book but—spoiler alert—no matter how fit, fast, or strong you are, you will eventually succumb to the relentless pull of gravity and become one with the Earth. Time will run out. Dust will return to dust etcetera. If Newton and Einstein are correct, this reality is true for every organism and atom in existence. Even the planets and stars themselves will one day collapse into a cosmic black hole of nothingness. Gravity is the master. Gravity always wins. But here's the silver lining in this existential cloud of doom: For a few fleeting moments, fueled by a rush of momentum, hormones, and human-powered propulsion, high-speed running allows you to harness the power of gravity, defy it, and find your place within it. High-speed running is the closest we bipeds get to the feeling of flying (without a mechanical aid). And, for an explosive 100-meter distance, that's exactly what elite runners like Usain Bolt are doing in an Olympic race: rhythmically firing massive amounts of force into the ground using ultrashort bursts of powerful ground contact so they can harness that energy to fly.

I mention all of this not for dramatic effect but to give you an accurate way to think about the concept of human speed and the biomechanics involved in creating it. The manifestation of speed is, at its core, the process of overcoming gravity by harnessing energy with every part of your body and directing that force at the ground to efficiently propel yourself in a specific direction through space and time. It happens on all three planes of motion simultaneously and requires multiple anatomical systems to coordinate in unison. That means training for speed is never about just one thing. It is complex and multidimensional and involves a near-endless set of variables—just like flying. As a result, if you want to help athletes achieve their full genetic potential for maximizing speed while minimizing their risk for injury, it's crucial you understand the different anatomical components involved and how they all work together.

Mass-Specific Force

Peter Weyand, the famed biomechanist and expert on human speed, published with his colleagues a Harvard study in 2000 comparing world-class sprinters with amateur field athletes on a high-speed US$250,000 treadmill outfitted with force plate technology. That study revealed that the most important factor in attaining maximum speed is not actually stride length or stride frequency. Instead, it is the amount of force an athlete can apply into the ground with each foot strike compared to their relative body weight (called mass-specific force). Gravity plays a role in this dynamic because the more you weigh, the more force you have to produce to overcome gravity. This means that, if you want to be fast, you need to be both relatively light and strong. A 2010 follow-up study on the subject, also led by Weyand, revealed that, in addition to the amount of mass-specific vertical force an athlete can apply on each foot strike, contact time is also a contributing factor. The research showed that top-speed velocity is determined by how fast you can apply large amounts of force into the ground (maximum force + minimum ground-contact time). This was demonstrated to be true for both forward and backward running as well as one-leg hopping. To put this in perspective, the ground-contact time for superelite runners is around eight hundredths of a second. Try starting and stopping your stopwatch in less than a tenth of a second and see if you can pull it off. Now, imagine applying more than twice your body weight in force at that speed with one limb.

This force–velocity relationship means that, when velocities are low—like when you're accelerating from a deadstart at the beginning of a race or charging forward at the initial snap of a ball—the amount of time your foot spends on the ground producing force is longer in order to create propulsion. But the faster your body moves, the less ground-contact time you have. And the ability to produce more ground force in less time to counteract gravity at high speed is what separates guys like Usain Bolt from everyone else in the human race. Elite sprinters are able to do that because in addition to being incredibly strong for their relative body weight, they can create extreme levels of stiffness (what Stu McGill calls "super stiffness") across the tissues and joints in their legs at ground strike and extend this stiffness through the hip complex and core to both reduce energy leakage and get the most return.

The acclaimed "Father of Function" Gary Gray describes running as a chain reaction of co-contractions that happens in three dimensions across multiple anatomical structures using the drivers of ground reaction, gravity, mass, and momentum. Basically, running is a chain reaction of reactive and proprioceptive events that starts below the ankle at the subtalar joint, which unlocks the tibia and fibula and transfers energy up the chain through the knee and hip joints. If the tissues around one or more of the joints in this kinetic chain are inhibited in any way, the effective and efficient transfer of force through the rest of the chain becomes limited. This means that the ability to create super stiffness in the joints of the lower body in an extremely short period of time is paramount to generating explosive levels of speed and reducing injury risk. Therefore, a high strength-to-weight ratio and the ability to create super stiffness at ground contact in the lower leg, hip, and core are the first factors to consider when looking at how to improve an athlete's speed. Another important consideration is how well balanced an athlete is in terms of their strength symmetry. We've become so hung up in the strength and conditioning world on the sagittal plane paradigm of doing squats, deadlifts, lunges, step-ups, etc., that we've lost sight of the fact that our bodies adapt and function omnidirectionally in three dimensions. Physical movement in the real world doesn't just happen on a single sagittal plane. As a sprinter, if you're not well versed in multiplanar movement and you don't have balanced omnidirectional tissue development, you increase your risk for injury. Without balanced structural integrity throughout your entire propulsion system, you will inevitably suffer an injury to some part of your body, such as the hamstring, for instance. But the hamstring in this situation might not have been the deficiency. If there's a deficiency or inefficiency somewhere else in the kinetic chain, that weak link can force the hamstring to overcompensate, which will eventually lead to injury. That's why understanding the anatomy of speed and applying a whole-system approach to developing personalized training prescriptions that safely increase power capacity is crucial.

What Is Speed?

Before popping open the anatomical hood and getting into mass-specific force and chain reactions, the first question to ponder is: What is actually meant when the word *speed* is used? The thing is, speed comes in many forms including pure acceleration, transitional acceleration, maximum velocity, deceleration, and multidirectional speed. Regardless of sport, if you want to be a great field or court athlete, they all matter. Assuming this is not your first rodeo on the subject, you are probably aware that there are key differences between the max velocity linear sprinting of a world-class track athlete and the multidirectional bursts of dynamic "game speed" required to excel in field and court sports. And while they each require different approaches to technical form and training, they also share fundamental components that can be strategically targeted based on individual sport, position, and body type. I'll start out by defining what each term means so we're all on the same semantic page before I get into the specifics of programming this elusive thing called speed.

Acceleration

Acceleration is an increase in velocity over a given period of time. When it comes to the discipline of running, there are two subcategories: pure acceleration and transitional acceleration. Pure acceleration is the process of initiating motion from a deadstart to overcome the inertia of gravity, like when a sprinter comes out of the blocks or a wide receiver takes off from the line of scrimmage when the ball snaps. Transitional acceleration occurs when an athlete who is already moving speeds up or rapidly changes direction and reaccelerates to outmaneuver an opponent, like when a basketball player cuts through a crowded lane of defenders to get to the basket. As a result, the ability to quickly accelerate is important in every sport from track and field to the gridiron to the tennis and basketball courts. It is the act of punching gravity in the face. During the acceleration phase, your feet spend more time applying a longer driving phase of force off the ground. This means that pure acceleration is very strength dependent. Simply put, stronger athletes can typically generate more force into the ground and cover more distance more rapidly.

A key component of acceleration is body angle. When you're overcoming static inertia to rapidly accelerate, optimal form is (1) leaning your body forward at an approximately 45-degree angle so that your feet are behind your center of mass and (2) propelling your center of mass horizontally while punching downward with enough force to overcome gravity vertically (see figure 1.1). This means that force is simultaneously being applied in both horizontal and vertical vectors that transition in a fluid way over the first three to six strides as you generate more speed and become more upright. At this point, you shift gears to apply more force downward vertically. The ability to overcome inertia and rapidly propel your center of gravity through space is the foundation of most field and court sports. Even in linear sprinting, research shows that how quickly you get out of the blocks—how powerful and fast those first three steps are—is critical to winning races. If you don't nail those first three steps, it's very hard to overcome that deficient acceleration over the course of the rest of the race. In other words, the ability to rapidly accelerate is the first skill necessary for optimizing individual athletic ability regardless of sport or position. And, as I mentioned, this skill comes down to being able to generate large amounts of force relative to your body weight both horizontally and vertically. The anatomy of these mechanics and the specific training protocols for improving acceleration is covered in chapter 6.

FIGURE 1.1   Proper acceleration form.

Maximum Velocity

Maximum velocity is the highest speed an athlete can achieve. As an athlete's running speed increases after initial acceleration, their ground-contact time for each foot strike progressively decreases until it is so brief that all of their force is now directed vertically into the ground to overcome gravity. At this point, the athlete achieves their maximum velocity and can no longer accelerate. Proper form and posture are critical for elite sprinting performance.

Sprinting at high speed requires a rapid cycling of the legs with minimal ground contact; neutral hips; a stiff, upright core that is balanced to minimize gravitational pull; and front-side leg action that allows the thigh to come up high so it can fire back into the ground with maximum force (see figure 1.2).

To put this in context, Usain Bolt's maximum velocity clocks in at around 27 miles per hour (or approximately 12 meters per second). According to World Athletics (formerly the International Association of Athletics Federations, or IAAF), it took Bolt 60 meters to reach his top running speed during the 100-meter race at the 2008 Beijing Olympics. This begs the questions (and frequent points of debate among strength and conditioning coaches): Does maximum velocity training matter for field and court athletes who are limited by the compact dimensions of their respective playing areas and seldom reach maximum velocity? Does maximum velocity

Upright body position (approximately 10 degrees)

Head and chest held tall and level

Hands travel from back pockets to chin

The hand on the front side of the body at or slightly above shoulder height with the elbow approaching 75-degree angle

Elbow on swing arm opens to approximately 95- to 105-degree angle

Front-side hip flexion that allows the thigh to approach a 90-degree angle near waist height

Neutral hips (no anterior tilt)

Rapid leg recovery with minimal backside swing

FIGURE 1.2 Proper max velocity form.

matter for "game speed"? My response to these questions is an unequivocal yes! And here's why: No other training stimulus compares to it. When an athlete sprints at maximum velocity, they are generating their maximum force production into the ground. Studies show that world-class sprinters generate force into the ground at more than 2.2 times their body weight, and amateur runners average around 1.8 times their body weight (Weyand et al. 2000; 2010). That's upward of 400 to 500 pounds (181 to 227 kg) of force per foot strike. Name any other movement that allows you to generate that much force with one limb. This means that max velocity sprinting provides unique benefits as a training stimulus when it comes to enhancing overall athletic performance. In fact, there is a growing body of scientific evidence showing that maximum velocity sprinting not only improves overall speed and agility in shorter distances but also helps reduce soft-tissue injuries in the groin and hamstring (Edouard et al. 2019). I'll provide a closer look at these studies and their anatomical implications for speed in chapter 7, but the short answer is that max velocity sprinting is unequaled as a training stimulus when prescribed in the right amounts. Also, while an elite track sprinter may take up to 60 meters to reach their maximum velocity, most trained athletes will exceed 80 percent of their maximum velocity within 20 meters. And this absolutely makes a difference on the field or court. Consider the following observations made by biomechanist Ken Clark on a study (Clark et al. 2019) he conducted at the NFL Combine comparing the acceleration profiles of athletes running a 40-yard dash.

"We tend to think of the 20-yard dash as an acceleration-only race," says Clark. "But the 20-yard dash isn't just impacted by acceleration capability. Top speed is also a factor. Let's say you've got a guy, we'll call him Athlete A, and he has a 20-yard acceleration profile with a top speed of 9.5 meters per second—that's about 21 miles an hour, give or take—and he runs a 20-yard dash in 2.74 seconds. It's not bad; it's not great. Now compare him to another guy, we'll call him Athlete B, who has an identical initial acceleration capability in the first five yards, but his top speed over the full distance is just slightly better [see figure 1.3]. His 20-yard dash will be a 10th-of-a-second faster at 2.64 seconds. Well, that small change in top speed translates to a one-yard difference in a 20-yard dash. That means that Athlete B will beat athlete A to the ball by a full yard. And in a game situation, that's a huge difference! So max velocity absolutely impacts acceleration and game speed."

As a coach, I think the importance of maximum velocity training is one of the biggest misconceptions in our industry. We all know that sprinting is the number one way to train and get faster. But the big questions are how much and how often should running be prescribed for each athlete and what else is there to do besides just running? Ultimately, the goal is to create rapid pulses of tremendous stiffness for extremely short periods of time punctuated just as quickly by extreme levels of relaxation. And that requires all of the body's systems—including the fascia system, musculoskeletal system, nervous system, endocrine system, and cardiovascular system—to be working in highly refined unison. This concept of speed being a product of both stiffness and relaxation is admittedly a bit of a paradox that can be hard to grasp even for experienced coaches, which is why both chapters 2 and 7 provide a deep dive into the concept.

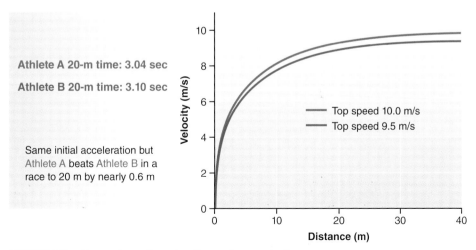

FIGURE 1.3 Comparison of acceleration and max velocity.

Deceleration

Speaking of paradoxes, it can seem counterintuitive to think of deceleration as a form of speed. Although the opposite of acceleration (how fast you can speed up), it's still a measurement of speed—how fast you can *slow down*. Just like a race car, the faster you can stop, the faster you can go—because you have more control. High-speed deceleration and the ability to control your center of gravity are paramount to executing rapid changes of direction and minimizing injury risk. Or, to use our flying metaphor, you wouldn't get on an airplane if you knew the pilot was great at accelerating, taking off, and flying but wasn't so good at landing. Deceleration is a fundamental skill for any athlete whether it's a point guard suddenly hitting the brakes to create space so they can pull up for a shot or a tennis player braking rapidly to set up for a return stroke after sprinting crosscourt. As a motor skill, deceleration comes down to being able to safely lower your center of gravity and manage the load with tremendous amounts of control so you can explode back out of it or come to a safe stop at the end of an effort. Studies (Delaney et al. 2015) show that the gravitational braking forces experienced by a decelerating athlete can be up to two times their body weight. As a result, eccentric strength and anterior chain strength both play a big role in safe deceleration.

Proper deceleration form involves lowering your center of mass and getting behind it. This means shortening up your strides and getting your feet in front of your center of gravity so you can quickly gain control over your momentum. The arms help maintain your center of balance by countering the braking forces created by flexion in the hips, knees, and ankles (see figure 1.4). In most competitive situations,

FIGURE 1.4　Proper deceleration form.

deceleration is immediately followed by a strategic task—whether that's changing direction to outmaneuver or tackle an opponent, catching a pass, or shooting a three-pointer. This follow-up task will also influence your hand and body positions. Often this follow-up action is explosive in nature, requiring the rapid storing and release of energy, which relies heavily on the body's elastic fascia system and the stretch-shortening cycle. The thing to keep in mind is that rapid controlled deceleration is a basic skill required for multidirectional speed changes of all kinds. And doing it improperly is how a vast majority of noncontact soft-tissue injuries occur. All of which makes training for deceleration a critical component in the design of virtually any sport-specific program. Chapter 8 covers these mechanics.

Multidirectional Speed

Multidirectional speed is a quick change of trajectory in any horizontal direction (forward, backward, lateral, diagonal, etc.). It is the difference between being fast and being quick. While it involves the basic elements of acceleration and linear speed—which is to say powerful force production, proper posture and body angle, and the ability to create rapid pulses of stiffness and relaxation—training for multidirectional speed is more complex and dependent on the sport or position. It requires a refined focus on skill-specific timing, movements, and pattern recognition.

Proper change of direction (COD) form involves maintaining a low athletic position with a slight amount of flexion in the hips, knees, and ankles with joint angles that are bent just enough to enable optimal force transmission and fast reacceleration (see figure 1.5). Maintaining this low position is crucial for cutting, sidestepping, pivoting, and other COD maneuvers. This means that multidirectional athletes need to have a solid foundation of both strength and technical form with an above-average level of coordination and movement literacy in their respective sports. Multidirectional speed is the most multidimensional manifestation of speed and also consists of three distinct subcategories that each require different approaches to training and assessment: change of direction, agility, and maneuverability. And, since they are the frequent subjects of debate regarding the best approaches for training and assessment, each subcategory warrants a brief explanation of the key differences.

Change of Direction

People often confuse change of direction (COD) and agility as being the same thing and frequently use the terms interchangeably to refer to rapid changes in trajectory, but there are a few important distinctions between the two. COD is a rapid *preplanned* change of direction or velocity. Also commonly known as "cutting," it is typically applied as part of an offensive strategy that is intentional—for example, a wide receiver who runs a pattern and then cuts to create space from their defender. Basically, with COD, you know where you're going, and you have a plan. You're in control of executing the neurological motor programs of move-

FIGURE 1.5 Proper change of direction form.

ment (motor engrams) you've developed and rehearsed as part of your training regime using cone drills, ladder drills, and other planned sequences. As a result, the training drills and technical demands involved are highly sport and position dependent. The mechanics of COD can be separated into three phases:

- *Braking or deceleration*. The muscles primarily contract eccentrically.
- *Planting or transition*. The muscles primarily contract isometrically.
- *Reacceleration or conversion*. The muscles primarily contract concentrically.

Agility

Agility, by contrast, is a rapid change of direction or velocity in response to external sensory stimuli. Agility is reactive, unplanned, cognitive, and requires the ability to both rapidly read visual and audio cues and respond with appropriate countermovements in the blink of an eye. Although offensive players use agility to respond to defensive movements, agility is primarily a defensive tactic for reading and responding to an opponent's foot movements, ball movements, shoulder angles, or other indicators so defenders can anticipate their opponent's next move. Agility involves a number of multidimensional factors, such as visual scanning, pattern recognition, decision making, and a highly tuned nervous system with acute reaction speed. As a result, agility has proven difficult for coaches and researchers to objectively assess in individual athletes. This makes it more of a challenge to measure an athlete's aptitude for agility and develop evidence-based training prescriptions for improving it. Some people will go so far as to say that agility is a natural talent that can't be efficiently targeted and trained. However, while some athletes are certainly more genetically gifted with agility, I believe it is a trainable skill.

Maneuverability

Maneuverability is the ability to manage the angular momentum of your body at discrete angles. It's like sprinting on a curved balance beam, meaning it combines elements of top speed and agility. Maneuverability is about managing your center of gravity while applying slight shifts in body angle, movement tempo, and trajectory in response to a stimulus. Think of a 200-meter indoor track sprinter running at max velocity on a banked track or a batter rounding the bases in a full sprint trying to turn a double into a triple and ducking under the third-base player's mitt as they slide into the base in an awkward position. This kind of running requires you to efficiently transfer force while your center of mass leans to one side. As a result, maneuverability takes a higher level of foot, ankle, and hip stability compared to traditional sprinting. It relies on super stiffness in lower-body joints, a high level of joint resilience, and three-dimensional spatial awareness (proprioception) that allows you to know how fast you can go based on the angle of the curve. The best way to develop this skill is to actually do curve running, which not enough athletes do.

Speed-Specific Warm-Ups

Since different forms of speed involve different anatomical systems, muscle groups, postures, and movement patterns, it's important to start each speed-specific training session with a warm-up routine that targets that day's activities—whether it's acceleration, max velocity, deceleration, or multidirectional speed. A speed-specific warm-up is not just about increasing body temperature, getting the tissues and joints lubricated, and getting blood flowing. It's also an opportunity to hone your skill set and refine neuromuscular coordination by working fundamental speed techniques, postures, and drills into the routine. Approaching the subject holistically, you want to start out by doing a general warm-up that prepares an athlete for movement before you do a targeted speed-specific warm-up. This general warm-up (covered in chapter 3) should be designed to activate the areas of the body that are essential for generating speed—the glutes, the core, and the lats. That glute–core–lats connection is important for sprinting and movement because those are the major muscle groups that combine to make an integrated whole-body connection that provides the stability needed to efficiently transfer force through the kinetic chain. Therefore, you want to start every session by activating those connections in order to (1) get the most benefit out of your targeted drills for the day and (2) reduce the risk of injury. As Ken Clark is fond of saying, the most important ability is availability.

PHASE 1: PRE–WARM-UP

The first stage of a pre–warm-up routine isn't practicing movement, it's finding and addressing any soft-tissue restrictions and adhesions in the kinetic chain using an appropriate mechanical aid such as a foam roller or lacrosse ball. The idea is to work through the anterior and posterior chains of the lower body—including the calf complex, IT band, quads, hamstrings, and glutes, as well as the bottom of the feet and the plantar fascia—ironing out tissue kinks that can limit mobility. Research indicates that this kind of direct pressure—known as self-myofascial release (SMR)—can help increase fluid flow to those areas due to tissue warming and changes in osmotic pressure (Cheatham et al. 2015). SMR has also been shown to temporarily increase joint range of motion and decrease perceived muscle pain for short periods of time. The goal isn't just "rolling" these areas but finding any tight spots or hot spots that exist and applying mechanical pressure to the trigger points adjacent to those areas to help them release.

Instead of applying pressure directly to the hot spot itself, it's recommended that you start by working the area around a tissue knot and slowly working toward the hot spot. The goal is to get the tissues to move, so you want to start out by loosening them up away from the tissue lesion or lump. Then, gradually get closer and closer to where the knot is. The goal is to get it to move from the inside, and the only way to get it to move from the inside is to loosen the tissues around it first. Basically, there's a block because the tissues haven't been moving, and you want to get the tissues to start moving again so you can gradually get closer and closer to the knot.

The next step of a general warm-up is getting the core, glutes, and lats engaged by doing things like the "McGill Big 3," the core activation sequences advocated by leading spinal biomechanist Stu McGill. These include the McGill curl-up, the side plank, and the bird dog. From there, you can progress into dead bugs, more advanced side planks, bird dog variations, and other plank exercises that fire the lats even more. Activating the small motor units of the feet is also an important general warm-up step for runners because you want to prepare them for high levels of ground-reaction force during your general warm-up.

I cover these techniques in more depth in chapter 3, but the important thing to remember is that a core activation warm-up is critical to safely getting the most out of any speed-specific training program.

PHASE 2: GENERAL ACTIVE DYNAMIC WARM-UP

The first step of an active dynamic warm-up (ADW) is doing exercises that help the body develop odd-position strength and overall shape stability by building up your internal armor. This is done by activating load paths across multiple joints and structures using loaded movements such as lunges with extended or overhead reaches on all three planes of motion. Loads should be submaximal and can be created by holding a medicine ball, kettlebell, or other loaded-movement tool. After working on shape stability and odd-position strength, a general ADW should transition into metabolic activation that uses calisthenics and plyometrics that incorporate different jumping exercises and dynamic oscillating movements such as jumping jacks. These sorts of exercises stimulate the nervous system, raise the heart rate, increase core temperature, activate the anaerobic energy systems, and help build local muscular endurance.

PHASE 3: SPEED-SPECIFIC ACTIVE DYNAMIC WARM-UP

In this last phase, you want to focus on doing movements that necessitate the specific postures required for that day's objective, since there's nothing better from a skill-training perspective than doing the skill itself. In this way, an ideal speed-specific warm-up should start with drills that roll directly into the training workout for that day. The goal is to have athletes do a progressive series of skill-based drills that slowly ramp up to doing the actual skill itself. Therefore, if you want to improve acceleration, you would start by working on the fundamental postures and drills needed for that skill until you are actually doing acceleration sprints and so on. We have a saying at the Parisi Speed School that "our warm-up is your workout," because our warm-up is fairly long. It could be as short as 12 to 15 minutes, or it could be as long as 20 to 30 minutes, depending on the physical condition of the athlete, the training goal that day, and the amount of time you get with them. But the warm-up should incorporate movement-specific drills that are going to help the athlete develop better form and build a more diverse set of neural pathways related to that specific movement. Most importantly, don't underestimate the value and importance of doing a speed-specific warm-up prior to any training session. In fact, we do very little weight training with our NFL Combine athletes because we get only four to six weeks to work with them. We don't want to break them down from a weight-training, eccentric-loading perspective. We want them to be fresh so they can optimize their performance in the skill tests. This is why generalized and skill-specific warm-up routines are huge building blocks for athletes when it comes to maximizing their performance.

Assessment of Strength-to-Weight Ratio

Before I bring this chapter on the many forms of speed to a close, let's take a moment to discuss speed-specific strength, since strength-to-weight ratio is the most important factor in all types of speed. When you're creating a speed-specific training program, you first need to determine an athlete's training age and history and which type of athletic animal you're dealing with—whether that's a lean, fascia-driven cheetah or a bigger, more muscle-driven rhino. I like to think of these category types as animals because it's an easy correlation to make and remember.

Olympic coach Dan Pfaff calls his process "mailboxing" athletes based on their body type, sport, position, and what their different movement drivers are. Whatever your approach to assessment is, mailboxing is an important first step for any coach or trainer, because training programs need to be customized for each individual to get the best results. A muscle-driven athlete is going to respond better to heavier lifting and traditional strength training (to a point) than a fascia-driven athlete who uses more elastic movement strategies to generate speed. Giving the same heavy-lifting prescription to a cheetah that you would give to a rhino will very likely end up slowing the cheetah down and increasing their chance for injury. Once you've identified what kind of animal you're working with, you'll want to assess their existing strength relative to their body weight before creating a program for them. Chapter 5 provides a more in-depth look at speed-specific strength, but some basic assessments for doing this include determining how many pull-ups an athlete can do, how much weight they can deadlift or squat, and how high they can jump. These three assessments will give you a quick snapshot of where the athlete is at this time and how much speed-specific strength training the athlete needs to get faster. These assessments will also give you an objective baseline for measuring the athlete's progress and determining the success of your training prescriptions.

When it comes to pull-ups, a good indicator for solid relative body strength starts at around 12 to 15 chins with an optimal target of 20. In my 30 years of anecdotal experience as a trainer, there isn't a lot of benefit north of 20 chins, and 12 is the minimum where I would consider an athlete to have good relative upper-body strength. In terms of measuring relative lower-body strength, being able to squat or deadlift two times your body weight is a solid baseline foundation, with a goal of working up to above two times your body weight. But this target range greatly depends on the individual body type, size, and weight of the athlete you're dealing with. Some athletes might be ready to go at two times their body weight, while others may need two and a half. Again, pushing more than two-and-a-half times your body weight in any of these movements has little, if any, added benefit when it comes to improving an athlete's ability to generate speed and may, in fact, slow them down by adding more bulk. Vertical jumping ability is typically measured from a flat standing start with 26 to 28 inches (66 to 71 cm) of height indicating a solid baseline. A good target goal is 30 inches (76 cm) or more. To put this measurement in perspective, only about a dozen players each year testing at the NFL and NBA Combines will top 40 inches (102 cm) in the vertical jump test.

Like I said at the beginning of this chapter, when it comes to training for speed, there is no one-size-fits-all approach. There is no magic ingredient. In addition to the fact that there are many different forms of speed, there are also many different ways for athletes to achieve speed. However, the most important thing for a coach or trainer to remember is that it all comes down to one word: *individualization*. Humans are incredibly diverse and unique creatures. Every one of us has different genetic traits, tissue compositions, injury histories, sleep patterns, diets, emotional motivations, and movement strategies. Many of these variables change on a daily, seasonal, or yearly basis. The art of coaching comes from understanding the basic anatomy and mechanics of speed as a skill and knowing how to apply those principles to each specific athlete. This means you need to regularly check in with your athletes and ask them how they feel, monitor how their body responds to different types of training, and do your best to understand the many nuanced variables that influence performance so you can accurately prescribe the optimal training activities for them, whether that's building more strength, fine-tuning form and symmetry, or just getting more rest. This starts with personally getting to know each unique athlete so you can really understand what they need to excel. If you want to maximize performance while mitigating injury risk, the days of having everyone do the same thing all the time because "that's what the program is" are over. To revisit our cooking metaphor in the preface, if you want to bring out the best performance in your athletes, you can't feed everyone the same cafeteria meal. You need to be an artisanal chef with an arsenal of ingredients at your creative disposal and have the ability to whip up whatever recipe is required. That's how you create lasting value as a trainer and coach.

SYSTEMS OF SPEED

Optimal speed comes from a symphony of biological systems firing harmonically in unison. There is no one system, one technique, or one approach that will get you there. Each system plays a significant role in the end result, and focusing exclusively on any one of them—such as the musculoskeletal or nervous systems—will inevitably compromise the contributions of the others, limiting performance and increasing chance of injury. If you want to achieve peak performance with maximum injury resilience, you need to understand the role each instrument plays in the symphony and how to tune each of them for combined maximum effect. This isn't open mic night. It's a sophisticated collaboration. Speed is complex, multidimensional, and based on each athlete's body type, movement strategies, emotional drivers, training history, and lifestyle choices such as rest patterns, stress triggers, and diet. Before we get into the practicalities of training, let's first take a look at how this symphony of different anatomical systems contributes to the manifestation of speed in its many forms.

Musculoskeletal System

The musculoskeletal system has probably received the most attention and focus over the past few decades of professional training and conditioning for good reason. I just explained how strength-to-weight ratio is one of the most important factors in creating speed. Being strong is essential to being fast, but I believe we've gotten too focused as an industry on training this one system at the expense of the others. The nervous, fascia, lymphatic, and energy systems play equally important roles in the creation of speed, but the musculoskeletal system is also the engine and foundation for movement. There are a number of anatomical overlays featured in the exercise segments of this book that highlight select active muscles. The labeled muscles aren't the only ones involved in these movements, but they are primary movers that work in conjunction with the other systems and myofascial structures.

Skeletal muscles are famous for their ability to create movement by contracting. They consist of integrated bundles of muscle fibers, nerve fibers, blood vessels, and three layers of connective fascia tissue that surround each individual muscle as well as the fibers within it. This dense sheath of connective tissue surrounding each muscle is called the epimysium, and it acts like an elastic powerlifting suit that increases the muscle's power to contract and maintain stability while integrating with the other muscles and structures around it. It also allows muscle fibers to slide smoothly against each other and other tissues. Muscle fibers are organized into bundles called fascicles, which are surrounded by a layer of connective tissue called the perimysium. This structure allows the nervous system to initiate precise muscle movement by activating a subset of fibers within the muscle, causing them to contract. Each muscle fiber inside of a fascicle is also sheathed in a connective fascia tissue called the endomysium, which contains the extracellular fluid and nutrients that sustain the fibers (see figure 2.1). When skeletal muscle fibers contract, the resulting tension transfers through several layers of elastic connective fascia tissue and tendons. This transference articulates joints and moves bones or creates systems of stiffness by using co-contractions of multiple musculoskeletal structures, such as the thoracolumbar aponeurosis, which comprises large sheets of connective tissue woven into the lower-back muscles.

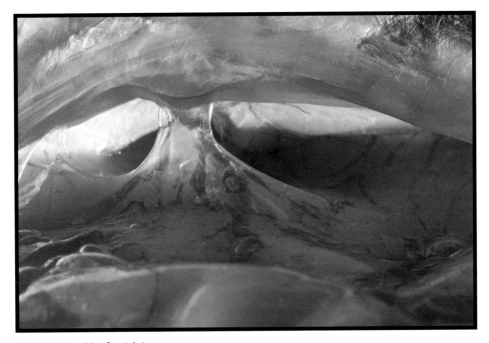

FIGURE 2.1 Myofascial tissue.

© Fascia Research Society. Photography by Thomas Stephan.

If it seems like I'm spending a lot of time talking about connective tissues in a subsection dedicated to the musculoskeletal system, it's because the two are literally intertwined. One doesn't work properly without the other. Also, the muscle system has been the focus for as long as textbooks about fitness and anatomy have been written but without a full understanding of how significantly the myofascial system works in conjunction with skeletal muscles to create movement. This is largely because the fascia system—which extends throughout your entire body like a hydraulic suspension system supporting every muscle, bone, and organ in you—is a single, interconnected web of collagen and pressurized fluid that only functions when you're alive. It is routinely discarded as part of the traditional dissection process. In fact, after more than 500 years of anatomical study, we still don't have a comprehensive, full-scale image of the fascia system like we do the musculoskeletal and circulatory systems. Recently, modern imaging technologies such as ultrasound and elastography have finally allowed us to see how this system actually works in the living body. More important to the subject of this book, studies conducted at the University of Tokyo (Kubo, Kawakami, and Fukunaga 2001) show that elastic connective tissues—not muscles—are actually responsible for more of the power generation in explosive actions such as acceleration, high-speed sprinting, and jumping than we previously thought. The data showed that muscle fibers contract isometrically and amplify the storage and release of elastic energy through the powerful tendons. This allows the muscles to rapidly contract and relax in a way that efficiently optimizes power output; for example, an archer firing a bow over and over or someone jumping on a pogo stick. Muscles play a critical role in speed but not in the way we've long believed. More about the important role the fascia system plays in human movement is covered later in this chapter.

Additionally, every skeletal muscle fiber is connected to a somatic motor neuron, which signals the fiber to contract (see figure 2.4 for more detail). Fun fact: The number of fibers in your skeletal muscles is genetically predetermined and doesn't change regardless of your training or diet (Pearson 1990). This is why some of us are born to be cheetahs and others to be rhinos. As you are probably well aware, three types of muscle fibers fall into two distinct categories: type I (slow-twitch) fibers and type II (fast-twitch) fibers. These fibers are distinguished based on how fast they contract and how they produce adenosine triphosphate (ATP)—the fuel that muscles run on. All three are present in virtually all skeletal muscle groups of the body with varying concentrations of each. Type IIA and IIB fast-twitch fibers are dominant in larger muscle groups that produce power for explosive movements and speed, while type I muscle fibers occur in a smaller format throughout the body to help maintain core stability and sustained endurance. When it comes to body composition and athletic predisposition, most natural-endurance athletes have a higher proportion of slow-twitch fibers, while quick-explosive athletes have a higher proportion of fast-twitch fibers.

Type I (slow-twitch, oxidative) fibers contract more slowly and primarily use aerobic respiration to produce ATP by metabolizing oxygen and glucose. They are slow to fatigue and are the dominant fibers used in sustained muscle activity such as core stabilization and endurance sports.

Type IIA (fast-twitch, oxidative) fibers contract quickly and use aerobic respiration but also have the ability to use anaerobic respiration (using glycolysis) to create ATP. They are dominant in activities that involve sustained power output such as 400-meter sprints or repeatedly lifting less than max weight.

Type IIB (fast-twitch, glycolytic) fibers contract very quickly and use anaerobic glycolysis to produce ATP. They are dominant in short, explosive bursts of power used for activities such as rapidly accelerating or doing clean and jerks, but these fibers fatigue rapidly.

The striated appearance of musculoskeletal fibers comes from the way myofilaments made of actin and myosin (myofibrils) are organized from one end of a muscle fiber to the other (see figure 2.2). Each bundle of these myofilaments and their regulatory proteins—troponin and tropomyosin—is called a sarcomere. Sarcomeres are the contractile units in muscle fibers. As myofibrils contract, the entire muscle cell contracts. Variable-loaded dynamic-movement patterns—medicine ball training, for example—prompt fast-twitch muscle fibers to produce pulses of short, powerful contractions. This increases the thickness of the activated muscle fibers by increasing their demand for structural proteins and fluid. It also stimulates three-dimensional collagen development in the associated connective tissues through a process called mechanotransduction. This increase in elastic connective tissue helps muscles produce more powerful contractions. Additionally, tendons that attach muscles to bones become stronger over time to offset the potential for tendon damage. How to apply these principles to optimize training programs for increased speed, power, and injury resilience is covered in later chapters. But the most important thing to keep in mind is that the contraction of skeletal muscles always begins with a signal from the peripheral somatic nervous system (SNS), which turns muscles on. In other words, no matter how strong or powerful your muscles are, the nervous system runs the show. If the musculoskeletal system is the engine, the nervous system is the driver.

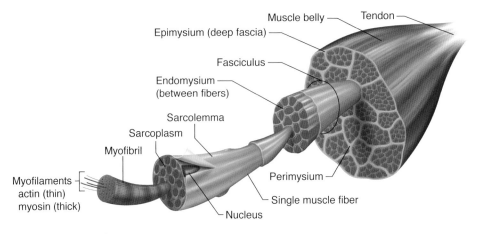

Muscle belly — Tendon —
Epimysium (deep fascia) —
Fasciculus —
Endomysium — (between fibers)
Sarcolemma
Sarcoplasm
Myofibril
Myofilaments — actin (thin) myosin (thick)
Perimysium —
Single muscle fiber
Nucleus

FIGURE 2.2 Muscle tissue.

Nervous System

The central nervous system (CNS) and peripheral somatic nervous system (SNS) control all the other systems in your body. If the nervous system is compromised, a cascade of other issues will manifest themselves. Performance will be inhibited, and the chance of injury increased. On the flip side, tuning and training the nervous system properly is essential to achieving optimal speed, precision, and power with the least amount of effort and risk. This is why learning to move with focused mental intention and programming your unconscious muscle memory properly by starting out slowly using optimal form are essential if you ultimately want to go very fast. You first need to encode the "motor engrams" for different movement patterns with good habits and form so your body can eventually recruit a greater number of muscle fibers to do it more quickly with more power.

Skeletal muscle fibers contract when they are innervated by a motor neuron, and a group of muscle fibers fired by a single motor neuron is called a motor unit. The size of motor units depends on the muscle or muscle group being activated. Small motor units consist of a motor neuron that activates only a small number of fibers within a muscle. Small motor units provide ultraprecise ocular control, which allows your eyes to change focus as they track a moving ball and enables your fingers to text someone at 2:00 a.m. to see if they're still awake.

Large motor units consist of a single motor neuron that activates a large number of fibers in a muscle. Large motor units are responsible for simple gross movements, such as extending your elbow to punch something. Large motor units in the thigh muscles or back muscles allow for a single motor neuron to activate thousands of fibers simultaneously.

All skeletal muscles are innervated with a diverse range of different motor units, giving the nervous system tremendously refined control over movement. Activation of smaller motor units results in a small amount of contractile tension in the muscle, while large motor units activate larger muscle fibers to create an increase in muscle contraction. This is known as recruitment. Muscle contractions become stronger as more units are recruited. The nervous system uses recruitment to efficiently use skeletal muscles. Variability in muscle fiber recruitment is what allows you to delicately pick a flower with minimal force using the same biceps muscle you'd use to lift a heavy kettlebell. When you explosively accelerate or lift a heavy barbell, your body recruits the greatest number of motor units available to produce maximum contraction force. This force production, however, only lasts for a short period of time due to the amount of energy required to sustain the contraction. To prevent complete muscle fatigue, motor units seldom fire simultaneously. Instead, the nervous system shares the load, relaxing some motor units while activating others. This allows for longer-duration contractions. Likewise, muscles are never completely relaxed. Muscles always retain some amount of contraction even when you're not moving to maintain action potential and contractile proteins and also to create the muscle tone that maintains your posture and stabilizes joints.

The key to expressing speed-specific force—whether it's through accelerating, changing direction, or sprinting at top speed—is training the nervous system so that it pulses multiple muscles in a rapid-fire sequence of contraction and relaxation. The symphony of your neuromuscular system has approximately 650 instruments in it. To play powerful, precise music, you need different instruments to fire at different levels, with different tones, at different times. They need to turn on with maximum recruitment for a beat and then turn off just as fast.

Renowned biomechanist, spinal expert, and author Stu McGill has shown the importance of this neurological pulsing cycle in studies involving six of the world's top UFC fighters from different weight divisions (McGill et al. 2010). In those studies, the fighters were measured using an EMG machine that recorded the electrical activity produced by their musculoskeletal system as they repeated a series of roundhouse kicks into a bag. The results showed that every fighter, regardless of weight class, had the same neurological pattern.

There was an initial pulse at the beginning of the whip action as each fighter's foot left the ground and their hips snapped down. Then, their bodies would go into a brief state of quiet neural relaxation as the brain signal momentarily relaxed to increase the closing velocity from the foot to the target. At this point, a second neural spike occurred as the foot struck the bag and their entire body locked into a state of super stiffness to deliver maximum force on the strike (see figure 2.3).

This clean, double-spike neural pattern would repeat smoothly and consistently until the fourth or fifth strike, at which point each fighter's neurology would begin to fall apart. With no beat of quiet relaxation between the foot kicking and contacting the bag, fighters began to tire. Instead of relaxing through the middle part of the whip action to increase momentum, they would use their strength to "muscle though" the motion and "push" their kick to the bag rather than letting it fly through the air with a crisp snap. Speaking of tuning instruments, the same on–off neurological pattern has been recorded in studies of some of the fastest drummers on the planet. This pulsing cycle of rapid contraction and relaxation

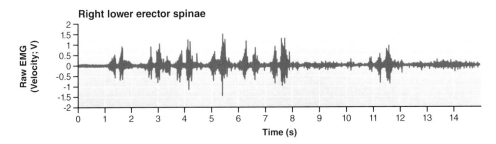

FIGURE 2.3 Neurological pulsing. UFC fighters were measured using an EMG machine as they repeated a series of roundhouse kicks into a bag. Every fighter had the same neurological pattern: an initial pulse at the beginning of the leg whip followed by a beat of neural relaxation and then a second neural spike as the foot struck the bag.

Adapted from S.M. McGill, J.D. Chaimberg, D.M. Frost, and C.M.J. Fenwick, "Evidence of a Double Peak in Muscle Activation to Enhance Strike Speed and Force: An Example With Elite Mixed Martial Arts Fighters," *Journal of Strength and Conditioning Research* 24, no. 2: 348-357.

is how you express force at speed. At foot strike, creating proximal stiffness in the core and distal stiffness in the ground-contact leg is essential to transferring energy into and off the ground when you're running, but the ability to relax between foot strikes is paramount.

A good way to think about this in terms of the leg movements involved in high-speed running is to imagine playing with a yo-yo. When you play with a yo-yo, you fire it down really fast with a lot of force. But to bring it back up, you just give it a slight upward flick. There are two different neural dynamics going on, and the timing is crucial to getting it right. The same thing happens when you're running at top speed. The idea is to fire each leg into the ground explosively while maintaining proximal stiffness in the ground-contact leg and core. The other leg unconsciously flicks up and maximizes the elastic stretch-shortening cycle in the hip flexor so you can harness the kinetic energy of that stretch cycle in the anterior chain before firing it down again. But one of the most profound things I've learned from Stu (and there have been many) is the overwhelming importance of the nervous system and mind when you're training for speed. We're so conditioned to focusing on training the muscles that we often lose sight of how important it is to "train the brain," as Stu says.

"The expression of strength always starts as a thought," says McGill. "In order to fire up the density of neural drive, you need to harness maximum strength from your entire body; you need to put your game face on; you need to trigger a bit of fight-or-flight response; you need to get a little angry, as if your life depends on it. All of that intention starts with a thought."

That said, too much thinking can really screw an athlete up. Intention matters, but a world-class sprinter isn't really thinking about the act of cycling his legs when running because they're moving so fast that their legs are just reacting to the ground contact. In this way, true speed is manifested almost unconsciously. To achieve this level of athletic mastery, you need to program your muscle memory, or motor engrams, to fire reactively and automatically by harnessing the primal power of your somatic nervous system using a phenomenon known as the gamma loop.

The SNS features afferent nerves (sensory nerves) and efferent nerves (motor nerves), which are located within the muscle spindles. Afferent nerves relay incoming sensations to the CNS about where you are in space and time (proprioception). Efferent nerves send out commands from the CNS to the body in response, stimulating muscle contraction. These nerves are mechanoreceptors that respond to changes in muscle length, which is then adjusted by gamma and beta (fusimotor) neurons. The gamma loop operates between the spinal cord and the muscles to expedite reaction time and automatically regulate the level of muscle tension in response to external stimuli before the conscious brain even gets involved (see figure 2.4).

For example, if you're running on a track versus on a grass field, it's going to change ground-contact time. Grass has a longer contact time than the hard surface of a track, and that will change your body's response, prompting a different

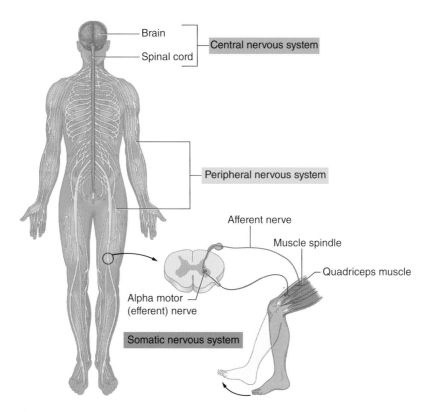

FIGURE 2.4 Nervous system.

adaptation in the nervous system. This is why changing your external training stimulus by sprint training on uneven surfaces that challenge your balance, running with a medicine ball held out in front of you, or running with dynamic variable loads like an aqua bag are effective. Using different forms of resistance stimulates the nervous system to fire and recruit muscles in ways that it normally wouldn't. This is also why the technique of high-speed sprinting (or doing anything at high speed, whether it's throwing, punching, or chopping vegetables) should first be rehearsed at slow speeds and then progressively ramped up to maximum speed and effort. Starting out slowly allows you to properly coordinate the firing order of the motor units involved and recruit more muscle fibers in the movement pattern. When you do something very quickly with improper form, your body will find ways to "cheat" the movement with inefficient muscle activity. Also, speed work should be conducted in the training week after a period of rest or light training to optimize neural firing. In a training session, speed work should be conducted after a skill-specific warm-up routine that incorporates those specific movements.

Cueing for Speed

One of the most powerful tools you have as a performance coach is the power of language. The challenge is trying to explain all the different postural landmarks and movement patterns for optimal acceleration or maximum velocity to an athlete. If you do, the athlete will inevitably overthink things and perform poorly. Movement is task driven and it starts with intention. The best strategy is to keep things simple and give your athletes movement cues that are easy to visualize like, "Spin the globe with your feet!" Cueing is a constantly evolving communication loop between coach and athlete. It is where a shared language is created and a bond of trust is formed. One of the frustrating paradoxes of language, though, is that we all have our own personal dictionaries. The same words mean different things to different people, and interpretation always depends on context. And, as coach Dan Pfaff is fond of saying, "Cues are like T-shirts. They all begin to stink after a while, and you need to change them to get good results." With that in mind, I've created a short sidebar section for a few of the upcoming chapters in this book: chapter 6, Acceleration; chapter 7, Maximum Velocity; chapter 9, Multidirectional Speed; and chapter 10, Agility. Each sidebar features some of the cues I have found to be successful with a wide range of athletes over the years. But these are just a starting point. Effective cueing is truly an art form that can be elusive even for experienced coaches. One of the world's top experts on the science of athletic cueing is Nick Winkelman, head of athletic performance and science for the Irish Rugby Football Union and author of the outstanding book *The Language of Coaching* (published by Human Kinetics). Some of the cues featured in the sidebars can also be found in Winkelman's book, along with an in-depth analysis of the science behind how to use them. If you are interested in the topic, I highly recommend you get a copy of his excellent book and take the time to really understand how you can use the information in it to become a better performance coach. The science-backed principles he covers will give you the conceptual tools you need to continually adapt your cueing language to the ever-changing needs of your athletes.

"I think of cueing as being synonymous with connecting," says Winkelman. "It is central to building an effective coach–athlete relationship and is as important to the training process as the program itself. However, the challenge with language is that the evidence for its effectiveness is far clearer to its recipient than to its creator. Thus, we depend on our athlete as a source of feedback to continually calibrate, update, and refresh language in line with their learning needs."

Energy Systems

The body generates ATP—the fuel required for muscle contractions—using three different energy systems: the ATP-PC system, the lactic acid system, and the aerobic system. The ATP-PC system provides the most immediate energy source. It gives your muscles about 10 to 15 seconds of explosive energy before the lactic acid (glycolysis) system kicks in to provide the energy needed for up to two more minutes of high-intensity output. After the glycolysis system is exhausted, the body switches from the anaerobic energy system to the aerobic energy system, and training efforts become more about endurance (see figure 2.5). The ATP-PC (composed of adenosine triphosphate and phosphocreatine) and lactic acid systems function anaerobically (without oxygen), and while all three matter in high-performance athletics, the anaerobic energy systems have the greatest impact on explosive acceleration, change of direction, and power. This is because anaerobic energy systems are responsible for fueling the first few seconds or minutes of power output. When you start sprinting, lifting, jumping, or punching, there simply isn't enough oxygen immediately available in the muscle tissues to fuel aerobic metabolism.

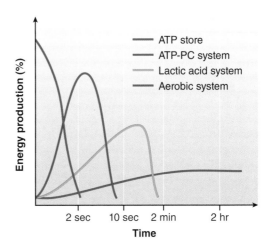

FIGURE 2.5 Energy systems. The body generates ATP, the metabolic fuel required for muscle contractions, using three different energy systems: the ATP-PC system, the lactic acid system, and the aerobic system.

ATP-PC System

The ATP-PC system is your body's instant fuel-injection system because PC (phosphocreatine) is a small, high-energy compound that the muscle cells store directly within themselves, making PC immediately available for sudden bursts of effort. But, since it is stored in very small amounts, it gives your muscles only about 10 to 15 seconds of high-octane fuel. After that, your lactic acid system kicks in to provide more energy for up to another two minutes of output until you become fatigued and start breathing hard because you need oxygen to continue. At this point, your body will switch to using the aerobic system. The chemical reaction in the ATP-PC system causes no fatigue by-products, and cells can quickly resynthesize PC. These advantages translate to providing you the ability to be ready to sprint, lift, jump, or punch again after a relatively short recovery period.

Developing this energy system for speed involves training sessions with reps of 10 to 15 seconds at maximum intensity, followed by approximately two minutes of rest between reps to allow the system to replenish itself. In sprinting, this system is best challenged as an athlete approaches max velocity between 30 and 60 meters at 95- to 100-percent effort. The general work–rest ratio for training the ATP-PC system is 1:10/20, meaning you should allow for 10 to 20 seconds of recovery for every second of work. For example, if you were to sprint as fast as you can for 50 meters, you would then follow up with a one- to three-minute recovery interval before repeating. The important thing to remember is that when you're designing training programs that condition the ATP-PC system, the rest cycle is critical. If there is a significant decrease in the quality of an athlete's movement or power output, that athlete should rest or stop the session because their fatigue indicates that the ATP-PC system has been depleted. If the athlete continues, they will switch to endurance-training modalities that are counterproductive to developing explosive power and speed. It's also important to consider that the speed component of anaerobic metabolism should be trained when no muscle fatigue is present (typically after 24 to 72 hours of rest).

Lactic Acid System

After your body exhausts the initial 10 to 15 seconds of ATP-PC energy, it taps into another ingredient—glycogen (glucose)—to continue producing energy, using a chemical reaction called anaerobic glycolysis, which creates ATP with lactic acid by breaking glucose down into pyruvic acid. The lactic acid system is the dominant energy system in exertions lasting between 10 to 120 seconds, and it replenishes itself relatively quickly, producing two ATP molecules per glucose molecule. The body stores an abundant amount of carbohydrates (around 500 grams) as glycogen in the tissues of the liver and muscles, which translates to a sizeable storage system of around 2,000 kilojoules of caloric energy. While lactic acid must get removed from the body, it's not technically a waste product because it's recycled into other useful chemicals, including lactate. Trainers, coaches, and athletes commonly use the terms *lactic acid* and *lactate* interchangeably and often believe (incorrectly) that lactic acid and lactate cause delayed onset muscle soreness (DOMS), so let me to clarify. Lactic acid interferes with muscle contractions and stimulates the free nerve endings within muscles that result in pain. But, contrary to popular belief, studies show that delayed onset muscle soreness actually comes from micro-tears in the muscle fibers, not lactic acid or lactate (Nalbandian and Takeda 2016). Lactate is actually an important part of both anaerobic and aerobic metabolism.

The main distinction between lactic acid and lactate is that, in order to be an acid, a substance must have an extra hydrogen ion to donate. When lactic acid donates its proton to create ATP, it becomes lactate—which your body then uses to delay fatigue and prevent tissue injury. When muscles contract intensely, they become more acidic and eventually interfere with their neural firing, which reduces muscle power. This is the muscle burn you feel when you reach your last rep. But lactate doesn't cause this acidity; instead, it serves as a signaling and protective mechanism in this process by preventing the body from damaging itself (Nalbandian and Takeda 2016). As your muscles begin to fatigue and become more acidic, lactate counteracts the depolarization of the cells. Your lactate threshold is basically the point at which lactate builds up in your bloodstream faster than the body can remove it. Therefore, the better an athlete can process lactate, the better they will perform.

The lactic acid system can be trained and improved by doing short bouts of intense exercise during which you push your body near its lactate threshold—such as high-intensity interval training (HIIT)—followed by a sufficient recovery phase. There are a number of ways to target your ideal lactic acid training threshold. Mark Sisson, author of the book *Primal Endurance*, established the ideal target heart rate range for training lactate threshold at 180 minus your age. For example, if you're 30 years of age, you would do short, intense bouts of exercise that push your heart rate to just under 150 beats per minute. A simpler way to gauge lactate production is to recognize that if you are breathing from your mouth while you're exercising, you're going too hard. This is because when you start breathing from your mouth, you begin tapping into your lactic reserves and going into a counterproductive catabolic state that breaks down both muscle and fat. It is also worth noting that it takes about an hour to remove lactic acid from the body when you do a cool-down session after your workout that incorporates low-level exercise. But it can take more than two hours if you don't. This is why incorporating cool-down and rest cycles into your training routines is important for rapid recovery and faster speed gains.

Fascia System

The fascia system, shown in figure 2.6, is one of the most important and least understood systems involved in creating power and speed. As previously mentioned, the science and research of the fascia system is relatively new. Since we can't see it with traditional imaging technology (such as MRI and X-ray), we're only just now beginning to understand its significance thanks to modern ultrasound, elastography, and other technologies. In fact, the International Fascial Research Congress—which convened in Berlin for only the fifth time in 2018—is still defining the exact parameters of the fascia system's features and properties. The terminology surrounding it continues to evolve as well. Professionals in the field commonly refer to it by different, often interchangeable names including the fascial system, the extracellular matrix (ECM), and the myofascial web, among others. Regardless of what you call it, modern research shows that the body's network of connective fascia tissue is greatly responsible for amplifying force for running, jumping, throwing, punching, and kicking. It does this using an elastic recoil dynamic called the catapult effect, which consists of cross-body co-contractions of myofascial structures that enable our ability to efficiently transfer energy through our kinetic chains by creating systems of stiffness in the limbs, core, and upper torso.

Researchers studying the amazing ability of kangaroos to jump more than 40 feet at a time in rapid sequence and achieve max velocity speeds of around 44 miles per hour (71 km) identified the catapult effect (Alexander 2003). Initially, it was assumed that kangaroos must have a higher proportion of type II (fast-twitch) muscle fibers. Upon further analysis, however, it turned out that kangaroos actually have the same basic muscle fiber composition as other marsupials, such as koala bears. Ultimately, the research showed that kangaroos are able to generate tremendous pulses of force for hopping because they have hyperdeveloped tendons in their hind legs that give them an unparalleled ability to store and release large amounts of kinetic energy. In fact, kangaroos burn more energy just using their muscles to walk around on their big, goofy feet than they do hopping, and the faster they hop, the less energy they consume (up to their cruising speed). The research revealed that when kangaroos hop, their muscles precontract to stretch the attached myofascial connective tissues—loading them like a stretched rubber band—and then quickly relax to release this stored elastic energy in a high-force pulse. Gazelles have this same anatomical feature. And recent ultrasound imaging has allowed us to see that humans are the only two-legged species on the planet that has this same type of kinetic energy storage system. Cross-body co-

FIGURE 2.6   Fascia.

contractions of elastic myofascial structures also account for why a professional MLB pitcher can throw a fastball at 100 miles per hour (161 km) when a chimpanzee can't even throw a rock through a window. Another important aspect of the fascia system is that we humans are born with our entire fascia system intact (just like our nervous system). It surrounds, supports, and connects every other organ, muscle, and cell in the body to enable a flexible combination of stability and movement in a constantly variable world. If you could magically extract your fascia system in all of its fluid- and collagen-filled glory, it would look something like the inside of a grapefruit after all the pulp and juice were sucked out, leaving just the internal mesh.

MYOFASCIAL SLINGS

The body's interconnected muscle and fascia network (myofascial system) creates whole-body chains of force transfer known as slings. Two of the most important for creating speed are the anterior oblique sling and the posterior oblique sling (see figure 2.7a and b), which work together with the longitudinal slings to compress and stabilize the sacroiliac joints to create force closure in the pelvic girdle. The pelvis consists of the sacrum and the iliac bones (ileum), which are held together by a deep collection of very strong ligaments via the sacroiliac (SI) joints. The SI joints serve as shock absorbers between the lower limbs and spine and provide proprioceptive feedback for coordinating movements between the trunk and legs.

The anterior oblique sling includes the pectorals, the external and internal obliques, and the transverse abdominis. When these muscles contract, they create core stability by tightening the abdomen and compressing the pelvic girdle, especially in the front.

The posterior oblique sling includes the latissimus dorsi, the contralateral gluteus maximus, and the biceps femoris. This sling provides stability through contraction of the lats and glutes by applying tension to the powerful ligaments of the SI joint, which increases compression.

"If there's not an intimately balanced relationship between the anterior and posterior slings, you're going to have severe dysfunction in the musculoskeletal system," says Evan Chait, physical therapist, acupuncturist, and creator of the Chait neuropathic release technique (CNRT). "In the anterior sling, the right external oblique on the right side works with the left internal oblique and adductors to create force closure at the pubic symphysis. When both sides contract at the same time, the pelvis rotates posteriorly. But when you're running in a single-leg stance, if you don't have the ability to counterrotate your thoracic spine with the abdominal wall, your pelvis can't lock down very well. This can cause common injuries such as adductor pulls, hamstring injuries, or hip flexor strains. Those are all very common injuries when the anterior oblique subsystem is not working as well as it should.

"What's interesting is that similar injuries occur with the posterior oblique subsystem, but they're prone to being back issues. With the posterior oblique subsystem, when the latissimus dorsi on the right side and the gluteus maximus on the opposite

As Thomas Myers, creator of Anatomy Trains, which is the mapping of the body's interconnected lines of myofascial force transmission, says: "We are accustomed to identifying individual structures within the fascial web—like the plantar fascia, the Achilles tendon, the iliotibial band, the thoracolumbar aponeurosis, and so on—but these are all just labels for zip codes within the singular fascial web. It's the same as thinking about the Atlantic ocean, the Pacific ocean, and the Mediterranean sea as being separate just because they have different names. There is really only one interconnected body of water in the world. Fascia is the same."

This is an important concept to understand because we've long been conditioned to identify individual anatomical structures by saying things like, "Oh,

side both contract, they create force closure at the SI joint. When someone has a discrepancy or dysfunction in their posterior oblique subsystem, the joints themselves actually become compressed. So the QL (quadratus lumborum) will go into overactivity. This creates increased muscle tone in the QL that results in muscle compensation. For example, the hamstring will often compensate for inhibited glutes or an inhibited lat. So, if you're an athlete who wants to create force production and these muscles are not working well, the system will become dysfunctional."

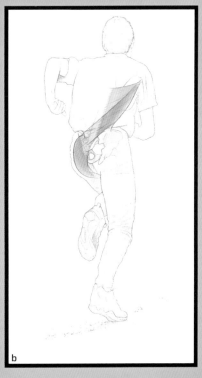

FIGURE 2.7   Myofascial slings: *(a)* anterior oblique sling and *(b)* posterior oblique sling.

you tore your biceps," forgetting that the word *biceps* is a scientific construct. The truth is that anatomical categorization of individual body parts creates a false impression of mechanical separation. Another important thing to keep in mind is that the collagen-based matrix of the fascia system constantly remodels itself three-dimensionally along the lines of load, impact, pressure, and stress by using mechanotransduction (Davis's law). This means that you develop and shape it throughout your entire life based on your unique movement patterns, injury history, and diet. As a result, no two fascia systems are alike. Recent studies also show that fascia tissue has approximately six to eight times more nerve endings than muscle tissue, making it a full-body sensory organ involved in proprioception (Schleip 2017). And we're just scratching the surface (all puns intended).

The best way to conceptualize the fascia system is to think of it as a tensegrity model. Tensegrity (tension + integrity), an architectural model Buckminster Fuller developed, creates flexible yet stable structures using a finely tuned balance between tension and compression. In this model, solid struts are suspended without touching each other, floating in a state of equalized tension that is created by a network of pretensioned cables or bands. Dr. Stephen Levin later expanded upon the concept and applied it to biological systems, coining the term *biotensegrity*. In biotensegrity, bones function as the struts of a tensegrity system by constantly pushing out, while the muscles and connective tissues provide a center-seeking pulling force. We're taught to think of our bodies as machines, but, in reality, our bones never really touch, and the body is a biologically adaptive organism, free of levers, that constantly adjusts to varying vectors of force by distributing it across the entire system. Biotensegrity has since become the foundation for a wide range of physical therapies, including yoga and Rolfing, as well as mechanical soft-tissue manipulations such as foam rolling and active release technique (ART). The body is designed to spread forces across this system through each joint and tissue in the body. The more effectively it can do that, the more power you can harness and the less prone to injury you will be. This giddyap comes with a hitch, though: It takes longer to develop and model fascia tissue with movement than it does to increase muscle size. This often leads to common connective tissue injuries (tendon, ligament, ACL, etc.) due to an imbalance between the different systems, frequently from improper training or overuse.

The Diaphragm

What's often overlooked with the anterior and posterior subsystems is their integral relationship with the diaphragm. The diaphragm is extremely important for cardiovascular and metabolic function. Improving your respiration efficiency is one of the best ways to improve your lactate threshold. But all of this relies heavily on the functionality of your diaphragm (see figure 2.8).

"In neurology, we don't call a muscle weak or strong, we call it facilitated or inhibited," says Chait. "For example, when you do a biceps curl, the biceps is facilitated, and it automatically causes an antagonistic relaxation response, called reciprocal inhibition, to the triceps. The same thing happens in the diaphragm.

With athletes who do a lot of aerobic endurance work or even a lot of CrossFit enthusiasts who do high-intensity interval training, the diaphragm is always facilitated. It's always working. When that happens, the TVA (transverse abdominis) becomes inhibited. Well, if the TVA is not working properly or is inhibited, it can't produce force. Also, when the TVA is not functioning well, the lat will typically become inhibited and so will the glute. Because the thoracolumbar fascia doesn't have enough tension on it. And that tension is what provides hydraulic lift in the lumbar spine and allows the lat and glute to communicate. So we get these athletes who have chronic hamstring issues, and they're going in to get acupuncture or ART to their hamstring when it's not the hamstring at all, it's their diaphragm.

"The diaphragm also has a pair of ligaments, called the crura ligaments, that run from T6 down to T12. Whenever we're running or walking, we need to have counterrotation at around the T7, T8, T9 area of the thoracic spine. For example, if my right leg is forward, my pelvis will rotate left while my torso rotates right. This counterrotation is what loads both the anterior and posterior subsystems. But if the diaphragm is facilitated or tight, we can't get proper counterrotation to occur in the thoracic spine. So then the lat becomes neurologically dysfunctional, the glute becomes dysfunctional, the internal and external obliques become dysfunctional, and so does the adductor. This leads to a disarticulation at both the pubic symphysis and the SI joint.

"That's why I really focus on getting the diaphragm working better. Because the diaphragm plays a huge instrument role. If you can get the diaphragm working better, then the pelvis sits in a better position and so does the cervical spine, and that helps improve your lactate threshold. But if your diaphragm is overworking or facilitated, it switches to being a postural stabilizing muscle instead of a true respiratory muscle, and you end up taking very, very shallow breaths. This means that you're breathing from the apex of your lungs, and you can't produce as much anaerobic threshold as you'd like."

According to Chait, there are three common factors that can often disrupt the diaphragm: how you eat, how you move, and how you think.

"If you're eating foods that are inflammatory to your gut, the diaphragm becomes facilitated. If you're moving in a way that's not based on your genetic requirements, the diaphragm becomes facilitated. And if you're thinking negative thoughts or consistently thinking bad thoughts about yourself or other people, the diaphragm will become facilitated," says Chait.

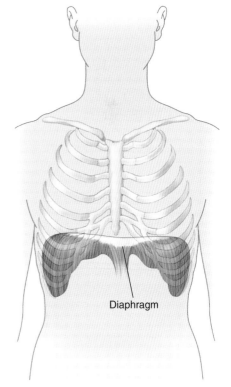

Diaphragm

FIGURE 2.8   Diaphragm.

Our bodies are so good at compensating for imbalances, the challenge becomes diagnosing when and where a dysfunction is occurring. Since Evan has helped thousands of athletes and nonathletes alike identify and solve these problems over the past 20-plus years of practicing physical therapy, I asked him how he diagnoses dysfunctions of the diaphragm.

"I love that question. There are actually a few different ways for us to assess it. One way is to do a muscle test to find a muscle that's weak. Nine times out of 10, the QL (quadratus lumborum) in the lower back is weak on both sides for most people. In the thousands of people I've tested, the QL is the most sensitive muscle to becoming inhibited. It's a pelvic and lumbar stabilizer that runs from the iliac crest up to the 12th 'floating' rib that also attaches to all of the lumbar vertebrae from L1 to L5. The sympathetic chain ganglia lie on top of it. The sympathetic chain ganglia are responsible for the body's adrenaline response. If an athlete has overtrained, they're going to be in a chronic state of fight or flight, and they will experience an inability to recover. So we can test the QL to know if somebody is fatigued or not. If the QL is inhibited or weak, chances are that the diaphragm has also become facilitated. So that's one way. If I muscle test the QL and it's weak, I'll have that person take a deep breath, hold it, and bear down. If the muscle gets stronger, it's the diaphragm that's causing the QL to become weak. Another way to do this is to muscle-test the gluteus maximus to see if the glutes are weak. In that case, you're testing the posterior oblique subsystem. If the glutes go weak, you have them take a deep breath and hold it. If the glutes become strong, it's a diaphragm problem. Those are some simple ways. You can also do the same thing with the lat, the obliques, and the adductors. If an athlete has pain when they squat, lunge, or do a single-leg squat, you can have them do a regular squat, take a deep breath, and bear down. If the pain gets better, it's a diaphragm problem, not a knee problem or a hip problem.

"A simple way to reset the diaphragm is with a cough. Just coughing actually causes a therapeutic reset of the diaphragm and its relationship to the anterior and posterior sling. This is because the diaphragm is opposed by the TVA and TS (triangularis sterni) muscles, which are both active on forced exhalation. When you cough, the diaphragm turns into this bridge that enables the respiratory diaphragm in the abdominal wall to communicate with the diaphragm in the pelvic floor. That relationship is intimately connected to the posterior oblique subsystem, the anterior oblique subsystem, the lateral subsystems, and everything above that, including the rib cage and the cervical spine. All of them are dependent on pelvic position. This means that conditioning the oblique subsystems is crucial to reducing pain and improving performance."

Lymphatic System

Postexercise recovery is also one of the most important and overlooked components to safely improving speed and injury resilience. The lymphatic system factors into this equation because it serves the function of removing waste from the body and maintaining fluid balance in the tissues and organs. Lymph fluid—

which is a form of blood plasma—collects waste from cells and transports it to the circulatory system via a network of lymph nodes and vessels. A blocked or restricted flow of lymph fluid leads to a buildup of waste and toxins that slow training recovery and contribute to tissue inflammation and disease. The lymphatic system is similar to the blood circulatory system in that it consists of an extensive network of vessels that traverse almost all of your tissues (see figure 2.9). But, unlike the circulatory system, lymph has no propulsion pump of its own. Lymphatic fluid moves through the vessels when we contract skeletal muscles or when we breathe. Manual manipulation, vibration therapies, cupping, hot–cold contrast bathing, gua sha (Graston), and other techniques can facilitate improved lymph flow to expedite the elimination of cellular waste and speed up recovery.

Overtraining is one of the main reasons the lymphatic system gets disrupted in many athletes. If an athlete is overtrained and not recovering as well as they should, there will be a cumulative injury response. This is because the body responds to any kind of injury—whether it's a muscle tear, a ligamentous injury, or a cartilage injury—with increased blood flow that brings white blood cells to the damaged area to clean everything up. For example, if you tweak your knee, it will swell up, and the fluid that flows back up to your heart will be constricted. This makes it difficult for the lymphatic system to drain.

"If an athlete has swelling anywhere in the body," says Chait, "it prompts a neurological phenomenon called arthrokinematic inhibition. *Arthro* means 'joint'

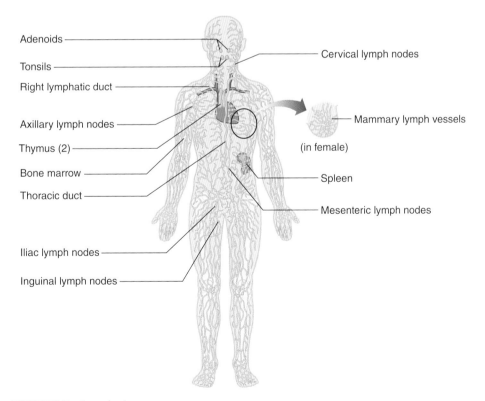

FIGURE 2.9 Lymphatic system.

and *kinematic* means 'movement.' Joint malalignment causes an inhibition to the muscles that surround that joint. For example, if you experience a mild MCL (medial collateral ligament) sprain in your knee, the muscles surrounding that joint will become inhibited. This means they won't fire as well as they should. If you compound that over time, and the MCL heals but the muscles remain inhibited because they were never reprogrammed not to be, then that athlete will be more prone to long-term injury or reinjuring themselves again. Also, acute injuries need to be treated completely differently than chronic injuries. If somebody has had pain for longer than four weeks, that's considered a chronic injury. If an athlete twists their ankle, gets a concussion, or has a low-back injury and they experience pain for longer than four weeks, their treatment has to change. What I found clinically is that the faster you get somebody the proper type of treatment, the faster they get better and the better the long-term results are. And the sooner you get the lymphatics cleaned, the faster the result is. Interestingly, when the lymph system drains, the right arm drains into the right thoracic duct while both legs and the left arm all drain into the left thoracic duct. I don't know why we have three extremities that drain into one thoracic duct in the chest cavity versus one in the right arm, but it's interesting to think about it. Because it means you could have an ankle sprain in your left ankle, and it would impact the lymphatic drainage of the left arm and the right leg. "

When it comes to improving speed (as opposed to injury recovery), the goal is to find a balance between punching the gas really hard during training bouts to improve your lactate threshold and using fast-track recovery techniques such as contrast baths, compression, cupping, and other modalities to accelerate lymphatic drainage and fluid flow.

"Acupuncture is extremely effective for the lymphatic system and improving circulation," says Chait, "because it dilates the blood vessels and allows new lymphatics to come in. Same thing with cupping. Cupping is a great way to drain lymphatics. Another way to move lymph is just doing trampoline work. It's low impact and low volume, which is great for improving recoverability."

The take-home point here is that rest, recovery, and diet are all critical to tuning the symphony for high-performance speed. I find this concept is often overlooked and underappreciated in our industry. But the reality is that if you want to help an athlete realize their maximum potential while minimizing their injury risk, then rest, recovery, and diet are just as important as training. You want to avoid overuse syndrome and give tissues time to rebuild. For a coach or trainer, this means the first step in tuning the symphony is to listen to it. Ask your athletes how they feel, if they're experiencing pain, if they're fatigued or tired, if they feel stressed out or sluggish. Watch how they move and respond to external cues. If you detect a problem or issue, those symphonic inhibitors have to be recognized and addressed before any real training work can be done. This is where the art of coaching and science intersect. Because, no matter how great of a conductor you are, you can't make great music if the instruments are out of tune.

3

PRE–WARM-UP FOR INJURY PREVENTION

A warm-up routine that is well structured is essential to maximizing performance and minimizing injury risk. Just like barbeques and baking ovens, if you want to achieve optimal results in training or competition, you can't skip the warm-up. Despite the scientifically backed wisdom of this fact, many coaches and athletes fail to give their warm-up routine the level of focus and structure it deserves. Sometimes they rush through it, or they'll just do some passive stretching and a light jog and call it good. Unfortunately, *good* is the enemy of *great*. If your activity involves any form of speed, then skipping a systematic warm-up specific to that activity is an invitation for injury. Speed is a manifestation of human movement at the highest levels, and the fast-changing variables, vectors, and forces your body experiences are not small. In fact, warming up is so important that you should do a pre–warm-up routine that prepares your body for movement even before you do your movement-specific warm-up for the day. That's right—you need to do a warm-up for your warm-up. I can hear you on the other side of the page right now thinking, "I don't have time for two warm-ups!" The good news is that you can complete an easy, highly effective pre–warm-up sequence in as little as 10 minutes and then roll it into the active dynamic warm-up (ADW)—general and speed specific—which I cover in the next chapter. To perform at top capacity and avoid injury, it's worth your time to show up a little early for training or competition and prime your body's systems for action. The enhanced performance and injury-resilience benefits of those few minutes of pre–warm-up before the day's efforts will be returned in dividends. Honestly, the term *pre–warm-up* doesn't do it justice. What you're actually doing from a biological standpoint is engineering a physiological process that primes your body's tissues to maximize their behaviors before you challenge them with activity. In this chapter, I discuss the important elements of a pre–warm-up routine and why they matter.

Soft-Tissue Prep

The first step of any pre–warm-up routine is to passively raise your core temperature and warm your body's tissues—both generally and locally. General whole-body warming can be accomplished in a number of ways, including sitting in a sauna or pedaling a stationary bike for five minutes. The main goal is to warm up the tissues and move fluids around the body.

"There is strong evidence showing that when you heat up the extracellular matrix, it behaves differently," says Michol Dalcourt, founder of the Institute of Motion and developer of the ViPR PRO loaded-movement training tool. "You're not changing the constitution of the ECM, but you're changing how it behaves. Studies show that when water binds to sugar receptors in fascia tissue, that tissue becomes more dynamic and injury resilient. So you're preparing the tissue to behave with more elasticity and with more shape stability. It's like cinching up your internal wetsuit so that it hugs you tighter, but it's still very elastic and provides for dynamic motion.

"When you watch an athlete who moves well, they've got dynamism but they're not floppy. Whether you're a competitive athlete or just training in the gym, you want your fascia tissues to have a stabilizing quality, and you want a dynamism in those tissues that allows for better athleticism and improved injury prevention. When your tissues are prepared, you get a more effective performance outcome, whatever that performance is," says Dalcourt.

After spending a few minutes warming up the whole body, Dalcourt advocates warming local tissues using a technique called the rub-and-scrub.

"The rub-and-scrub is exactly what it sounds like," says Dalcourt. "You make a fist and then take the front side of that fist—the digits that are bent in front—and use it like a scouring pad to rub around key areas and joints. What you're going to feel in the digits on the palm side of your hand is heat. So you would rub around the soft-tissue aspects of your knee and warm them up. Then you would move on to the foot and ankle, going around the medial and lateral malleolus, the arch of the foot, and then the top part of the foot. The point is to heat up those local areas so they can physiologically move better. This is one of the steps for engineering your pre–warm-up so that your tissues can rev up slowly and be ready to go by the end of it."

Fluid Dynamics

Once your body's tissues are warm, the next step is to spend a few minutes improving their fluid dynamics. This is where using tools can be highly beneficial. These tools accelerate the movement of fluid, including water, blood, and lymph, through the body.

Foam Rolling

Foam rolling, in particular, has been the subject of a tremendous amount of hype, misinformation, and debate about its efficacy as a training tool. Although foam rolling is useful for facilitating fluid movement and self-myofascial release (SMR), its long-term benefits are relatively limited and hard to scientifically validate. Foam rolling certainly has a place in a well-rounded pre–warm-up routine, but that place takes a very short period of time. Foam rolling is great for enabling fluid movement and doing SMR on larger areas such as the back or hip complex, as shown in figure 3.1, but the amount of time dedicated to it should be relatively short—a couple of minutes is plenty. Studies (Pearcey et al. 2015) indicate that foam rolling is most effective as a postexercise recovery tool for improving fluid flow to restricted tissues and reducing delayed onset muscle soreness (DOMS).

FIGURE 3.1   Foam rolling improves fluid flow through changes in osmotic pressure. Rolling large structures, such as the hip complex, helps warm the tissues and increase the flow of blood, lymph, and water in the extracellular matrix (ECM).

Vibration Guns and Plates

The same is true for vibration guns and plates, which are less common than foam rollers but use optimal vibration frequencies for targeted SMR and improved fluid flow. It feels good to use these tools because they stimulate tissues that are rich with proprioceptive nerve endings, but a couple of minutes is plenty to get the desired results. That said, spending a few minutes of your pre–warm-up using vibration and pressure tools to facilitate fluid movement can enhance tissue behaviors in ways that prepare you for high-level activities.

Self-Myofascial Release

Working through a progressive sequence from general to specific, the next step of fluid dynamics optimization is to spend a few minutes doing some self-myofascial release (self-massage). The basic idea is to find tight spots, adhesions, and trigger points in your body and apply gentle, sustained pressure to those areas. Again, while SMR can increase the range of motion in joints, research indicates that the benefits are short-lived (Cheatham et al. 2015).

"If you have a trigger point, that's because it's an area of high neurological activity," says Dalcourt. "You can temporarily alleviate that sensitivity using self-myofascial release through what's called autogenic inhibition. But it's more of a nerve thing. When you put low-grade pressure on a trigger point, it reflexively acts through the muscle spindles and proprioceptors. Basically, it uses the sensory motor pathways to tell the nervous system to turn the muscle off. The problem with this is that if there is a threat—which is to say an instability in your body—your nervous system is not going to want to release the muscle even though it has a trigger point because releasing the muscle creates more instability. So it's going to keep the muscle tight as a safety mechanism. It doesn't matter how much you release it or add flexibility or try to roll things out; your nervous system is going to keep things tight. A good analogy is to try walking on ice. No matter how much you want to relax, your body's nervous system is going to say: 'Forget it. We're unstable. We're going to keep everything tight because you're on a frictionless surface and we don't want to fall.' What you want to do is address the underlying instability, and you do that through small motor unit recruitment."

The process for SMR is to take a lacrosse ball, tennis ball, foam roller, or other similar tool and roll it around, finding the tender spots in your torso, legs, or feet, as shown in figure 3.2. When you locate a trigger point, apply sustained pressure to the area until the pain or tenderness subsides by about 75 percent. Then work on that spot for about 30 to 60 seconds while breathing deeply, using your diaphragm. This part of your pre–warm-up routine should take less than five minutes and target one to three muscle groups. While SMR has been shown to increase range of motion in joints for short periods of time, as Michol pointed out, releasing those trigger points over the long term and restoring optimal mobility ultimately comes down to balancing the system. This starts with working on recruitment of small motor units.

FIGURE 3.2 Self-myofascial release (SMR) can be done using a lacrosse ball, tennis ball, foam roller, a vibration tool, or even just your hands.

Recruitment of Small Motor Units

The goal of recruiting small motor units is to activate type I muscle fibers because they are faster than type II muscle fibers at reaching their threshold of activation in anticipation of movement. Type I comprises smaller, tonic-based muscles (as opposed to phasic-based muscles) that are typically close to the joints and generally slow to fatigue. Their job is to help stabilize and guide joints. They also play a significant role in the core stabilization required for speed.

Core, Lat, and Glute Activation

Dr. Stuart McGill, author of *Back Mechanic* and *Ultimate Back Fitness and Performance*, is recognized as one of the world's leading spinal experts. He developed a method called the McGill Big 3, a series of isometric exercises that safely activates, strengthens, and prepares the core and lats for athletic activity. It is one of the most research-validated approaches to activating and strengthening the core and lats. Dr. McGill advocates holding each isometric position for 8 to 10 seconds in a descending pyramid of reps to improve core stability without overly fatiguing the body (e.g., six reps, then four reps, then two reps). The three exercises are the curl-up, side plank, and bird dog.

FORCED INHALATION AND EXHALATION

A powerful technique for improving small motor unit recruitment during isometric exercises like the McGill Big 3 is to incorporate forced inhalation and exhalation into the exercise. Forced diaphragmatic breathing helps activate tonic (postural) muscles like the intercostal muscles between the ribs and the transversospinales that run along the spine (see figure 3.3). These type I muscles are slow to fatigue and important for stabilization. One of the challenges of getting athletes to fire these deep tonic muscles is that they are not as obvious as phasic muscles like the glutes or lats. If you tell an athlete to fire their glutes, they intuitively know what to do. But if you tell them to fire their multifidus muscles—which are thin, fascia-rich tonic muscles located on either side of the spinous processes of the vertebrae—they will look at you with great confusion. The good news is that muscles are task driven. Telling the athlete to incorporate forced breathing into their pre–warm-up exercises gives them a task that will activate these deep core muscles for improved core stability without the athlete needing to know their scientific names.

To incorporate forced exhalation into the McGill Big 3 (and other pre–warm-up exercises), breathe in deeply through your nose and fill your lungs with air as you extend into the isometric hold. Then exhale with control using your diaphragm as you hold the position and push all of the air back out of your lungs. When your lungs are completely empty, keep exhaling forcefully, as if you're trying to blow out five more candles on a birthday cake. Continue forced exhaling as long as comfortably possible. Then inhale again as you return to the starting position. When done correctly, you will feel the deep tonic muscles along your spine, neck, and ribcage activate.

Forced inhalation is slightly more challenging but is essentially the opposite action. Exhale the air from your lungs before you start the isometric hold. As you extend into the hold position, inhale through your nose as deeply as you can and hold the breath as long as comfortably possible. Forced diaphragmatic breathing helps activate the deep core muscles in an athlete's body for more efficient muscle recruitment, better stabilization, and increased injury resilience.

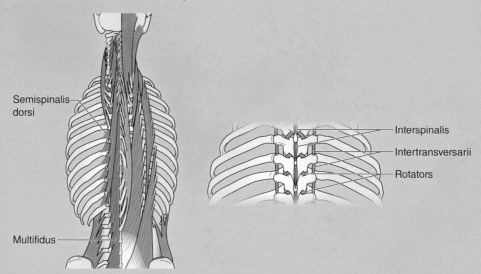

Semispinalis dorsi

Interspinalis

Intertransversarii

Rotators

Multifidus

FIGURE 3.3 The transversospinales muscles of the back are type I tonic muscles that maintain posture and spine stability. They are also involved in rotation and extension of the spinal column.

Activated and balanced glutes are important for speed because if the hip complex is not stabilized, your running stride will be uneven. This imbalance leads to reduced speed and an increased risk of injury. In fact, most foot, ankle, and knee problems actually originate from a dysfunction in the hips. Injuries such as runner's knee and Achilles tendinopathy usually result from a lack of pelvic control in the frontal plane due to weak or inhibited glutes—particularly the gluteus medius, the muscle located on the outer edge of the buttocks.

While the more well-known gluteus maximus, the largest muscle in your body, is responsible for extending the hip and assisting with abduction and outward leg rotation, the other gluteal muscles are just as important for speed. If they're weak or imbalanced, other muscles overcompensate, and this is where lower-leg injuries begin to manifest. The gluteus medius is the primary abductor muscle responsible for external rotation of the hip, while the gluteus minimus helps with abduction and medial rotation of the hip and thigh. See figure 3.4 for musculature of the gluteus maximus, gluteus medius, and gluteus minimus.

In addition to the McGill Big 3, the clamshell is one of the best warm-up exercises for activating your glutes and improving the balance between your pelvic floor and thighs (Selkowitz, Beneck, and Powers 2013). I'll be the first one to admit that it both looks and sounds a little goofy, but if you want to move fast on multiple planes with lower injury risk, the clamshell should be a consistent part of your pre–warm-up routine. You can do a number of variations and progressions with the clamshell to help improve core strength and stability, such as using a resistance band, which further challenges the glutes and hamstrings.

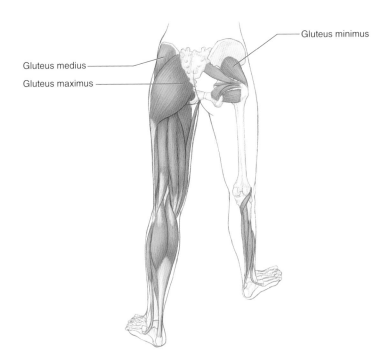

FIGURE 3.4 Glute muscles: gluteus maximus, gluteus medius, and gluteus minimus.

CURL-UP

1. Lie on your back with one leg straight and the other knee bent. Place your hands under your lower back to help your spine remain in a neutral, slightly arched position (see figure a).

2. Brace your core as if someone is about to punch you in the stomach. Lift your shoulders off the ground as if someone is sliding a piece of paper under them. Keep your head and neck in a neutral position, as if you are holding an apple in place under your chin. Allow only your head to come a few inches off the ground and hold the position without moving your lower back (see figure b). Avoid raising your head and shoulders to the point that your lower back starts to curve (like a normal crunch), which transfers excessive forces to the spine and is counterproductive.

3. Hold the position for approximately 6 to 10 seconds and return to the resting position. Perform 3 to 6 reps and rest for 1 to 2 seconds between each rep.

4. To increase difficulty by decreasing stability, raise your elbows off the ground before lifting your head off the ground. Dr. McGill recommends increasing the number of reps rather than the duration of the holds as the exercise becomes easier. This allows you to increase endurance without cramping.

SIDE PLANK

1. Lie on your side with your legs bent and your top leg forward in front of your bottom leg. Support your upper body with your elbow. Place your free hand on the opposite shoulder (see figure *a*).

2. Raise and extend your hips and support your body weight using only your feet and arm (see figure *b*). Be sure the hips are forward and in one straight line.

3. Hold this position for 6 to 10 seconds and return to the resting position.

4. Repeat 3 to 6 reps an equal number of times on each side. The side plank activates the lateral oblique and quadratus lumborum (QL) muscles on the challenged bottom side and activates the stabilizing muscles of the hip complex.

BIRD DOG

1. Assume a quadruped dog position on all fours with your back in neutral alignment (see figure *a*).

2. Kick one leg straight back while raising the opposite-side arm until both extremities are fully extended (see figure *b*). Do not allow your back to move. You can increase muscle activation in the core by contracting the muscles in your arm and clenching the extended arm into a fist.

3. Hold this position for 6 to 10 seconds and return to the flexed position in a flowing type of action for a second or two, and then extend back into the extended position.

4. Repeat 3 to 6 reps an equal number of times on each side. The key is to maintain a stiff core throughout the entire movement while hinging at both the hips and shoulder joints.

CLAMSHELL

1. Lie on your side with your legs stacked and your knees bent. Your heels, hips, and shoulders should form a straight line. Rest your head on your lower arm and use your top arm to steady your torso (see figure *a*).

2. Keep your feet together as you raise your top knee and open your legs like a clamshell—hinging at the hip (see figure *b*). Be sure your hip bones are stacked on top of one another (the top hip wants to roll backward, but don't let it).

3. Focus on squeezing your glute muscles and engaging the small motor units to increase recruitment. Hold the position at the top for 4 to 6 seconds and return to the resting position.

4. Target a rep scheme of around 15 to 20 reps on each side.

RESISTANCE BAND CLAMSHELL

1. Lie on your side with your legs stacked and your knees bent. Place a resistance band around both legs, just above the knees (see figure *a*). Your heels, hips, and shoulders should form a straight line. Rest your head on your lower arm and use your top arm to steady your torso.

2. Keep your feet together as you raise your top knee without moving your hips or pelvis (see figure *b*). Contract your abdominal muscles to activate the core and spine.

3. Hold the position at the top for 4 to 6 seconds and return to the resting position.

4. Perform 1 to 2 continuous sets of 15 reps on each side with 2 to 3 seconds of rest between each set.

Assessment Exercises

Going through a pre–warm-up routine before the workout is like prepping the engines and controls of an airplane prior to takeoff. You want to go through a series of physiological and neurological exercises like a pilot going through a pre-flight checklist and making sure all of the computers, electronics, and engines are warmed up and operating smoothly. Our checklist of movements and exercises is done in a way that allows you to see if everything is moving freely through the full range of motion and to find where the limitations are on a day-to-day basis. In addition to ramping up the systems progressively until they are operating at full intensity, this sequence allows you to assess an athlete's range of motion and movement capability so you can identify issues that need to be addressed before advancing into the day's workout routine. Often an athlete will have tissue or joint restrictions that can be improved with some foam rolling or mechanical manipulation that helps release possible trigger points. A well-structured pre–warm-up routine can melt tightness away just by warming up tissues and pumping fluid through them, because many of these movement limitations come from a tightness within the connective tissue of the fluid-filled fascia system. It can also be a case of certain muscle groups not turning on or off. For example, as discussed in chapter 2, a diaphragm that is "turned on" all the time (i.e., hyperactive) and functioning as a structural muscle instead of a respiratory muscle will inhibit activation of the glutes and erectors and compromise your ability to achieve maximum hip activation and stability. This is why we end the pre–warm-up with a squat progression; it serves not only as an easy warm-up drill for the whole body but also an assessment tool that helps a coach or trainer identify imbalances and movement restrictions. If issues are identified, go back to doing some foam rolling or self-myofascial release techniques to address those restrictions. Then use ground-based activation drills for the small motor units to target imbalanced areas—the glutes, core, hips, feet, and so on.

POWER SQUAT

1. Start with your hands behind your head, a strong neutral spine position, and feet about shoulder-width apart with the toes in line with the knees (see figure *a*).

2. Hinge at the hips and lower your torso, maintaining a neutral spine while keeping your hands behind your head. Do not allow the spine to round (see figure *b*). Be sure to keep your knees over or behind your toes.

3. Focus on squeezing your glute muscles and engaging the small motor units to increase recruitment.

4. Hold the bottom squat position for 1 to 2 seconds and perform 8 to 12 reps.

RESISTANCE BAND OVERHEAD SQUAT

MODERATE

1. Start with your hands overhead at arm's length stretching an elastic band (you can also use a PVC pipe, dowel, or whatever is on hand), a strong neutral spine position, and feet about shoulder-width apart with the toes in line with the knees (see figure *a*).

2. Hinge at the hips and lower your torso, maintaining a neutral spine while keeping your hands behind your head. Do not allow the spine to round (see figure *b*).

3. Focus on pulling the band apart isometrically while squeezing your glute muscles and engaging the small motor units to increase recruitment.

4. Hold the bottom squat position for 1 to 3 seconds and return to the starting position. Repeat for 8 to 12 reps.

Performing hip stretches like the prone hurdler as part of your pre–warm-up routine helps activate the hips and increase range of motion and flexibility. It is also a good opportunity to identify potential restrictions or problem areas before moving on to an ADW.

MODERATE

LYING PRONE HURDLER

1. Start lying face down on your stomach with your legs straight and your arms outstretched at your sides in a T position (see figure *a*).

2. Keep your chest flat to the ground and bend one leg as you pull the knee up toward your elbow without overrotating your hips or letting your knee touch the ground (see figure *b*).

3. Return to the starting position without letting any part of the moving leg touch the ground.

4. Repeat on the opposite side.

5. Perform 1 to 2 sets of 8 to 12 reps on each side.

As a gentle yet important reminder, your pre–warm-up routine should take about 10 minutes. It's worth the small investment of time and focus if you want to achieve maximum speed with reduced injury risk. The point is to engineer a physiological process that maximizes your body's tissue behaviors and allows you to rev your systems up slowly so they're ready to go by the end of it. Once you've completed a pre–warm-up routine, move into a general ADW routine that then rolls into a speed-specific ADW that is targeted for the day's training activities. These principles are covered in the next chapter.

4

SESSION-BASED ACTIVE DYNAMIC WARM-UP

Three major phases comprise a complete warm-up: first, a pre–warm-up (covered in the previous chapter); second, a general active dynamic warm-up; and third, a speed-specific active dynamic warm-up that includes exercises targeted at the day's training objective. This chapter focuses on these last two phases.

When you add these three phases together, the complete warm-up will run about 20 to 30 minutes, and as I mentioned previously, I recognize that the thought of spending 20 minutes at minimum on a warm-up might dissuade some coaches who feel like they don't have that much time. But for an athlete who really wants to achieve optimal performance, the reality is that they need to find the time. They need to get to practice early if that's what it takes. When structured correctly, the warm-up is the catalyst for a successful workout. The concept of active dynamic warm-up (ADW) is not new to most trainers and athletes, but it was when the Parisi Speed School began pioneering the approach more than 35 years ago. Back then, doing static stretches with prolonged holds was the norm for most athletes in every sport, and the concept of an ADW was revolutionary. Modern research is finally explaining why ADW is superior to static stretching and how too much static stretching at the wrong time can actually make you slower, less explosive, and more prone to injury. But when I first started promoting ADW as a training practice, I just knew that it worked because of the results I was seeing and the way it made my body feel.

I was originally exposed to the concept of an active dynamic warm-up during my college years in 1985 under coach Tony Naclerio and again while training in Finland with some of the best javelin coaches and throwers in the world. As a stocky, five-foot-nine Italian trying to throw a javelin 240-plus feet (73 m), I needed to get every ounce of power and speed I could out of my body, and the last thing I wanted was to be nonexplosive. After learning ADW techniques from Coach Naclerio and the Finns and seeing firsthand how effective these techniques were at improving my performance as a Division I javelin thrower, I realized they were applicable to *all* sports, and so ADW became one of the foundational elements of the Parisi Speed School.

In fact, Parisi Speed School made the first training videos on ADW techniques in the United States and released them on VHS tapes back in 1998. Those VHS tapes eventually became top-selling DVDs through the National Strength and Conditioning Association (NSCA). In 2000, we started training NFL Combine athletes under an exclusive partnership with Manhattan-based SportStars, one of the biggest athlete representation agencies in the NFL, with more than 100 professional NFL players. Over the course of the next 10 years, we used ADW techniques to help produce numerous first-round draft picks—many of whom overachieved so well at the Combine that they increased their draft value. High-level players from all over the country would travel to New Jersey to train with us and prepare for the NFL Combine. Many of these guys were coming off the season pretty beat up. So, when we got a hold of them, we didn't spend much time doing heavy lifting in the weight room. Instead, we took an extensive look at the condition of each athlete and decided what their inherent body composition was. This assessment of their physical condition helped us to determine what they really needed in order to improve. And, without a doubt, one of the most important things we taught them was our ADW techniques. The key is that every element of our warm-up includes a speed-specific objective and learning progression for which each drill flows into the next part of the routine and is targeted at the movement goal for that day—whether it's acceleration, maximum speed, or multidirectional speed. And as mentioned before, that's why we say, "Our warm-up is your workout"— because our warm-up drills and exercises are foundational and roll directly into the rest of the workout.

ADW Versus Static Stretching

Before getting into outlining the basic menu of drills and exercises for an effective ADW routine, let's take a short detour to look at why traditional static stretching at the wrong time is counterproductive and what the research is telling us. This detour is important because, surprisingly, many people still operate under the misguided assumption that static stretching is highly beneficial. In fact, according to a 2016 study of 605 personal trainers—most of whom had certifications from the NSCA or the American College of Sports Medicine (ACSM)—80 percent still prescribed traditional static stretching to their clients (Waryasz et al. 2016). Now, before you sit down to write me a very thoughtful, well-crafted email about the value of static stretching and the importance of flexibility, let me be clear that I'm not saying that static stretching is bad. It certainly has its place in the world of sports training. The important thing to understand is that an athlete's need for flexibility comes down to the ranges of motion required for their sport. Therefore, we must begin by assessing the individual athlete's ranges of motion to see if they fall into the ranges required for their sport or position. For example, a 100-meter high-hurdler obviously needs more flexibility in their hamstrings and connective tissues than a basketball player. But, at the same time, you don't want to stretch away the strong, tight springs a basketball player needs to excel in their sport. So the first thing to consider is: What kind of athlete are you dealing with, and what are the ranges of motion they need for their respective movements? With that caveat in place, let's consider what the research says.

A study conducted in 2008 on a group of NCAA Division I track athletes comparing static stretching to ADW revealed that static stretching impaired 40-meter sprint performance and slowed athletes down (Winchester et al. 2008). Another study conducted on Division I football players using a vertical jump test showed similar results (Holt and Lambourne 2008). In both studies, the researchers hypothesized that the reduction in performance from static stretching came from reduced stiffness of the body's myofascial system combined with an inhibition of proprioceptive response and a reduced ability to recruit motor units. Conversely, they found that doing an ADW routine enhanced performance for both sprinting speed and vertical jumping.

Essentially, it comes down to the behavior of neuroreceptors such as the muscle spindles and Golgi tendon organs (GTOs) found in the muscle and muscle–tendon junction, respectively. In addition, it is now known that there are up to 8 to 10 times more proprioceptors in the fascia than in muscle. These mechanoreceptors are known as Pacinian corpuscles and Ruffini's corpuscles, among others. The body is an adaptive organism. It has different types of muscle and tendon receptors that are designed to adapt and respond to both the inputs of load, stretch, and stress and the speed—how quickly or slowly—at which these inputs take place. In addition, there are different receptors in the fascia that identify inputs such as vibration, stretch, and pressure and respond to these inputs based on the speed of the inputs. If you're warming up by doing slow, static stretching and holding positions for long periods of time to increase your range of motion, which changes the plasticity of your myofascial tissue, then you're presetting those tissues and the nervous system to respond by contracting slowly. The neuroreceptors responsible for sending signals to those motor units are not only being desensitized in a way that makes them react slowly but also decreasing the activity of the stretch reflex. In fact, the evidence shows that holding a static stretch for a minute or more can temporarily decrease strength and speed for up to an hour. Holding static stretches programs the nervous system to contract muscles slowly because the neuroreceptors responsible for sending signals to those motor units become desensitized to the stretching of the tissues (see figure 2.4 in chapter 2).

Muscle spindles, the sensory receptors in the belly of a muscle, primarily detect changes in the length of that muscle and how fast those changes in length occur. A dynamic known as the alpha-gamma loop, a continuous loop of feedback and response that determines the body's reaction to force and motion, transmits this length-change information back and forth to the central nervous system. Muscle spindle responses to changes in length also play an important role in force production and super stiffness, which is created by the co-contraction of multiple muscles in order to resist muscle stretch. But what about improving flexibility and range of motion? The sit-and-reach test—sitting on the floor with your legs outstretched and seeing how close you can get to touching your toes—is a common way to measure static flexibility. Static stretching—pushing a position to the edge of your range of motion and holding it for 20 to 30 seconds—has been shown to increase static flexibility. But this is very different from the kind of movement-specific range-of-motion flexibility you experience in a dynamic warm-up or on the field in competition. And this is an important difference. The reality is that too much static stretching can weaken the plasticity of connective tissues and increase your chance of injury by making joints too flexible. This is especially true for sprinters and other athletes who need to maintain joint stiffness and stability upon ground contact under tremendous amounts of load. So yes, contrary to the once-popular belief that static stretching helps protect you from injury, in some cases, it can actually make you more susceptible to injury.

This concept wasn't always revolutionary. In fact, doing a dynamic warm-up routine was common back in the 1960s and 1970s; however, people were doing explosive dynamic warm-up movements without first having a raised core temperature and proper blood and fluid flow to the local tissues, and this resulted in people getting injured. That's how static stretching became popular. And this is why it's important to begin with and follow a well-planned, sequential *pre–warm-up* routine that physiologically prepares the tissues for movement. The goal is to raise your core temperature, increase your heart rate and fluid flow, do some self-myofascial release to improve range of motion, and activate the stabilizing small motor units in your core and glutes.

Once the body is warm from your pre–warm-up, you can go through sport-specific ranges of motion that improve mobility in a way that programs the muscle receptors to respond rapidly, as opposed to slowly. But you first want to get the joints, muscles, and fascia tissue lubricated and sliding effortlessly during pre–warm-up. You also want to get the proprioceptors within those systems to contract at the rate you're actually going to contract them during the day's workout or competition. The key is to do this in a progressive fashion using a logical sequence that allows the muscles and joints to ramp up by going through the ranges of motion required for the sport or training goal, depending on whether it's linear speed or multidirectional speed.

Warm-Up Progression: General to Specific

For each speed-specific training category of focus—whether it's a linear-speed day, a multidirectional day, or a strength-training day—we're always going to do a sequence that starts with a pre–warm-up, followed by a general active dynamic warm-up. Then, we do a speed-specific active dynamic warm-up based on the training goal for the day. After these three phases of warm-up, we transition into anchor drills and exercises (loaded motor-learning drills or exercises) followed by application drills and exercises (gamelike drills or exercises at full intensity) targeted at the specific goal (acceleration, max velocity, multidirectional speed, or strength).

This section will serve up a menu of general ADW drills we've developed as part of the Parisi Speed School curriculum that have been demonstrated to be effective for starting any speed-related training day. This chapter includes a basic "starter" menu of ADW drills, but you can use the menus in chapter 12 to find more drills in each category that can be adapted to the needs of your particular sport, program, or athlete. In the subsequent chapters that cover each speed category, I've charted out the specific anchor and application drills to transition into after doing the general ADW drills listed in this chapter.

The underlying premise of the general active dynamic warm-up is to work at submaximal intensity to prepare the tissue and develop fundamental movement skills and muscle memory, allowing you to progressively ramp up to the point where you're moving with a super-high level of efficiency, or movement literacy. Then, as you reach higher levels of intensity with more-specific drills, you progress into anchor drills. This is the transitional point when the warm-up turns into the workout itself. Anchor drills are movement-specific drills that are either loaded or use the body's leverage in a very specific way or are a combination of both. The idea is to put the body in highly targeted, movement-related positions, or use added load, with the goal of programming the motor engrams for that specific movement or skill. Once you get to the anchor drills, the real workout has technically started. Progressing from anchor drills, you then do application drills, such as taking the loaded drills and unloading them in a more realistic, gamelike way. After this, you move directly into the day's speed-specific workout by focusing on which particular needs will improve your performance. When the sequence is done correctly, athletes don't even realize when they have transitioned from the warm-up to the workout routine because each step feels like a natural progression. While there are several ways you can structure an ADW routine to meet your needs, after experimenting with many progressions and athletes, this is the approach I've found to be most successful, especially for speed.

General Active Dynamic Warm-Up

According to Gary Gray, founder of Applied Functional Science (AFS) and CEO of the Gray Institute, one of the fundamental truths of human motion is that the body moves through three-dimensional space using the drivers of ground-reaction force, gravity, and mass momentum. Another truth of AFS is that human movement is a subconscious reaction to a conscious task. This means that we want to do task-driven warm-up drills and exercises with conscious intention. That's why it is highly beneficial to use functional training tools such as medicine balls, bands, kettlebells, and loaded-movement tools. For example, holding the ViPR PRO at odd positions while squatting or lunging provides a task-driven form of resistance and load, activating myofascial trains, or load paths across the entire body on all three planes of motion—the sagittal plane (front to back), the frontal plane (side to side), and the transverse plane (rotational)—not just over a local joint or segment. Another example, such as repeatedly bouncing a medicine ball off a wall or floor, engages multiple anatomical structures with variable loads and vectors that stimulate the fascia system to lay down fibers omnidirectionally for increased shape stability and elasticity while also priming the nervous system and pumping fluid through the appropriate tissue. You can also use simple whole-body movements like jumping jacks that use the functional drivers of ground-reaction forces, gravity, and mass momentum to raise the core temperature, fire up the body's elastic response, and prime the nervous system. The idea is to subject the body to different load paths that engage multiple joints, tissues, and structures in a three-dimensional way. Therefore, you want to start an ADW routine with task-driven drills and exercises that require you to proprioceptively sense timing, tension, and load on all three planes of motion and respond accordingly. In addition to preparing athletes for the day's workout, it will help them develop the balance of stability and mobility needed for optimal speed performance and injury resilience over the long term.

GLUTE SHIFT KNEE LIFT

The glute shift knee lift helps develop odd-position strength by activating whole-body load paths and co-contractions in three dimensions on all three planes, focusing on the hip, leg, and foot structures.

BASIC

1. Start in an athletic stance, holding a ViPR PRO at the midline with an offset grip (see figure *a*).
2. Step back and lunge down (see figure *b*). Drive the ViPR PRO down and away while shifting the hips in the opposite direction.
3. Drive the rear knee up and toward the ViPR PRO while balancing on the other leg (see figure *c*).
4. Repeat an equal number of reps (4 to 6) on each side.

SIDE LUNGE LIFT

The side lunge lift helps develop odd-position strength by activating whole-body load paths and co-contractions in three dimensions on all three planes.

1. Start in an athletic stance, holding a ViPR PRO by the center grips at the midline (see figure a).
2. Step into a side lunge (see figure b).
3. Turn the ViPR PRO vertical and lift it up, extending the opposite-side arm up to full extension while lifting (see figure c).
4. Repeat an equal number of reps (4 to 6) on each side.

JUMPING-JACK PROGRESSION

I really enjoy the fact that when we go to work with a school or team—regardless of whether it's high school, college, or pro—people are shocked when I say that we're going to start out by relearning every aspect of the jumping jack in great detail. They're always like: "Wait a minute . . . did you say we're teaching the jumping jack?" And then I get to explain that the beauty of the jumping jack is that you're always getting better or worse at it—and getting better is all about mastering your ground-reaction forces.

HALF JACK

As an athlete, you really need to understand the importance of the ankle complex and its relationship to ground response. In order to do this, we literally re-educate people on how to do the jumping jack by having athletes start out doing half jacks with their hands on their hips.

Half jacks work on activating the calf complex—along with the ankle joint and Achilles gap—and harnessing the stored elastic energy created at foot contact.

a   b

BASIC

1. Start with your hands on your hips and feet in a spread stance with the foot in a dorsiflexed, toe-up position and your weight on the front part of your foot (see figure *a*). By starting legs apart, athletes can really understand their range of motion and how wide they want their legs to spread.

2. Close and open your legs in a jumping-jack fashion with your hands on your hips and without bending at the knees (see figure *b*).

3. Focus on popping off the ground at each foot contact, using the stored elastic energy in your calf and Achilles tendon. Don't consciously extend at the ankle; rather, allow the up-and-down momentum to facilitate the movement through a slight knee-and-hip flexion and extension.

4. Repeat for 10 to 15 reps.

FULL JACK

The full jack is a whole-body plyometric exercise that activates muscles across multiple structures on the frontal plane (in the torso as well as the ankle and calf complex) and requires rhythmic timing. As a coach, I'll have everyone in the group I'm working with simultaneously fire their arms down from this position when I say the word: "Down!" And everybody's arms will come down in one big, dynamic movement. Usually, this causes a loud clapping sound as everyone's hands hit the sides of their hips simultaneously. It's pretty cool. And then, boom, when another coach watches you do that, and they see their team respond like it's some sort of military exercise, it immediately sets the tone that you are a professional strength and conditioning coach. They often say things like: "Wow! I just learned a bunch of stuff with a drill that's been around for thousands of years, but how it was taught changed everything." That's how you start gaining real credibility with your athletes and other coaches—by using a simple jumping jack and explaining the science behind it.

1. Start with your legs in an open stance and reach both hands overhead as high as you can (see figure *a*). Reach up high to find your range of motion for a full, open jumping-jack position.

2. Jump up and bring your legs together while firing your arms down and slapping your hands down to your side (see figure *b*).

3. Repeat the sequence slowly, reaching high overhead to stretch the lats and then firing your arms down and bringing your feet back together in one powerful motion.

4. Ramp up to doing full jumping jacks with dynamic, elastic movements—popping off the ground dynamically—just like with the half jack.

5. Repeat for 10 to 15 reps.

SEAL JACK

Speed is not just about training your legs. Your arms are also part of the equation (just try sprinting without them). This means you also want to move your arms through their dynamic ranges of motion as part of your warm-up. While jumping jacks provide that on the frontal plane, the seal jack gives you a way to warm up your dynamic range of motion on the transverse plane. It allows you to dynamically stretch the pecs and lats and gets those joints and proprioceptors moving through their ranges of motion in a dynamic fashion that programs them to be fast.

1. Start with your hands extended in front of you with your palms and feet together (see figure *a*).
2. Open your hands widely to the sides as you jump out into a jack stance (see figure *b*).
3. Slap your hands together in front of you like a seal as you bring your feet back to center.
4. Repeat for 10 to 15 reps.

ICE SKATER LUNGE

The ice skater lunge loads tissue paths across multiple vectors on all three planes of motion in a dynamic way that increases elastic recoil and neural engagement.

ADVANCED

1. Start in an athletic stance, holding a ViPR PRO at the midline.
2. Quickly jump from side to side, alternating feet with a rhythm of an ice skater (see figures *a-c*). Swing the ViPR PRO across your body to the drive-side foot with each bound.
3. Repeat an equal number of reps (4 to 6) on each side.

FORWARD OVERHEAD MEDICINE BALL THROW

The forward overhead medicine ball throw activates the core, specifically the rectus abdominis, erector spinae, and lats, in a dynamic fashion not only through flexion of the spine but also extension when catching the ball on the rebound from a wall or a partner returning the throw. The goal is to create a stretch-shortening action in the anterior core muscles and lats that opens up the thoracic spine in a dynamic fashion.

1. Start by standing with one foot forward while holding a medicine ball overhead.
2. Brace the core and pull the ball backward over your head with both hands (see figure *a*).
3. Using the core and lats, engage the ball and pull it forward and then throw to a partner or against the wall (see figures *b* and *c*).
4. Repeat for 10 to 15 reps and then reverse the feet position and repeat.

KNEELING ROTATIONAL MEDICINE BALL THROW

The kneeling rotational medicine ball throw is a loaded movement that dynamically activates the core in the transverse plane and engages the internal and external obliques as well as the transverse abdominis in a rotatory action that creates the stiffness needed to stop momentum. Upon the reversal of the rotatory action, muscles and connective tissues work to decelerate the rotatory action in the opposite direction.

ADVANCED

1. Start by facing parallel to a wall or partner, resting one knee on a pad or soft surface and holding a medicine ball firmly with both hands. Brace your core and rotate 45 degrees to the side that you have your knee on the floor (see figure *a*).
2. Throw the ball at the wall or toward a partner (see figure *b*).
3. Repeat on both sides for 8 to 15 reps each.

OVERHEAD SQUAT MEDICINE BALL THROW

The overhead squat medicine ball throw dynamically activates the erector spinae first by prestretching with the squat hip and knee hinge using the anterior load of the medicine ball followed by a quick reversal of hip and spine extension that is facilitated by the lower back and hips.

1. Start by standing with your feet a little wider than shoulder-width apart and holding a medicine ball with both hands between your legs.
2. Squat down, hinging at the hips and knees while keeping your arms straight (see figure *a*).
3. Explode upward with your legs only and let your arms act as "hooks" holding onto the ball (see figure *b*) and then, once the legs and hip are just about fully extended, pull with your arms to throw the ball upward and backward overhead (see figure *c*).
4. Repeat for 8 to 12 reps.

Speed-Specific Active Dynamic Warm-Up

When it comes to speed training, it's either going to be a linear day or a multi-directional day. This is because you want to maximize the body's specific tissue adaptations for that day. If it's a linear day, you're typically going to focus on either acceleration or maximum velocity. On some days, you might focus on both. It really depends on the deficiencies and needs of the individual athlete.

The takeaway here is that after doing a general ADW, the speed-specific ADW for the day should be targeted at the day's training goal, whether it's a linear-speed day, a multidirectional-speed day, or a strength-training day. So the workout for each day would be based on those needs (linear, multidirectional, or strength)—which I've addressed in their respective chapters. These speed-specific ADW exercises precede the anchor and application drills found in each of the discipline-specific chapters. You can expand on the general and speed-specific ADW exercises (as well as the anchor and application drills) by using the programming menus in chapter 12.

BASIC

FORWARD SKIP

Skipping is one of the most fundamental movement skills all athletes need to practice if increased speed is their goal, but don't be surprised if you start working with a new athlete and they do not know how to skip. Broken down into its simplest form, skipping is basically transitioning from hopping twice on one leg to hopping twice on the opposite leg. The focus on the skip can be one of two areas: the drive phase or the recovery phase. The goal of skipping is to accentuate the sprinting action at the hip and shoulder joints. The primary internal cue I like to give is to extend one hip and drive the foot down as fast as possible while not even thinking about the opposite leg. Allow the hip to flex and raise the knee to about the height of your waistline and strive to let this happen naturally. I describe this action similar to playing with a yo-yo. When you play with a yo-yo, you flick the round disc down with force as fast as possible to create a fast spin. Then, at just the right time, you slightly flick the disc back up and it returns rather quickly. This is the kind of action that should happen at the hip.

1. Start by standing tall with one foot forward and one foot back (see figure *a*).
2. Hop off the front foot onto the same foot (see figure *b*). As the foot lands, immediately drive the opposite foot down toward the ground under the hip as fast as possible. Be sure to keep the ankle in dorsiflexion (toes up) the entire time during this exercise.
3. Be sure to sync up your arms with your legs, keeping the elbows bent at 90 degrees and focusing on striking the same arm and elbow backward, matching the knee that is forward and up (e.g., the right arm and elbow are backward while the right knee is forward and up).
4. Do 2 sets of 10 to 20 yards (9 to 18 m).

STRAIGHT-LEG SHUFFLE BOUND

The straight-leg shuffle bound is designed to activate the hamstrings and generate horizontal and vertical driving force off the ground. Keeping the legs straight and knees locked forces the hamstrings to do more of the work as opposed to the quad and glute muscles. The hamstrings are a complex, two-jointed muscle responsible for hip extension and knee flexion, so it is commonly injured. Pay special attention to ensuring it is warmed up properly.

1. Start by standing tall with both legs firmly locked at the knee joint.
2. Shuffle your legs while taking short strides forward, keeping your knees locked and legs straight. Then fire them back behind you and slowly increase the intensity of the force production off the ground on each stride (see figures *a* and *b*).
3. Stay leaning slightly forward with a strong active anterior core while syncing your opposite arms and legs to maximize force production into the ground.
4. Do 2 sets of 20 to 30 yards (18 to 27 m).

A-WALK TRIPLE EXTENSION

During the drive phase ("A" phase) of a sprint, the ground-contact leg is in triple extension where the hip, knee, and ankle all extend slightly outward and downward. Likewise, all three of those joints in the opposite swing leg will be bent at 90 degrees. A-walk drills help develop co-contractions across the lower body and core while improving basic motor skills and balance.

1. Start standing tall in the A-position and hold it for 1 to 2 seconds (see figure *a*).
2. Walk forward one step driving the lifted leg down forcefully directly under the hip and then balance in the A-position on the other leg (see figure *b*).
3. Check your form to make sure your toes are pointed up toward your shin (dorsiflexed) and that there is a 90-degree angle at the hip joints.
4. Do 2 sets of 10 to 15 yards (9 to 14 m).

WIDE OUT

A wide out dynamically activates the gluteus medius and maximus and adductor group. By staying low and abducting and then immediately, upon ground contact, adducting the legs in a jumping fashion while maintaining balance and a low athletic position, this exercise is a great challenge and preparation tool.

BASIC

1. Start in a wide-stance squat position with knees in line with your toes and hands behind your back (see figure *a*). Think about isometrically pushing your feet apart for 5 seconds as if you were spreading a bathroom floor mat.

2. Without increasing your jump height, bring your feet close together by adducting the legs in a synchronized jump. Land softly, maintaining a strong core without increasing the height of your head or hips (see figure *b*).

3. Immediately upon landing, jump again, abducting both legs and separating them back to the starting position.

4. Repeat the jumps continuously for 2 sets of 8 to 12 reps.

CROSSOVER LUNGE

The crossover lunge is ideal for dynamically stretching the abductors, especially the glutes, tensor fasciae latae, and sartorius. It is important to not only activate these muscles but also put them through a full range of motion because they play an important role in the ability to generate force, which is determined by our range of motion from different body positions and angles.

1. Start by standing tall and facing straight ahead (see figure *a*).
2. Move to the left by crossing your right leg over, across your body to the left. Try to keep both feet pointing straight ahead in the sagittal plane throughout.
3. Once your right leg touches the ground, sink down to transfer your body weight to your right foot and drop into the stretch (see figure *b*). Return, moving in the same direction up the track or field, and repeat.
4. Repeat an equal number of reps on both sides for 2 sets of 6 to 8 reps.

HIGH-KNEE CARIOCA

The high-knee carioca develops the dynamic crossover action needed when busting into a lateral change of direction. The synchronization of the arms and leg drive is an important part of this drill. The focus is to actively drive the leg down after each synchronized hip flexion and shoulder extension. Timing the opposite shoulder and hip extension action is critical to maximizing the force production and outcome of this drill. Coaches can evaluate the distance the athlete covers with each rep while moving laterally when performing this drill to determine if maximum efficiency is being achieved.

ADVANCED

a   b

1. Start by facing straight ahead with your elbows at a 90-degree angle (see figure *a*).
2. Keep both ankles dorsiflexed and toes up while dynamically driving your right foot and knee upward and across your body so that the knee comes to the midline at your navel (see figure *b*).
3. Once your knee reaches midline, immediately fire your foot and knee back down to the ground by extending your hip. At the same time, extend and fire the opposite shoulder by driving the right elbow backward. Keep the core stiff and create a side-to-side rhythm.
4. Repeat an equal number of reps on both sides continuously for 2 sets of 15 to 20 yards (14 to 18 m).

BASIC

RESISTANCE BAND OVERHEAD RAISE

The resistance band overhead raise is an activation exercise that uses accommodating resistance to target the shoulder muscles, specifically the deltoid muscles, as well as the upper and lower trapezius and the serratus anterior.

1. Stand tall and place an elastic resistance band securely under both feet, holding it with your hands using a pronated grip (see figure *a*).
2. Raise the band upward until overhead maintaining straight arms (see figure *b*). Then lower the resistance band back to the start position.
3. Perform 2 sets of 10 to 15 reps.

SUPINATED PULL-APART

A supinated pull-apart requires external shoulder rotation, but it's not about range of motion. It's about activation. The athlete should hold a neutral posture throughout the exercise to activate the posterior rotator cuff, rear deltoids, rhomboids, middle traps, and lats.

1. Stand in an athletic position with a band in both hands and your palms facing up. Bend elbows to a 90-degree angle with your upper arms pressed against your sides (see figure *a*).
2. Pull the band apart, keeping your upper arms pinned against your sides, and maintain tension in the band throughout the exercise. Press your armpits toward your hips to maintain neutral shoulders throughout the exercise (see figure *b*). Exhale as you pull the band apart to help maintain a neutral spine and prevent you from compensating through hyperextension.
3. Perform 2 sets of 10 to 15 reps.

DUMBBELL HANG CLEAN

The dumbbell hang clean is a free-weight exercise that primarily targets the quads and, to a lesser degree, the hamstrings, hip flexors, lower back, outer thighs, biceps, glutes, and shoulders.

1. Stand with dumbbells at your sides. Your feet should be about shoulder-width apart (see figure *a*).
2. Bend at the knees in a squat motion, allowing the dumbbells to go just below your knees (see figure *b*).
3. Explode up from the squat position while flipping the dumbbells up to your shoulders (see figures *c-d*). Then bring the dumbbells back to the starting position.
4. Repeat 10 reps for 1 to 2 sets.

These sample exercises for general and speed-specific ADWs are just examples—you can modify exercises to fit your own needs using the programming menus in chapter 12. But one thing to keep in mind is that you want to mix things up. If you serve the same training meal every day, people will get bored and disengage—especially young athletes. Regardless of whichever exercises you use, the basic prudence is to go from general to specific, and from whole-body loaded movements like ViPR PRO–loaded lunges to low-intensity plyometrics like jumping jacks to mobility drills like double- and single-leg bridges to higher-intensity drills that prime the nervous system like skipping or acceleration sprints, and all of them should be targeted at the day's workout goals. Structured correctly, you can transition seamlessly into the day's training routine without your athlete ever knowing exactly when the warm-up ended and the workout began. It's how our warm-up becomes your workout.

5

SPEED-SPECIFIC STRENGTH

Since research shows that mass-specific force is an essential component of speed, it logically follows that being fast requires being strong relative to your body weight. But this brings us to the notorious speed and strength paradox. In reality, some of the fastest humans on the planet are not what you would consider weight-room strong. In addition to having great running form and solid foundational strength, their genetics give them an inherent biological advantage for speed. As a result, they can generate tremendous amounts of force very quickly without a lot of muscle mass. The fact is that too much strength training could be detrimental to their speed because carrying too much muscle mass can actually slow athletes down and increase their risk for injury.

Muscle power is also metabolically expensive. While it's true that getting foundationally stronger will make most athletes without much training history faster, there is a point of diminishing returns when it comes to speed after the initial strength gains are achieved. In respect to speed-specific strength, the real question is: How strong is strong enough? The immediate follow-up question to that is: And strong enough for what? Punching the ground with explosive force to rapidly accelerate requires a different kind of strength than quickly decelerating to rapidly cut and change direction. Every person's body is unique: We all have different compositions of muscle and fascia tissues, movement biases, anatomical proportions, and psychological drivers. There's never a one-size-fits-all answer; the answer is always, "It depends."

Stronger Doesn't Always Mean Faster

The idea that heavy weight training can improve speed took hold in 2000 after renowned human locomotion expert Peter Weyand, PhD, published a ground-breaking Harvard University study revealing that the swing time of a runner's recovery leg was virtually the same for both superfast athletes and slower athletes (Weyand 2000). The difference is that superfast athletes can generate significantly more force into the ground than slower athletes. This finding resulted in an overemphasis on heavy lifting in the weight room by coaches who believed that getting stronger was the primary strategy for getting faster. Suddenly, squats and deadlifts were the new go-tos for speed training.

However, one of the biggest challenges with applying traditional strength training to speed is that force production is multidimensional. While trainers and coaches have long conceptualized the body as a highly refined machine made of component parts that can be trained in isolation, our bodies are actually more like plants than machines. They operate according to biological laws more than Newtonian laws. The body's interconnected fascia system and neurological system play significant roles in the expression of force. It's not just about levers, pivot points, and muscles. Therefore, to see meaningful results, we must apply a multidimensional, whole-system approach to strength training.

Speed requires a balance of proximal concentric strength and stiffness at the hip and core combined with distal force transmission to a stiff lower leg and ankle–foot complex for the punch. If there are energy leaks in the core and hip, the legs don't have the solid anchor they need to produce maximum distal force at ground strike. To go fast, you need a solid foundation of strength relative to your body weight, a strong and stable core, powerful elasticity in the tendons and myofascial tissues of your lower legs, and a highly tuned nervous system. These features can be enhanced in the weight room, but often not in the ways we have traditionally approached them. Part of the reason is that strength trainers tend to focus on individual muscle development without understanding the important role both the fascia and nervous systems play in expressing explosive force. To be fast, you need Bruce Lee strength, not Arnold Schwarzenegger strength. You don't want giant muscles; instead, you want the ability to quickly produce violent amounts of force using your entire body. This starts with having a super strong and stable core. No matter how strong your lower body is, being able to create proximal stiffness limits your ability to transfer distal force. When there is instability in the core, you not only leak energy and lose speed but also increase the risk for injury because your body compensates across the rest of the kinetic chain.

Training the core, however, involves a lot more than the traditional ab routine or the ancillary benefits your core gets from doing squats and deadlifts. While these exercises can help, the essence of core strength comes from the ability to co-contract multiple myofascial structures to create a mechanical composite of tissues that make the whole stronger than the sum of its parts. This ability to create pulses of super stiffness in both the core and ankle–foot complex is a skill that requires neurological and tissue adaptations that traditional, sagittal plane heavy lifting doesn't sufficiently address. To be clear, I'm not saying that heavy lifting is bad. The problem is that it has become too much of the focus for too long in many high school and college weight rooms.

How Strong Is Strong Enough?

It should surprise no one reading this book that if you want to be fast, you need a well-balanced foundation of strength relative to your body weight. There are a number of ways to define foundational strength, but rather than having you take my word for it, I reached out to William "Bill" Kraemer, PhD, one of the world's top researchers in resistance training, to ask his thoughts on the subject. Dr. Kraemer is currently head of the Neuroscience and Neuromuscular Laboratory at Ohio State University and has co-authored more than 400 peer-reviewed publications and a dozen books. In addition to being an experienced researcher and professional training consultant, he is also the editor in chief of *The Journal of Strength and Conditioning Research*. I rang him up and asked him the million-dollar question: When it comes to speed, how strong is strong enough?

"Well, I can simplify this for you because we've done multiple studies looking at college athletes in different sports, and we have the data to back it up," says Kraemer. "The main thing we found is that—at least for college athletes—if you're trying to develop power and speed, men should be able to squat two times their body mass, and, for women, it's around 1.8 times. When you compare guys who can squat two times their body weight with guys who can only squat about 1.3 or 1.4 times their mass, there is a dramatic difference in power output. So being able to squat two times your body weight is what I would consider the gateway strength level for being fast. Obviously, you also need good running mechanics and flexibility and all the other things that go into speed. But the data say that if you can't squat two times your weight, your power potential will go down."

This begs the question: Why is the squat used as a benchmark for speed-specific strength, as opposed to a trap bar deadlift or other weightlifting exercise? And the answer is that, when you're running, the center of mass is above the pistons of your legs. This makes the squat more relevant for assessing foundational strength for speed because it better mimics the direction of force production applied when you're punching the ground at max velocity (as opposed to a trap bar deadlift, where you are lifting a mass from the ground). Of course, this metric is dependent on each athlete and their body type—there's no one magic number for everyone. Once you achieve the foundational strength needed to squat between two and two and a half times your body weight, there are many additional speed benefits to be gained by going above that. The goal is to maximize your relative strength-to-weight ratio—not to become a competitive powerlifter. A solid foundation of strength has also been shown to help reduce injury risk (Young 2006). The key is knowing what dosage to prescribe for each person based on their body type, deficiencies, and sport. And that's where the importance of assessment comes in.

Measuring and Assessing Strength for Speed

Since you can't improve what you can't measure, the ability to conduct accurate assessments is one of the most valuable skills any coach or trainer can have. It's where the art meets the science. A wide variety of tools are available that provide objective data on where an athlete's strengths, weaknesses, and imbalances are—including force plates, motion capture technology, and video analysis—but visual assessment is the simplest and, for experienced coaches, one of the most useful tools. Regardless of which tools you use, conducting an initial assessment followed by regular benchmark testing to monitor progress is crucial to knowing what an athlete needs and if your prescriptions are working as intended. Assessment and benchmark testing also creates more buy-in with your athletes because they can see progress toward their goals in a measurable way.

In addition to squat assessments, when it comes to speed, one of the most relevant assessments you can do is the vertical jump test. Vertical jump testing is a reliable and scientifically validated measurement of explosive, lower-body power and faster sprint times (Loturco et al. 2015). It can be done practically anywhere using a tape measure, some chalk, and a wall. You can also use a video camera to film vertical jumps from the posterior, anterior, and lateral sides. Observing an athlete's vertical jump can help a coach determine whether they need more anterior strength, posterior strength, core strength, or a combination of all three. Obviously, the first thing you're measuring is the height of the jump. But, more importantly, you want to assess the *quality* of the jump. This means looking at the joint angles. Is there valgus at the knees? Are they stable at the core? Are they hinging at the hips correctly? Are they using their arm swing? Are they fully extending at the hip through the jump? Are they eccentrically loading the jump with speed on the initial downstroke? Are there any asymmetries? All of these observations can provide indicators for where an athlete is strong, weak, or has mobility limitations or imbalances. Once you identify those issues, you can create a targeted training program to address them. Of course, there are also a number of vertical jump assessment technologies that can provide objective data on force production and movement symmetry.

A reliable, research-based solution in this category includes force plate technologies, such as Sparta Science's platform. In fact, doing a vertical jump test on Sparta's platform is now a required assessment test at the NFL Combine. Literally every major sports league in the United States and elite U.S. military units use it. What makes the platform unique is that, in addition to providing a numeric measurement of force production (called a Sparta Score) for all three variables of a vertical jump—categorized as "load," "explode," and "drive" (see figure 5.1)—the platform also combines machine learning with an anonymous database of over a million jump scans to identify movement imbalances and biases and predict injury risk with a high degree of accuracy.

I mention Sparta Science not only for its state-of-the-art technology but also because its terminology is useful for conceptualizing the different phases of force production. This gives us a framework for targeting deficiencies and prescribing strength-training programs to address them—whether it's the eccentric loading phase of a jump, the concentric exploding phase, or the drive phase, which is the continuation of the concentric exploding phase. Based on those three-dimensional values, you can assess if an athlete's anterior chain is weak, relative to their posterior chain and core stability. For example, if they have a weak anterior chain, we'll prescribe more front or back squats where there is less of a hinge at the hip and more at the knee. Anterior chain strength plays an important role in the ability to decelerate and eccentrically load. If the issue is a weak posterior chain, we prescribe more single-leg Romanian deadlifts or rear-elevated split squats and so on.

Sparta's platform measures the load variable as the eccentric rate of downward force. This value has a lot to do with the anterior fascia chain. Load scores tend to be very high in athletes who squat for long periods of time, such as linemen, catchers, and slalom skiers. Its explode variable is a measurement of concentric force production—the transition athletes make when uncoiling for a jump. This value tends to be the hardest to improve because it's more of a genetic neural ability, but research has shown that core stiffness and strength both play an important role in minimizing energy leaks to maximize explosiveness. While it can be improved through training, gains in explosiveness are much fewer than gains in the other two values. The drive variable is a measurement of concentric impulse, and it is the only measurement that multiplies force by time (the other two divide it). Athletes with high drive scores tend to have posterior chains that are more developed and the ability to recruit and use those muscles throughout the entire jump.

FIGURE 5.1 Sparta Science's platform provides a three-dimensional measurement of the three variables of a vertical jump—load, explode, and drive—which can be used to identify deficiencies and imbalances that affect both injury resilience and performance.

Adapted from Sparta Science, "Sparta Jump Scan 101: Load, Explode, and Drive," 2018, accessed April 26, 2021, https://spartascience.com/sparta-101-load-explode-and-drive/.

The fact is traditional resistance-training routines typically aren't the best prescription; this is why regular benchmark testing is crucial to the process. You need to know if your training prescriptions are working the way you intend. For example, according to Dr. Phil Wagner, founder and CEO of Sparta Science and developer of its platform, the company's research team was surprised to find that doing overhead squats turned out to be one of the best ways to improve drive scores.

"That realization kind of shattered our previous thinking," says Dr. Wagner. "Because we'd been pushing a lot of single-leg stuff, under the assumption that it was going to improve drive, and overhead squats are a double-leg movement. Initially, we thought it was all about the posterior chain strength. Which, in theory, means that if you want to improve drive, you should do things like split squats, lunges, and Romanian deadlifts, which all have a very noticeable impact on the musculature and create a ton of delayed-onset soreness. But, when you think about it, a simple overhead squat makes you go through a full range of motion in both your lower and upper body. And when you do it, you don't really get sore, because there's not a lot of weight involved. It's also not focused on any one particular muscle group. That was a powerful realization for us about the significance of the fascia system. When you understand that fascia is a connected, body-wide system and then think about how to best activate that system, there's probably no better movement than an overhead squat. I think that speaks to how much the entire body is connected and how critical fascia is to movement. But it's this ability to classify the effects of different exercises that allows us to prescribe different training approaches based on a vertical jump test."

According to Dave Tate—an elite powerlifter, strength trainer, and founder of EliteFTS—another valuable assessment tool in the weight room is looking at the bar speed of a lift. A former protégé of Louie Simmons and trainer at the legendary Westside Barbell in Columbus, Ohio, Tate has been working with competitive strength athletes for more than 35 years.

"I want to see a barbell move with force, and I rely very heavily on watching the bar speed," says Tate. "The way my eye is trained, I'm looking for the bar speed to be about 0.8 of a meter per second. Based on that, I can determine if an athlete needs more absolute strength or more repetition strength. If their bar speeds just suck, then I know they need to do more plyometric and dynamic work because they don't know how to express force."

At Parisi Speed School, we've found that chin-ups are also a valuable assessment tool for speed. This may seem counterintuitive at first but, as I mentioned, core strength is a huge contributor to speed. The upper body and especially the lats play a major role because the superficial back line and spiral line of the fascia system are crucial for stabilization. The superficial back line runs from the bottom of the foot over the top of the head to the brow in one continuous myofascial net that can be dissected as a single entity (see figure 5.2).

Common postural compensation patterns associated with the superficial back line include limitations of ankle dorsiflexion, knee hyperextension, hamstring shortness, and anterior pelvic shift—all of which influence speed performance.

When you extend your left hip, you're also extending your right shoulder and vice versa. The connected fascia slings of the superficial back line and spiral line work together in this exchange to distribute force and stabilize movement. This is one of the reasons why upper-body strength training can aid in speed development. In fact, with our young and even sometimes older, more experienced athletes, the ones who can do more chin-ups in our Parisi evaluation tests are almost always faster. The take-home point is that successful programming starts with doing a comprehensive assessment and then using that assessment as a baseline for tracking progress as an athlete goes through their training so you can adjust accordingly. The catch is that there is no such thing as an ideal assessment for everyone. Every athlete has a unique body composition, movement bias, and injury history. And there are a lot of assessment tools available that can tell you different things. Regardless of which tools you use, if there's no increase in performance, the athlete may very well need to rest or the training program needs to be adjusted.

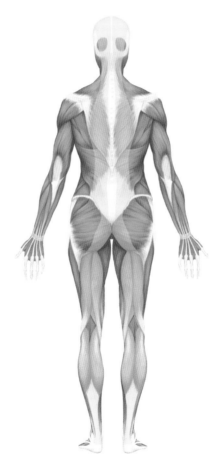

FIGURE 5.2   The superficial back line originates at the bottom plantar surface of the foot and travels up the back of the body, over the head, and terminates at the brow.

Strength Training Form and Technique

When it comes to strength training, the importance of form and technique cannot be overstated. This is probably the most important thing I can communicate in this chapter. Strength training is a technical skill that needs to be properly instructed and mastered. Form matters—a lot. If you do heavy weight training with improper form, you are promoting injury. And the unfortunate truth is that too many injuries that happen on the field, court, or track often start in the weight room because coaches don't realize when their athletes are lifting with faulty mechanics that promote muscle imbalances.

One of the most common lifting-related injuries is to the annulus fibrosus of the spinal discs in the lower back. The annulus fibrosus surrounds the soft inner core, known as the nucleus pulposus, of the intervertebral discs (see figure 5.3).

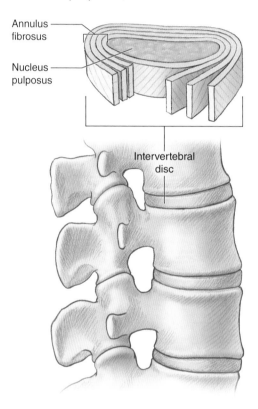

FIGURE 5.3 The elastic inner core of the intervertebral disc that allows the disc to withstand compression and torsion forces is called the nucleus pulposus. It is composed of a jelly-like material mostly consisting of water and collagen fibers.

This dense outer section of protective tissue consists of ligament fibers that encase the inner core and connect the spinal vertebrae above and below each disc. It is a rubber-like donut of connective tissue that supports the rotational stability of the spine and helps resist compressive stress. According to "Dr. Back Mechanic" Stuart McGill, PhD, if you don't keep your lumbar spine locked into a neutral position when squatting, lunging, or doing other loaded movements, you are delaminating the fibers of the annulus fibrosus and creating cumulative damage over time that is slow to heal and can result in more serious injury. This means that if you don't help your athletes master proper lifting technique from the outset and train them to use proper form, you are promoting injury. One of the challenges is that faulty form can sometimes be hard to spot. For example, an athlete may be lifting with slightly improper form that you can't see because their T-shirt may be ballooning out. And if the spine is slightly out of neutral and the load is heavy relative to the athlete, this will become a problem. This is why athletes should wear tighter clothing when they weight train. It makes it easier for their coach or trainer to assess and correct their form.

Lifting is a technical skill that has to be mastered, and it starts with proper back hygiene. Teach your athletes to pick up a barbell off the floor properly and return it to the rack with good form. This will emphasize the ever-so-important point of always working to maintain a strong neutral spine. This is a spine hygiene paradigm that every athlete needs to buy into. If they are not showing me that they get it, then I don't want to see any loading of the bar at all. Athletes—especially young athletes—want to see success. They want to see progression. If you're going to handcuff them by not giving them the proper technical skills to get stronger in the movement, then they're going to become frustrated very fast and eventually get injured. They'll make their beginner gains, but then after six or eight weeks, they're not going to progress anymore. But if you can fix the mistakes in their technique early, you can add 50 pounds (23 kg) to somebody's lift without them even getting stronger.

The caveat here is that proper lifting form depends to some degree on the individual athlete. The length ratios of different body segments create different leverage mechanics, and different depths of hip sockets determine how far someone can squat before their pelvis tucks and begins to stress their lumbar discs. What is ideal for one athlete may not be right for another. But there are some basic principles that can be followed to find the sweet spot. One way Dr. McGill helps lifters find their correct form is the shortstop squat.

1. Start with feet apart and do a few knee bends to adjust the internal and external rotation of the hips and find the correct hinge tracking for the knees and ankles. Look at the turnout of your feet. Remember this angle and start in this position.

2. Stand tall and place your hands on the tops of your thighs while making a V between your thumbs and index fingers (see figure 5.4*a*). Keep your arms straight and push your hands down the thighs, hinging at the hips. Do not allow the spine to bend.

3. Lower and stop as your hands reach just above the kneecaps and grab around the knees (see figure 5.4*b*).

4. Imagine a vertical line dropping down from each knee. It should fall between the balls of the feet and the heels. This ensures that your hips are well positioned. Focus on the curves in your torso. If they are the same as when you were standing, you have good form. If not, adjust them back to their natural curves.

5. To rise from this position, you don't want to shrug—you should do what McGill calls an anti-shrug by compressing the shoulders down into your torso while co-contracting the pectoral and latissimus dorsi muscles. Stiffen your torso while keeping the normal curves.

6. As you go back up, do not think about lifting your torso with your back. Think about *stiffening* your back and torso. The rising motion will happen simply by pulling your hips forward as you push through the ground with both feet and slide your hands back up your thighs.

FIGURE 5.4 Using the shortstop squat to help find correct lifting form.

To transition this to a lifting motion, assume the shortstop position with your hands on your thighs. Grip the ground with your toes and heels. Do an anti-shrug and grab the bar with a double overhand grip. Then try to bend the bar with the external rotation of your shoulders. Tighten and stiffen your back and squeeze the bar hard while applying force with all 10 fingers. Imagine spreading the floor with your hips, legs, and feet as you pull the hips forward. This will enable you to safely lift a heavy load from the floor with proper form.

The other side of the form equation is that dialing in an athlete's technique is an easy way to help them achieve rapid gains. Technique improvements are low-hanging fruit that must be addressed before you can add more weight and complexity to a training program. We recommend starting out using 40 percent of one-repetition maximum (1RM) so you can practice grooving into a movement until a lifting skill is mastered. Then you can gradually ramp up the weight and speed to safely achieve gains.

Speed-Specific Strength

Before you can improve an athlete's speed capabilities, you must first develop their capacity to generate force. Developing speed-specific strength begins with developing an athlete's foundational strength. These gains can be made fairly quickly in athletes without much training history and are harder to improve as athletes reach the target zone of being able to squat two and a half times their body weight. Developing core strength is also paramount to optimize power transfer, minimize energy leaks, and improve injury resistance. And, of course, developing good lower-body strength is essential for achieving peak speed performance.

Foundational Strength

Developing the foundational strength needed for men to squat twice their body weight and women to squat 1.8 times their body weight is best done by mastering the squat technique over time. There are variations on the squat and the deadlift techniques that can be used based on an athlete's limb length and bone anatomy. The most important factor is that they are done with proper form as part of a strategically structured program. Squats and deadlifts can enhance speed when an athlete is new to strength training as they work their way up to developing the appropriate strength-to-weight ratio. But this is just one of the pieces to the speed enhancement puzzle. These exercises help to develop a solid foundation of strength for optimal force production and reduced injury risk, but they are not the be-all and end-all. Too many coaches put too much emphasis on these movements at the sacrifice of other training modalities that build the tremendously important body-wide myofascial spring suspension system.

PULL-UP

Pull-ups are a great foundational-strength exercise that require elbow flexion, shoulder extension, and scapular retraction with downward rotation. The primary muscles involved include the latissimus dorsi, middle and lower trapezius, and rhomboids.

Middle trapezius

Latissimus dorsi

Biceps brachii

Rhomboids

a

b

Primary Muscles Activated

Pull phase (same muscles work eccentrically during return phase):
- *Elbow (flexion):* biceps brachii, brachialis, brachioradialis
- *Shoulder (adduction):* latissimus dorsi, pectoralis major lower fibers, teres major, subscapularis, coracobrachialis
- *Shoulder girdle (adduction, downward rotation, depression):* middle trapezius, lower trapezius, pectoralis minor, rhomboids

---

1. Start by grasping the bar slightly wider than shoulder-width apart with hands pronated (palms facing away) and hang from the bar with straight arms (see figure *a*).

2. Pull your upper chest toward the bar until your chin is above the bar. As you pull your body up, try to imagine your shoulder blades moving toward your back pockets (see figure *b*).

3. Depending on the training phase, do anywhere from 2 to 12 reps for 3 to 8 sets. Common variations include holding the top and bottom position of the exercise for 15 seconds, eventually building up to 60 seconds. Assisted and resisted options also regress and progress this exercise.

BACK SQUAT

Back squats simulate the direction of vertical force application involved in running where the legs are under the mass. Body weight should remain over the midfoot with the heels and toes in contact with the floor throughout the exercise. Midfoot pressure promotes co-contraction of the hamstrings and quadriceps, resulting in better stability and force production.

Gluteus maximus

Biceps femoris

Gastrocnemius

Vastus lateralis

a   b

MODERATE

Primary Muscles Activated

Descent phase (same muscles work concentrically during ascent phase):

- *Hip (flexion)*: gluteus maximus, biceps femoris long head, semitendinosus, semimembranosus
- *Knee (flexion)*: rectus femoris, vastus lateralis, vastus medialis, vastus intermedius
- *Ankle (dorsiflexion)*: gastrocnemius, soleus

---

1. Start with the bar set at midchest height inside a squat rack or stands. Facing the bar, set your hand grip on the bar as close to shoulder width as possible. Press the elbows toward the hips and set the elbow position underneath the bar. This position helps the athlete create the upper-body tension to maintain a neutral trunk and spine at an angle that places the bar vertically in line with the midfoot throughout the exercise. Spread feet to at least hip-width apart, feet facing forward if possible or slightly externally rotated.

2. Take the bar out of the rack with it resting on your rear shoulder muscles (see figure *a*).

3. As you lower the hips down and back, imagine you are pulling yourself down with your lower body. Proper squat depth is the lowest point the athlete can achieve without flexion of the lumbar spine or posterior pelvic tilt, which will vary for each athlete (see figure b).

4. Return to a tall standing position by pushing through the midfoot and consciously activate the glutes as you near a tall position.

5. Depending on the training phase, do anywhere from 2 to 5 reps for 3 to 5 sets.

TRAP BAR DEADLIFT

Trap bar deadlifts are a staple for training foundational strength. Body weight should remain in the midfoot with the heels and toes in contact with the floor throughout the exercise. Midfoot pressure promotes co-contraction of the hamstrings and quadriceps, resulting in better stability and force production.

Gluteus maximus
Rectus femoris
Biceps femoris

a   b

Primary Muscles Activated

Descent phase (same muscles work concentrically during ascent phase):

- *Hip (flexion)*: gluteus maximus, biceps femoris long head, semitendinosus, semimembranosus
- *Knee (flexion)*: rectus femoris, vastus lateralis, vastus medialis, vastus intermedius
- *Ankle (dorsiflexion)*: gastrocnemius, soleus

1. Stand inside the trap bar and grip the bar with each middle finger over the line at the center of the handles and vertically in line with the midfoot. The bar path should remain vertically in that line throughout the exercise. Hips should be low with your chest up and a neutral spine before lifting the load (see figure *a*).

2. Maintaining straight arms, lift the bar by pressing your feet down through the midfoot to create upper-body tension until you're standing tall (see figure *b*). Consciously activate the glutes as you near a tall position.

3. As you lower the hips down imagine you are pulling yourself down with your lower body. Maintain or release tension at the bottom depending on your goal.

4. Depending on the training phase, do anywhere from 2 to 5 reps for 3 to 5 sets.

ADVANCED

Core Strength

Training the body to become a powerful elastic spring that results in faster speeds starts at the core. Over the past few decades of training athletes of all types for faster speed, the biggest deficiency we've consistently seen at the Parisi Speed School is in the athletes' cores. Obviously, most athletes need to get stronger in their lower and upper bodies too, but the core is usually the biggest deficiency. In some ways, I think the core gets forgotten in a lot of high school and college weight rooms where they spend too much time focusing on squats and deadlifts. Those exercises help activate and train the core if proper core bracing is applied to the lifting technique, but they are also limited in application. They can increase muscle recruitment by providing the ability to work with high loads, but it's with very limited degrees of freedom and only on the sagittal plane. The trunk and core provide the stable foundation for efficient distal force transfer to the limbs. But the trunk and core also need to be neurologically programmed to activate quickly and provide stability on all three planes of motion. This is where Newtonian mechanics come up short as a model for thinking about human movement.

New Jersey Italians get a pass for repeating themselves to make a point, so I'll say it again with feeling: Humans are more like plants than machines. We are not robots assembled from a box of component parts that can be trained in isolation. We biologically self-organize in response to the stress of our environment—just like trees. I'll give you a core-related example. When trees grow in the wild, the wind forces their limbs to move constantly. This multidirectional loading from wind creates stress that is distributed through the limbs and trunk of the entire tree all the way down to the roots. Trees respond to this stress by internally growing what is known as reaction wood (or stress wood), which is mechanically different than structural wood in terms of cellulose content and how it is composed. Cellulose is a polymeric fiber that self-organizes in reaction wood in a triple-helix pattern along the lines of stress in much the same way collagen does in fascia tissue. Reaction wood responds to loading by creating a mechanical composite that provides structural stability in trees just like rebar does in concrete. It's what allows trees to grow toward the best light in contorted ways and survive extreme loads even in awkward shapes that would cause a Newtonian building to collapse.

The multidimensional submaximal loading that wind creates makes trees strong enough to support their own weight as they grow. In fact, when scientists tried to grow trees in the fully enclosed Biosphere 2 research facility in Arizona, they were surprised to find that, while the trees grew faster than they did in the wild, they would collapse before they fully matured because they were never exposed to the stress of wind. As a result, they didn't develop the shape-stabilizing reaction wood that makes them strong. Our bodies, and specifically our core–trunk complex, require similar multidimensional submaximal loading to develop the resilient myofascial connections that create stability.

This is why it's important to understand Stu McGill's concept of mechanical composites and Michol Dalcourt's concept of developing odd-position strength. No one muscle group is responsible for core strength. Proximal stiffness in the core comes from the simultaneous co-contraction of multiple agonist and antagonist muscles working together as a single composite that makes the whole stronger than the sum of its parts. And this mechanical composite feature is enabled by the mesh of myofascial tissues that surround and connect every muscle in the body.

So how do we train the core multidimensionally? Well, it starts in the pre–warm-up with the exercises in the McGill Big 3, which activate and fire the small muscle motor units of the core (see chapter 3) and planks of all types. In addition, ab rollouts are also great for the core because they engage the rectus abdominis, glutes, lower back, and obliques while forcing the entire kinetic chain to work together in coordination. Loaded isometric carries, such as the suitcase carry and the farmer's carry, are also valuable for core activation; and antirotational exercises, such as the Pallof press, are beneficial for strengthening the core on the transverse plane. While isometric exercises are integral for developing core strength, ultimately you also want to program the core to fire and co-contract quickly in ways that transfer to the field and court. This is where dynamic medicine ball and plyometric exercises that require whole-body movements with greater degrees of freedom and lighter loads excel at engaging the kinetic chain while programming the neuromuscular system for rapid gamelike response.

FARMER'S CARRY

The farmer's carry is a whole-body exercise that involves carrying equal weights in each hand while walking. It engages your entire upper body and core as well as your arms and lower body, including the trapezius, obliques, transverse abdominis, rectus abdominis, quadriceps, hamstrings, and calves. It is one of a series of moving carry exercises that include the suitcase carry and the overhead carry.

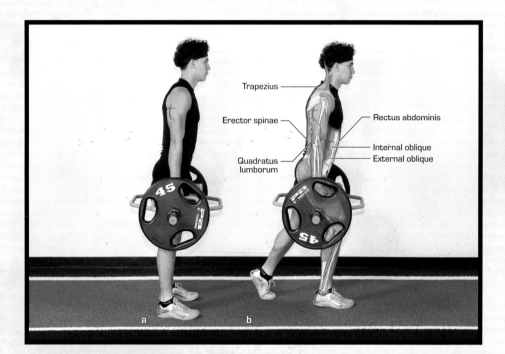

Primary Muscles Activated

Isometric phase (front foot flat on ground):

- *Shoulder girdle (isometric elevation)*: rhomboids, levator scapulae, trapezius upper fibers, trapezius middle fibers
- *Elbow (isometric flexion)*: biceps brachii, brachialis, brachioradialis
- *Wrist (isometric flexion)*: flexor carpi radialis, palmaris longus, flexor carpi ulnaris, flexor digitorum superficialis, flexor digitorum profundus, flexor pollicis longus
- *Trunk (isometric neutral)*: transverse abdominis, rectus abdominis, internal oblique, external oblique, erector spinae, quadratus lumborum
- *Front hip (isometric flexion)*: gluteus maximus, biceps femoris long head, semitendinosus, semimembranosus
- *Front knee (isometric flexion)*: rectus femoris, vastus lateralis, vastus medialis, vastus intermedius
- *Front ankle (isometric flexion)*: gastrocnemius, soleus

1. Start by holding a trap bar or a pair of equally weighted kettlebells or dumbbells, one in each hand (see figure *a*). Begin with a light weight of approximately 50 percent of your body weight (25 percent in each hand). Align and brace your back and bend your knees to pick up the weight.

2. Walk slowly in a straight line with control for 20 to 40 yards (18 to 37 m; see figure *b*).

3. You can turn around to travel the 20- to 40-yard distance but do not turn around with the weight if you're carrying a trap bar. Stop, place the bar on the ground, turn around inside the bar, and pick the bar back up to return to the starting point. The momentum of the trap bar when turning the body can torque the lower back in a way that can be a risk for injury. You can turn around with kettlebells or dumbbells as long as you do it slowly and under control.

4. As you gain strength in your arms and core, you can increase the weight to up to 50 percent of your body weight. Perform 2 to 4 sets of walks.

MODERATE

PALLOF PRESS

The Pallof press is a highly effective antirotational core stabilization exercise that helps athletes resist spinal flexion, extension, and rotation. It isometrically challenges the obliques and the rectus abdominis to resist spinal and pelvic rotation and the sheer forces generated in rapid turning, change of direction, and agility movements.

Primary Muscles Activated

Isometric phase (with handle in right hand):

- *Shoulder (horizontal adduction on side holding handle)*: biceps brachii, pectoralis major upper and lower fibers, coracobrachialis, deltoid anterior fibers
- *Trunk (isometric flexion)*: rectus abdominis, erector spinae, internal oblique, external oblique
- *Hip (isometric external rotation)*: gluteus maximus, gluteus medius posterior fibers, piriformis, gemellus superior and inferior, obturator externus and internus, quadratus femoris

1. Start with a cable machine or a band with a manageable amount of resistance attached to a fixed object and grab the band or cable handle at chest height.

2. Step away and to the side of the cable machine or where the band is attached so the cable or band forms a 90-degree angle from your arms and the resistance is on your core.

3. Keep a slight athletic bend in your knees and brace your core by slightly bringing your rib cage toward your pelvis.

4. Hold the handle close to your chest to begin (see figure *a*) and then press the handle away from your chest while maintaining a braced core (see figure *b*). The goal is to keep the core stable and not move from this pressed position.

5. Hold the extended position for 4 to 10 seconds.

6. Perform 2 to 5 reps on each side of the body for 2 to 4 sets.

BASIC

AB ROLLOUT

The ab rollout is basically a rolling plank with the added variable of a roller (or stability ball) that makes the core muscles work harder. It also requires more core strength and balance than a plank, making it more of an advanced exercise. The ab rollout targets the rectus abdominis, obliques, and erector spinae.

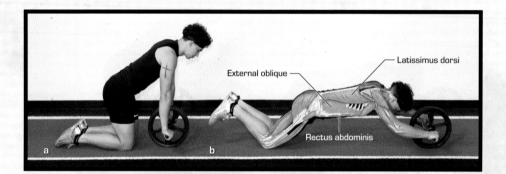

Primary Muscles Activated

Flexion phase:
- *Shoulder (extension)*: latissimus dorsi, teres major, triceps brachii long head, pectoralis major lower fibers, deltoid posterior fibers, infraspinatus
- *Trunk (flexion)*: rectus abdominis, internal oblique, external oblique
- *Hip (flexion)*: rectus femoris, iliacus, psoas major, pectineus, tensor fasciae latae

Extension phase:
- *Shoulder (flexion)*: deltoid anterior fibers, pectoralis major upper fibers, coracobrachialis
- *Head and trunk (extension)*: erector spinae, quadratus lumborum, splenius capitis and cervicis, sternocleidomastoid (extension of head)
- *Hip (extension)*: gluteus maximus, biceps femoris long head, semitendinosus, semimembranosus

1. Start on your knees and put both hands on the ab roller (see figure *a*). If you're using a stability ball, place your forearms on top of the ball with loose fists.

2. Brace your core by inhaling deeply and extend your arms and body forward slowly.

3. Extend out to a point that is a challenge to hold yet a stable position that you can hold for 4 to 10 seconds (see figure *b*). Extend out farther as your strength allows. Do not to collapse or sag at the core!

4. Slowly return to the starting position and rest for 1 to 3 seconds between reps. Be sure to control your breathing during this exercise without unbracing your core.

5. Start with 6 to 8 reps of 4- to 6-second holds and slowly progress to 8 to 15 reps of 6- to 10-second holds for 2 to 4 sets.

Lower-Body Strength

When it comes to lower-body strength, the most important muscles for speed are the hip extensors, hip flexors, and knee flexors (see figure 5.5). An MRI study comparing the strength and muscle composition of Division I sprinters to average humans demonstrated that, in addition to having solid foundational body strength, strong hip and knee flexors and extensors are crucial for speed (Handsfield et al. 2016). Additionally, analysis of sprinting biomechanics has revealed that the hip flexors and extensors express more proximal concentric strength, while the knee flexors rely on more eccentric strength (Chumanov, Heiderscheit, and Thelen 2011). The gluteus maximus and gluteus medius stabilize the pelvis and hip complex to help resist swinging, dropping, and excessive rotation. During the ground contact phase of a stride, the glutes shorten and contract isometrically. This means that a speed-specific resistance-training program should include glute exercises that require peak contraction at short muscle lengths.

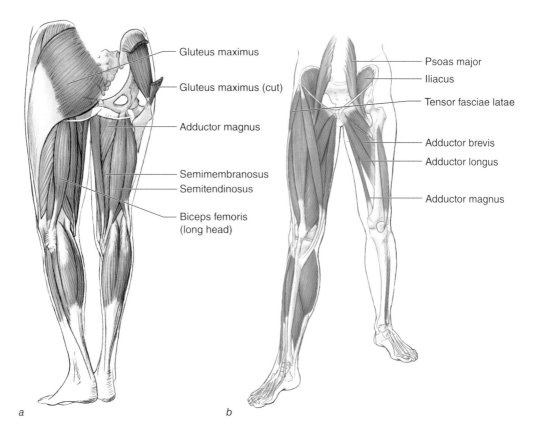

FIGURE 5.5   Strong hip and knee flexors and extensors are essential for speed, stabilization, and injury resilience.

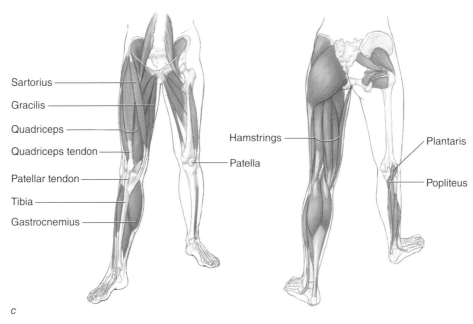

Sartorius

Gracilis

Quadriceps

Quadriceps tendon

Patellar tendon

Tibia

Gastrocnemius

Hamstrings

Patella

Plantaris

Popliteus

c

FIGURE 5.5   *Continued*

The main propulsive muscles used for sprinting are the hamstrings, which consist of the biceps femoris, semitendinosus, and semimembranosus. The hamstrings work eccentrically at the knee and concentrically at the hip and use a lot of stored elastic energy during ground preparation. They basically store elastic energy during the lengthening phase and release it at ground contact. As a result, hamstring force is higher during ground preparation and lower during ground contact (unlike the glutes). At the beginning of the ground preparation phase (during maximal hip flexion), the hamstrings concentrically contract locally while eccentrically contracting distally. This eccentric action of the hamstring group during ground preparation plays a significant role in speed, but it is also a contributor to injury risk.

A study of hamstring sprinting mechanics revealed that the biceps femoris experiences the greatest amount of muscle and tendon strain—which is likely why it's the most commonly injured hamstring muscle—while the semimembranosus does most of the concentric and eccentric work and generates the most power (Schache, Dorn, and Pandy 2012). Multiple studies have shown that having stronger hip extensors can improve sprinting speeds (Beardsley and Contreras 2014). Additionally, studies indicate that eccentric-specific training programs are effective for improving maximum running speeds and aiding injury prevention (de Hoyo et al. 2015). On that note, a Norwegian study conducted in 2004 found that using bands with Nordic hamstring curls is more beneficial than traditional hamstring curls for developing eccentric hamstring strength (Mjølsnes et al. 2004).

NORDIC HAMSTRING CURL

Nordic hamstring curls are an advanced exercise that is challenging to do. Athletes should build up their eccentric capacity prior to attempting them by working on only the eccentric lowering phase over the course of 4 to 6 seconds until they develop enough strength to perform the concentric phase of the exercise.

Primary Muscles Activated

Extension phase:

- *Knee (flexion)*: biceps femoris short and long head, semitendinosus, semimembranosus
- *Hip (isometric external rotation)*: gluteus maximus, gluteus medius posterior fibers, piriformis, gemellus superior and inferior, obturator externus and internus, quadratus femoris
- *Trunk (isometric extension and flexion)*: erector spinae, quadratus lumborum (extension); rectus abdominis, erector spinae, internal oblique, external oblique (flexion)

1. Lock your heels under a weight (you can also have a partner hold your feet) and kneel on a pad facing away from the weight (or partner; see figure *a*).

2. Slowly lower yourself forward while keeping the spine neutral and chest upright until you are in a parallel position with the floor and there is a stretch in the hamstrings (see figure *b*).

3. Flex your hamstrings and pull yourself back up to the starting position while holding your torso in a straight line. Keep your hips extended throughout and don't allow them to take tension off of your hamstrings.

4. Repeat 4 reps for 1 to 3 sets.

BASIC

CALF RAISE

Calf raises are one of the simplest lower-body exercises for runners to incorporate into a workout. This exercise requires foot and ankle stability, plantarflexion, and dorsiflexion. The primary muscles involved are the gastrocnemius and soleus.

Gastrocnemius

Soleus

a   b

Primary Muscles Activated

Raise phase (same muscles work eccentrically during lower phase):

- *Ankle (plantarflexion)*: gastrocnemius, soleus

1. Stand up straight with the balls of your feet on an elevated surface such as a weight plate placed flat on the ground (see figure *a*). The elevated surface increases the range of motion, so that the plantar flexors, Achilles tendon, and plantar fascia are in a lengthened starting position. To increase strength, add resistance with dumbbells or kettlebells.

2. Push through the balls of your feet, raising your heels off the floor as high as you can control until you are standing on your toes (see figure *b*).

3. Slowly lower back to the starting position. When lowering your heels, imagine that they are being pulled back down to the floor.

4. Do 6 to 12 reps for 3 to 5 sets.

SINGLE-LEG SQUAT

Single-leg squats target unilateral strength, which helps coaches identify strength imbalances and can help correct them. Also, many movements in field and court sports involve the athlete transferring force from one leg to the other.

Gluteus maximus

Vastus lateralis

Gastrocnemius
Soleus

a   b

Primary Muscles Activated

Descent phase (same muscles work concentrically during ascent phase):

- *Hip (flexion)*: gluteus maximus, biceps femoris long head, semitendinosus, semimembranosus
- *Knee (flexion)*: rectus femoris, vastus lateralis, vastus medialis, vastus intermedius
- *Ankle (dorsiflexion)*: gastrocnemius, soleus

---

1. With a bench or box behind you, stand tall on one foot with your body weight held in the midfoot and elevate the other foot so it is hovering 2 to 4 inches (5 to 10 cm) above the floor and in front of (not touching) the stance foot (see figure *a*). Keep your chest up with a neutral spine and strong core throughout the exercise.

2. As you squat while standing on one foot, imagine that your stance foot is pulling you down. When your glutes contact the bench or box (see figure *b*), push through the midfoot to return to a tall position.

3. Repeat 5 reps for 3 to 5 sets on each side.

4. If needed, add a heel lift under the planted foot by standing on a small plate. This will help technique for those who have tight Achilles. You can also add a dumbbell in each hand to increase exercise intensity.

Odd-Position and Deadstart Strength

Odd-position strength is the ability to generate force from uncommon body positions. Athletic movements in field and court sports often require proficiency in specific and uncommon postures. Training with submaximal loads in odd positions requires multiple joints and structures to work together three dimensionally. It builds shape stability in the connective tissues and develops an athlete's internal armor. Odd-position strength can be trained from various body orientations (standing through ground based) for a variety of tissue responses. Deadstart strength is the ability to produce high levels of force with less contribution from the elastic components of connective tissue. It begins from a stationary position with little initial motion (dead position) and creates only a very small mechanical prestretch when moving from relaxed positions, as seen in ground-to-standing movement (e.g., deadlift, Turkish get-up), and preset positions, such as most sprint starts and Olympic lift pulling patterns.

LATERAL STEP SHOVEL

The lateral step shovel is a multidimensional loaded-movement drill that focuses on odd-position strength.

Primary Muscles Activated

Landing phase:

- *Shoulder (top hand; abduction)*: pectoralis major upper fibers, deltoid anterior fibers, deltoid middle fibers, deltoid posterior fibers, supraspinatus
- *Shoulder (bottom hand; adduction)*: latissimus dorsi, pectoralis major lower fibers, teres major, subscapularis, coracobrachialis
- *Hip (stationary leg; abduction)*: gluteus medius, tensor fasciae latae, gluteus maximus upper fibers, gluteus minimus
- *Hip (stepping leg; abduction, flexion)*: gluteus medius, tensor fasciae latae, gluteus maximus upper fibers, gluteus minimus, (abduction); gluteus maximus, biceps femoris long head, semitendinosus, semimembranosus (flexion)
- *Knee (stepping leg; flexion)*: rectus femoris, vastus lateralis, vastus medialis, vastus intermedius
- *Ankle (stepping leg; dorsiflexion)*: gastrocnemius, soleus

1. Hold the ViPR PRO with a shovel grip at your midline in front of your body (see figure *a*).
2. Lift the ViPR PRO over one shoulder as if you're shoveling dirt up and away while taking a lateral step in the opposite direction (see figure *b*).
3. Hold the extended position for 2 to 3 seconds and then return with control to the starting position.
4. Repeat 4 to 8 reps for 1 to 3 sets on each side.

TRANSVERSE PLANE LUNGE WITH ARC

The transverse plane lunge with arc is a multidimensional loaded-movement drill that focuses on odd-position strength.

Deltoid

Rectus femoris

Vastus lateralis

Vastus medialis

a   b   c

Primary Muscles Activated

Landing phase:

- *Shoulder (top hand; abduction)*: pectoralis major upper fibers, deltoid anterior fibers, deltoid middle fibers, deltoid posterior fibers, supraspinatus
- *Shoulder (bottom hand; adduction)*: latissimus dorsi, pectoralis major lower fibers, teres major, subscapularis, coracobrachialis
- *Hip (stationary leg; external rotation, flexion)*: gluteus maximus, gluteus medius posterior fibers, piriformis, gemellus superior and inferior, obturator externus and internus, quadratus femoris (external rotation); gluteus maximus, biceps femoris long head, semitendinosus, semimembranosus (flexion)
- *Knee (stationary leg; flexion)*: rectus femoris, vastus lateralis, vastus medialis, vastus intermedius
- *Ankle (stationary leg; dorsiflexion)*: gastrocnemius, soleus

1. Hold the ViPR PRO with a neutral grip overhead (see figure *a*).
2. Step back in a transverse lunge and shift the ViPR PRO vertically over the front leg as if you're holding a log in front of you (see figure *b-c*).
3. Hold the extended position for 2 to 3 seconds and then return with control to the starting position.
4. Repeat 4 to 8 reps for 3 to 5 sets on each side.

LATERAL BIG ARC DEAD SHIFT

The lateral big arc dead shift is a multidimensional loaded-movement drill that focuses on deadstart strength.

Pectoralis major

Contralateral external oblique

Ipsilateral internal oblique

Rectus femoris

a   b   c

Primary Muscles Activated

Lift phase (same muscles work eccentrically on lower phase):

- *Shoulder (top hand; abduction)*: pectoralis major upper fibers, deltoid anterior fibers, deltoid middle fibers, deltoid posterior fibers, supraspinatus
- *Shoulder (bottom hand; adduction)*: latissimus dorsi, pectoralis major lower fibers, teres major, subscapularis, coracobrachialis
- *Hip (front leg; extension)*: gluteus maximus, biceps femoris long head, semitendinosus, semimembranosus
- *Knee (front leg; extension)*: rectus femoris, vastus lateralis, vastus medialis, vastus intermedius
- *Ankle (front leg; plantarflexion)*: gastrocnemius, soleus

Rotation phase:

- *Trunk (rotation)*: ipsilateral erector spinae, contralateral external oblique, ipsilateral internal oblique
- *Hip (bilateral external rotation)*: gluteus maximus, gluteus medius posterior fibers, piriformis, gemellus superior and inferior, obturator externus and internus, quadratus femoris

1. Set a ViPR PRO upright on one end and stand next to it at arm's length in an athletic position. Squat and grab the ViPR PRO by the handles (see figure *a*).
2. Lift it overhead as you turn and pivot (see figure *b*).
3. Set it down with control on the other side of you, taking a lunge step as if you were moving a large log from one side of you to the other (see figure *c*).
4. Repeat 4 to 8 reps for 3 to 5 sets on each side.

Strong Enough for What?

Having answered the first question (How strong is strong enough?) earlier in this chapter, it brings us to the second question: Strong enough for what? When talking about acceleration and sprinting, the answer to this question is being able to apply large amounts of force into the ground literally faster than you can blink (ground-contact time for elite runners is around eight hundredths of a second, while the average time it takes to blink an eye is a tenth of a second). Side note: If you just read that sentence without blinking, you are probably an android. That punch of force also needs to be applied over and over in near-perfect rhythm like a drummer. Enhancing these abilities in the weight room takes a more targeted approach than just doing squats and deadlifts. And it starts with training the neuromuscular system. Since neurological and tissue adaptations are both specific to the stress of training, the first thing to keep in mind when talking about getting speed specific is that, if you want to be fast, you need to train fast. Why? The faster you move something, the more your neuromuscular system gets involved. When you do a squat with heavy weight, the muscles and fascia tissues of your body respond to handle high force at slow speed primarily in the sagittal plane, but they respond very differently when you are accelerating or cutting to change direction on multiple planes at speed. This is part of the reason why simply doing squats and deadlifts doesn't always translate to increased game speed (once foundational strength is achieved). The sudden changes of vector, load, and velocity that happen in field and court sports require a very different neuromuscular response. Another example is doing loaded single-leg balance exercises and calf raises in order to increase ankle stability and lower-leg stiffness. Ankle stability and lower-leg stiffness are crucial for speed, but when you're decelerating and cutting, the muscles, tendons, and connective tissues around your ankle fire in very different ways than when you're just maintaining your center of gravity in a loaded stance. They must transmit force into the ground while also stabilizing and protecting the joint from rotational injury on different vectors. As a result, focusing on mental intention and timing is critical to athletic training. The ability to rapidly co-contract muscles and harness the elastic storage power of tendons and fascia to transfer force at just the right moment in the rhythm is more important to speed and explosiveness than just being strong. And as an athlete gets more advanced, generalized resistance training becomes less impactful on their speed. Once a solid level of foundational strength is established, speed gains can be better achieved through high-velocity, sport-specific training with submaximal loads, dynamic plyometrics, and accommodating resistance modalities that mimic the biomechanics of running.

Muscle Slack

One of the most important training principles for improving speed and power is what renowned speed coach Frans Bosch describes as "eliminating muscle slack." According to Bosch, the ability to quickly eliminate muscle slack and create tension in the system is more important than the maximum amount of force you can produce. A good analogy for the concept of muscle slack is trying to tow a car with a rope. In order to apply the force necessary to move the car, you have to get the slack out of the rope first. Removing muscle slack is why doing the countermovement loading phase of a vertical jump results in a higher jump than just jumping from a static squat—even though you can produce more force starting from the static squat position. If you don't pre-tense the muscles with a countermovement that quickly removes the slack, you generate force too slowly. According to Bosch, elite athletes are able to make smaller countermovements that efficiently maximize the elastic storage capacity of their tendons and fascia tissue, while slower athletes tend to have larger countermovements when running or jumping because they're trying to take the slack out of the system. I always come back to the javelin throw because it's where I started, and throwing is one of the most whole-body movements you can do. When you throw a javelin, you plant your forward foot after the penultimate step of the run-up and cock your throwing arm back to get all of the slack out of the muscles with a brief isometric contraction, which helps harness the elastic whip of your tendons and fascia to maximize that throw. But if you have too much slack in your muscles, you're not going to be elastic enough, and it will take longer to generate force. This means that dynamic plyometrics that involve rebounding movements (e.g., depth jumps) and absorption movements (e.g., depth drops) can be beneficial for speed-specific strength training because they prompt the muscles to co-contract and create tension quickly. The caveat with these exercises is that, while they have the potential for high reward, they also involve higher levels of risk and should only be done after you have developed a solid level of foundational strength with experienced trained athletes.

The ability to remove slack from the system quickly is also why bar speed matters in the weight room and why research shows that high-velocity Olympic lifts such as hang cleans and snatches can also be beneficial for improving power and speed (Ayers et al. 2016). The challenge with Olympic lifts is that they too are technical movements with a higher risk for injury. For that reason, they should be limited to one-on-one or small-group training sessions with an experienced coach.

There's a psychological side to this dynamic as well. Research studies show that, at least with high-velocity strength training, the mental intention to produce force quickly is more important than the actual speed of the action (Balshaw et al. 2016). This is one of the reasons why training with submaximal loads is beneficial for speed. Current evidence suggests that resistance exercises done rapidly using between 40 and 60 percent of an athlete's 1RM are the most effective for improving power, high-velocity strength, and sprinting performance (Mora-Custodio et al. 2016). Ultimately, you're programming the neuromuscular system, and that starts with a thought.

DUMBBELL PUSH PRESS

The dumbbell push press is a variation of the traditional barbell push press that develops lower-body power. You should use your lower body to generate upward momentum and focus on keeping your core tight as you pump the dumbbells overhead. Keep your chest up with a neutral trunk and spine throughout the exercise.

Triceps brachii

Pectoralis major

Primary Muscles Activated

Lift phase (same muscles work eccentrically during lower phase):
- *Shoulder (flexion)*: deltoid anterior fibers, pectoralis major upper fibers, coracobrachialis
- *Shoulder girdle (upward rotation)*: serratus anterior, trapezius upper, middle, and lower fibers
- *Elbow (extension)*: triceps brachii all heads, anconeus

1. Stand with your feet hip-width apart holding a dumbbell in each hand at shoulder height with your palms facing inward and your forearms directly under the dumbbells (see figure *a*).

2. Maintaining a tight core and neutral spine, preload the movement by dipping down slightly and bending at your hips and knees (see figure *b*).

3. Explode upward and drive the dumbbells overhead by extending your hips, knees, and ankles and pushing the dumbbells up with your arms until your elbows are straight (see figure *c*). Hold the dumbbells overhead for a beat and then lower them back to the starting position with control.

4. Repeat 2 to 5 reps for 3 to 5 sets.

BARBELL CLEAN

The barbell clean is a complex, whole-body Olympic lift. It requires your body to work as a connected unit and demands complete focus. On that note, one of the most important things to learn when doing the barbell clean (or any Olympic lift) is how to drop the bar safely if you fail. When you miss a clean, the bar will fall forward. Keep your hands on the bar as it falls, but don't try to slow it down. Just guide its path, pushing the bar away from you and releasing it when it's about two or three feet from the floor. When the bar hits the floor, it will bounce and roll. After it bounces, keep it from rolling too far. It's important to take time to learn the skill before adding load and intensity. A great way to learn the clean is to start out using an empty Olympic bar (or lighter fixed barbell) until you master the movement sequence.

MODERATE

Primary Muscles Activated

Lift phase (same muscles work eccentrically during return phase):

- *Ankle (plantarflexion)*: gastrocnemius, soleus
- *Knee (extension)*: rectus femoris, vastus lateralis, vastus medialis, vastus intermedius
- *Hip (extension)*: gluteus maximus, biceps femoris long head, semitendinosus, semimembranosus
- *Trunk (extension)*: erector spinae, quadratus lumborum
- *Shoulder (flexion)*: deltoid anterior fibers, pectoralis major upper fibers, coracobrachialis
- *Shoulder girdle (elevation)*: rhomboids, levator scapulae, trapezius upper fibers, trapezius middle fibers
- *Elbow (flexion)*: biceps brachii, brachialis, brachioradialis
- *Wrist (extension)*: extensor carpi radialis longus, extensor carpi radialis brevis, extensor carpi ulnaris, extensor digitorum, extensor pollicis longus

1. Stand over the barbell with your feet hip-width apart. Engage your core and keep your spine neutral as you squat down and lift the bar to a standing position. Keeping your core tight and your knees bent slightly, allow the bar to rest against the front of your thighs (see figure *a*).

2. Begin the movement by forcefully driving the hips up and forward as you straighten your legs. As soon as your hips are fully extended, quickly drop your body under the bar and catch it in the front-rack position (across the front of your shoulders with elbows as high as possible) in a quarter squat and extend to a full standing position (see figure *b*).

3. Lower the barbell back to the starting position (standing with bent knees).

4. Depending on the training phase, do anywhere from 2 to 5 reps for 3 to 5 sets.

KETTLEBELL SNATCH

The kettlebell snatch is a truly whole-body exercise. It is also a technically demanding lift that requires the entire body to work together to get the sequence right and reap the most benefits.

Pectoralis major — Quadratus lumborum — Vastus medialis

a   b   c   d

Primary Muscles Activated

Explode phase (same muscles work eccentrically during lower phase):

- *Ankle (plantarflexion)*: gastrocnemius, soleus
- *Knee (extension)*: rectus femoris, vastus lateralis, vastus medialis, vastus intermedius
- *Hip (extension)*: gluteus maximus, biceps femoris long head, semitendinosus, semimembranosus
- *Trunk (extension)*: erector spinae, quadratus lumborum
- *Shoulder (flexion)*: deltoid anterior fibers, pectoralis major upper fibers, coracobrachialis
- *Shoulder girdle (elevation)*: rhomboids, levator scapulae, trapezius upper fibers, trapezius middle fibers
- *Elbow (flexion to extension)*: biceps brachii, brachialis, brachioradialis (flexion); triceps brachii all heads, anconeus (extension)

1. Stand with feet about shoulder-width apart, brace your core, and hold a kettlebell in one hand between your legs (see figure *a*).

2. Hinge at the hips and hike the kettlebell between your legs keeping a strong braced core and neutral spine (see figure *b*).

3. Imagine your arm is a hook with the kettlebell attached to it and explode upward by extending the hips, knees, and ankles, accelerating the kettlebell up vertically (see figure *c*). Use the momentum from your hips to punch your fist straight up (see figure *d*).

4. Lower the kettlebell back to the starting position by bending your forearm inward toward your midline while simultaneously extending your elbow. Control the kettlebell's descent as gravity pulls it toward the floor.

5. Repeat 2 to 5 reps for 3 to 5 sets.

Isokinetic and Accommodating Resistance

While relative strength is important for athletic performance, the musculoskeletal system is only part of the symphony. The entire body is involved in creating speed. The kinetic energy storage and elastic recoil properties of the tendons and fascia system give muscles their ability to express strength as power. The nervous system runs the show, and that's why traditional weightlifting has limited application when it comes to improving speed. While heavy lifting can increase hypertrophy and motor unit recruitment, it also limits your degrees of freedom in movement. In competitive sports, most movements are done with high degrees of freedom, low load, and fast speeds. To get to the next level, your training program must cater to the multidimensional way the body actually moves at speed. That's where isokinetic and accommodating resistance exercises can make a huge impact on performance. They allow you to mimic sport-specific movements under load with greater degrees of freedom and higher speeds.

Another factor to consider is the importance of eccentric loading in force production. While most traditional weightlifting exercises have both an eccentric and concentric phase to them, an athlete's ability to produce force eccentrically at 1RM is significantly greater than their ability to produce force concentrically at 1RM (Kelly et al. 2015). With most traditional weightlifting exercises, you can produce more force at the beginning of a lift because the joint angles provide greater leverage, but as the muscles lengthen and the joint angles decrease at the end range of the motion, so does your ability to apply force. Additionally, you have to decelerate the weight at the end of a movement to control the momentum required to lift it (unless you want to throw it). No matter how much weight you're lifting, there's always momentum carrying the weight up or riding with it down. Consequently, many traditional lifting exercises don't develop an athlete's eccentric strength at the same rate they develop their concentric strength because the weights and reps are limited by the athlete's maximum concentric abilities. This is why using some form of accommodating resistance by adding bands or chains to the bar or using isokinetic modalities has been shown to increase power and speed (Joy et al. 2013). By training with an isokinetic form of accommodating resistance, you can maximize your efforts all the way through the power stroke to the very end range of the motion.

To illustrate this concept, the Parisi Speed School conducted force plate studies with Ken Clark, PhD, at West Chester University of Pennsylvania's Exercise Science Lab looking at the force signatures created during a traditional trap bar deadlift as compared to an isokinetic OHM machine (see figure 5.6). Those studies showed that force output decreases once you get past the halfway point of a traditional trap bar deadlift. In contrast, when you use an isokinetic machine to do the same exercise, you are able to continue increasing force output all the way to the very end of the motion. This is black-and-white force plate data.

Accommodating resistance is proven to enhance strength, power, and explosiveness for all types of athletes, but it is especially relevant for speed athletes.

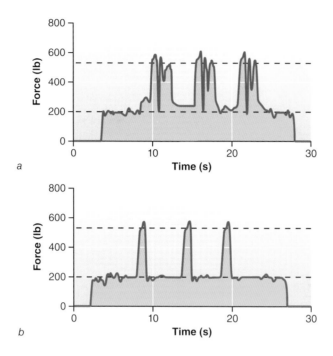

FIGURE 5.6   Force plate signatures comparing (*a*) a traditional trap bar deadlift to (*b*) a deadlift on an isokinetic OHM machine show a stark difference in force output with the OHM machine resulting in a much smoother stroke that optimizes the end range of movement.

© Kenneth P. Clark. Used with permission.

In addition to needing the lower-leg complex to be stiffer at ground contact for maximum force production and speed, the entire core and hip complex needs to be stiffer at ground contact as well. And you need to be able to take the slack out of the system quickly. Isokinetic training with loaded movements allows you to use your whole body to produce force in natural ways that directly translate to the field, court, or track. When you train with this kind of modality, you're recruiting more motor engram units at every stage. This includes doing dynamic resisted jumps on a Vertimax Platform or doing short, resisted sprints on an isokinetic OHM Run machine (see figure 5.7). Of course, many athletes and trainers don't have access to these types of advanced tools, but the same principles can be executed using traditional exercises such as sled drags, resisted bounds, or dynamic medicine ball pushes out of an acceleration position. Once you understand the basic concepts, there's a lot of potential available in adding some type of loading stimulus to acceleration and deceleration drills such as bands, weighted vests, medicine balls, or sandbags (which we'll delve into in the subsequent chapters). The idea is to do loaded sport-relevant movements in very specific body positions that require balance, core stability, and rapid force production. In addition to helping increase speed-specific strength, this approach also strengthens tendons and ligaments and increases neuromuscular engagement.

FIGURE 5.7   The OHM Run's "Delta Kinetic" platform provides an isokinetic form of accommodating resistance that allows athletes to maximize efforts working against a responsive load all the way through the very end range of motion, where force production matters most.

There are multiple schools of thought, books, and opinions on how to best structure a strength-training program for speed, and the terminology can quickly get deep. Wading into those waters is not the purpose of this book. I've outlined some evidence-based training and periodization protocols in the menus in chapter 12 that will give you the basics so you can apply these principles to your own program. But one of the most important things you can do for your athletes is to keep it simple. If you keep your program relatively simple and explain things in clear terms as you go, your athletes will buy into the programs more easily and they'll better understand why they're doing things. You also need to remind them that (somewhat ironically) speed training is a slow process. Early gains are easy for inexperienced athletes to achieve, but advanced gains take time. And it's critical that you stay consistent. You have to trust the process, one that can take six months to a year before significant gains are realized. Too often, I see trainers or athletes change course like they're changing shirts. A good analogy is that speed training happens in much the same way hair grows: It's a biological process. Your hair grows every day, but you don't really notice it. Then, all of a sudden, you wake up one day and realize you need a haircut. A lot of times, that's what happens with speed training—you work harder and harder and don't see your times change, so you get frustrated. But if you stick with the process and strategically time your rest periods, eventually you take a couple of days off and then boom! You wake up the next day to find you've got that added pop. It's just like waking up one day and realizing you need a haircut even though your hair's been growing for the last six weeks. The secret is to chart a solid training course based on individual need, do regular assessments to monitor progress, and, above all, trust the process.

6

ACCELERATION

I'll say it again for the people in the back: Intention matters in all things, and the nervous system runs the show—especially when it comes to acceleration. I could get you to run the fastest 40-yard dash you've ever run in your life with zero training or preparation simply by putting a very hungry, very angry grizzly bear in a cage 10 yards behind you and opening the cage the moment the starting gun went off. *But that's a primal instinct, fight-or-flight response,* you say, *not a race.* Fine. Instead of tapping into the raw survival instincts of your limbic animal brain, let's tap into your more logical, business-minded cerebral cortex by putting a big, red button 40 yards away that lights up for four and a half seconds as soon as you leave the starting line. If you hit the button before the light turns off, you get $10 million dollars (which is kind of how the NFL Combine works). I'm not saying you would escape getting eaten by a bear or win $10 million (or not injure yourself in the process of trying), but your nervous and adrenal systems would ensure that you ran the fastest 40 you've probably ever run.

That said, give me six months of focused training and I guarantee I can significantly increase your chances of winning the bear lottery without injuring yourself. This is because speed, in all of its forms, is a skill that research has proven can be developed and improved through targeted training and optimal mechanics. The science of how we improve speed has rapidly evolved over the past few decades as well. Thanks to pioneering research and increasingly advanced analysis tools, we now know far more about the functional biomechanics of sprinting, acceleration, maximum velocity, and multidirectional speed than when I first started in this industry over 30 years ago. And one of the top researchers leading the charge toward this new knowledge is Ken Clark, PhD, a former Parisi Speed School athlete whose passion to understand the science of speed began when his dad brought him into the Parisi facility as a young, relatively slow high school football player who just wanted to get faster so he could become a better running back.

"Genetically, I could probably run the 40 in like 5.2 seconds back then, which was too slow to be a good high school football player or even play at the Division III college level," says Clark. "My dad started coaching me and taking me to different speed coaches and performance programs, including the Parisi Speed School. That's when my passion for understanding the mechanics of speed really began. During that time, I learned two important things. I learned that (1) you can make people faster. I mean, you're not going to get everyone to be Usain Bolt—but you can certainly make people faster through targeted training. And (2) some training methods work better than others."

Since then, understanding the biomechanics of speed has become Ken's lifelong obsession. After becoming an All-Conference Division III running back while attending Swarthmore College, he went on to work as a strength and conditioning coach at a number of high schools, colleges, and private sector settings around the nation. In 2014, Ken received his PhD in Applied Physiology and Biomechanics from Southern Methodist University where he worked on groundbreaking research with renowned speed expert Dr. Peter Weyand, studying some of the fastest sprinters on the planet at the most advanced human locomotion lab in the country. Today, Ken teaches biomechanics, kinetic anatomy, and motor learning at West Chester University of Pennsylvania and is recognized as an expert on the subject of speed mechanics. I tell this story not just because I enjoy a nostalgic trip down memory lane, but because it underscores how you can change the world simply by deciding you want to be great at something that you're not naturally gifted at—which, coincidentally, was also my experience throwing the javelin in high school and college. Intention matters. To achieve that kind of goal, you don't get to coast on charm and good genes. You need to work harder than everyone else. More importantly, you need to work *smarter*. You need to learn everything there is to know about the how and why of your chosen discipline from people who are much smarter than you and then keep pushing until you break new ground. That's how you get from novice to expert, from basic to advanced. I also tell this story because I had the opportunity to interview Ken at length for this book and I wanted you to know that his content is grounded in rigorous science conducted with some of the top researchers and athletes in the world. It's not just something we came up with because it sounds cool. If you want to reach your full genetic potential for speed, you need to understand how the engine works—also the transmission, suspension, drivetrain, electrical system, and everything else under the hood.

A WORD ON THE DATA

It's worth noting that much of the linear speed research referenced in this chapter and the next chapter (on maximum velocity) comes from the world of track and field. While field and court sport athletes will run differently in game situations than track athletes, it's important that they understand the rules of acceleration and sprinting so they can break those rules based on the constraints of their sport. Some of the data cited in this chapter also comes from studies conducted at a unique testing facility located at the National Institute of Fitness and Sports in Kanoya, Japan, where research teams led by Ryu Nagahara and others have access to a state-of-the-art running track embedded with 50 meters of instrumented force plates combined with a synchronized motion capture system that gathers incredibly detailed data for every stride.

"An athlete can start at the starting line, and every single step of their entire sprint generates three-dimensional force data, including ground-contact times, flight times, stride rate, stride length, and speed," says Clark, referring to the test track in Kanoya. "When you have that type of experimental setup, every research publication you produce is going to be a worthwhile contribution because it's all new."

Phases of Acceleration

Figure 6.1 looks at sprint phases and stride variables as an athlete performs a 20-meter acceleration from a three-point stance. The start and initial acceleration phase of a sprint lasts from zero to approximately 10 meters, with ground-contact times that are relatively longer, flight times that are relatively shorter, and a body position that's leaning forward. The transitional acceleration phase occurs from approximately 10 to 20 meters, with intermediate ground-contact and flight times and a body position that's becoming gradually more upright with each step. The top-speed phase begins at around the 20-meter mark where the ground-contact times are much shorter, flight times are longer, and the body position is almost entirely upright. By the 20-meter mark, the runner will be displaying near-maximum velocity mechanics. This has important training (and game) implications that I'll get into later in this chapter and the next.

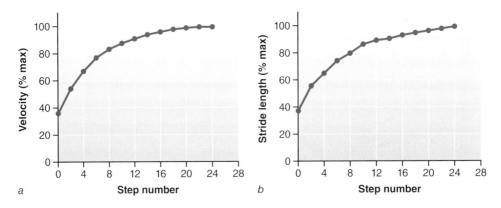

Phase	Distance	Contact time	Flight time	Body position
Start + initial acceleration	0-10 m	Longer	Shorter	Forward lean
Transitional acceleration	10-20 m	Intermediate	Intermediate	Becoming upright
Approaching top speed	20+ m	Shorter	Longer	Upright

FIGURE 6.1   The start and initial acceleration phase of a sprint lasts from zero to approximately 10 meters; the transitional acceleration phase happens between 10 to 20 meters; and the top-speed phase begins at around the 20-meter mark, at which point the athlete will be displaying upright max-velocity running mechanics.

© Kenneth P. Clark. Used with permission. Adapted from R. Nagahara, T. Matsubayashi, A. Matsuo, and K. Zushi, "Kinematics of Transition During Human Accelerated Sprinting," *Biology Open* 3 (2014): 689-699.

"It's important to know that from a stimulus and mechanics standpoint, if you're having an athlete do sprints of 20 or 30 meters, you are touching on top-speed qualities," says Clark. Data also show that an athlete reaches a high percentage of their maximum step frequency by about 10 meters, meaning they will be at near-maximum step frequency by steps six to eight. After the 10-meter mark, the increases in stride length will be nearly proportional to increases in velocity (see figure 6.2*a* and *b*). In short, as an athlete progresses through the phases of acceleration from a static start, their ground-contact times gradually decrease as their flight times increase with every step in a smooth, rhythmic crescendo until they reach max velocity (Nagahara et al. 2014).

FIGURE 6.2   An athlete accelerating from a deadstart will achieve a high percentage of their maximum step frequency by about 10 meters, which means they will be at near-maximum step frequency by steps six to eight, after which their increases in stride length will be proportional to increases in velocity.

© Kenneth P. Clark. Used with permission. Adapted from R. Nagahara, T. Matsubayashi, A. Matsuo, and K. Zushi, "Kinematics of Transition During Human Accelerated Sprinting," *Biology Open* 3 (2014): 689-699.

Cueing for Speed: Acceleration

Acceleration can be broken down into different phases, such as front- and backside mechanics and transition. While coaches can cue individual elements of acceleration based on what an athlete needs to work on, the athlete, however, experiences them all as one connected action. Cues are powerful because they provide a task-driven metaphor for the athlete to visualize and feel. Coaches should work on one point of focus at a time with simple, short cues. Once that target goal is achieved, move on and revisit the cue only as necessary. Also, there are endless possibilities. I've listed a few proven acceleration cues here to get you started, but you should experiment with what works for you and your athletes and remember—every situation is unique.

Imagine your entire body is a switchblade folded at the hips. Open the switchblade in a dynamic, spring-like action that centers at the hips.

Scissor the thighs as if they are a pair of scissors opening.

(continued)

Cueing for Speed: Acceleration *(continued)*

Push the ground away and think about driving the ground back with full force.

Punch the knees forward as if you're a boxer throwing a jab punch with your knees.
Short version: Punch the knees!

Mechanics of Acceleration

Good acceleration mechanics involve a balance of propulsion and braking forces (where you need more of the former and less of the latter) applied horizontally and vertically (with more horizontal force and longer contact times in the first few steps, shifting to more vertical force and shorter contact times as speed increases). It also requires a combination of explosive strength and elastic recoil that efficiently harnesses the power of the stretch-shortening cycle.

Propulsion and Braking

Acceleration is classically defined as the rate of change in velocity over time. It is not limited to how fast you can accelerate from a static start. If you are running at 10 miles per hour (16 km), acceleration is the measurement of how quickly you can go from 10 to 20 miles per hour (16 to 32 km)—in other words, your rate of change in velocity. The question is: How fast can you get to maximum velocity?

"When a runner is accelerating from a static start, there is a net increase in velocity during the course of each step," says Clark. "But after the second step, the runner's foot will start to land slightly out in front of the center of mass [COM]. From step three onward, the foot lands slightly in front of the center of mass. That's just how it works for everyone. This causes a braking force (technically known as a 'braking impulse') to occur. When your stance foot is out in front of your center of mass, you put on the brakes in the same way you decelerate when you're trying to stop. Then, as your center of mass moves in front of the foot during the second half of ground contact, you generate a propulsive force (technically known as a 'propulsive impulse'). Basically, you have a braking force happening during the first part of ground contact and a propulsive force happening during the second part of ground contact. This means that how much you increase velocity with each step comes down to the ratio of your propulsive forces to your braking forces [see figure 6.3]. If you don't have much braking force at the beginning of the step, and you have a lot of propulsive force during the second portion of the step, you will accelerate more during that ground contact."

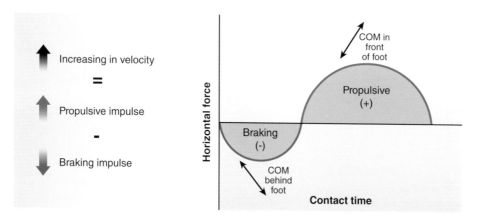

FIGURE 6.3 Athletes need to apply greater propulsive impulses than braking impulses to increase velocity during acceleration.

In the initial steps of a sprint—steps one, two, and three—the braking impulses are small because the foot is landing close to underneath the center of mass, and the propulsive impulses are very big because there's a long push-off time. This translates to high acceleration (big increases in velocity) with each step at the beginning of a sprint. As a sprinter progresses and their body becomes more upright, the braking impulses increase while the propulsive impulses decrease due to their body posture and where the foot strikes relative to the center of mass. The faster you go causes your foot to land farther in front of you, braking impulses to become bigger, and propulsive impulses to get smaller. When you are running at top speed, the braking impulses and propulsive impulses become equal, and there is no net change in velocity per step because you are now running at your top speed. Simply put, to increase velocity with each step, you need to apply greater propulsive impulses than braking impulses. In fact, a study by J.B. Morin and colleagues (2015) comparing world-class sprinters with average sprinters found that their braking impulses were relatively similar in the first few steps of a sprint, but the big difference is that world-class sprinters are able to apply greater propulsive impulses in slightly shorter ground-contact times than slower runners. This is especially relevant in the first few steps of a sprint. Elite sprinters strike behind their center of mass at initial ground-contact for the first two to three steps. As a result, their entire ground-contact time comprises propulsive impulses with almost zero braking impulses. This ability to rapidly accelerate comes from having both optimal strength relative to their body weight and good acceleration mechanics (body position).

Vertical and Horizontal Forces

Speed requires the application of both vertical and horizontal forces. The goal of a runner during the initial acceleration phase is to apply enough vertical force to support their body and lift their center of mass into the next step while they direct the rest of their forces horizontally so that the action–reaction forces can propel them forward. When you're starting from a static position, you want to start with a forward lean of approximately 45 degrees. This position allows you to project the maximum amount of force horizontally for increased acceleration with minimal braking impulse. Of course, the optimal starting angle is unique for every athlete based on different factors, including body dimensions; relative strength; and whether it's a two-, three-, or four-point starting stance. But 45 degrees is a good baseline for aligning the center of mass. The goal with initial acceleration is to project the center of mass up and out so that you maximize the propulsive force of the first step while also putting your body in a position to successfully execute the following steps.

With the first step, your foot strikes underneath your body. So the braking force is small, and the propulsive force is large. After the first step, there should be an acute forward body angle as the center of mass rises progressively with each sequential step. Typically, an athlete will reach a nearly fully upright maximum-velocity posture somewhere around steps 12 to 14, or roughly 20 to 25 meters into the sprint. This gradual rise allows the legs to have the swing space necessary to reposition for the increased stride length that results in increased velocity. As a runner increases velocity, there is a gradual decrease in ground-contact times, along with a corresponding increase in flight times and a gradual increase in stride length. During the first half of ground contact, the athlete must rotate their center of mass so that it's in front of the stance foot and the vector of ground-reaction force. This means that aiming to strike underneath the body and keeping the center of mass ahead of the foot for a majority of the ground-contact time will result in optimal mechanics that minimize braking forces and maximize propulsive forces. As velocity increases and ground-contact times decrease with each step, the amount of vertical force that needs to be applied downward to support body weight increases with every step.

"From a general physics standpoint, the requirements for a static sprint start are that you need to apply enough vertical force down to support your body weight, and then whatever force reserves you have remaining get directed backward," says Clark. "Athletes who are stronger and lighter have no problem applying enough vertical force to support their body weight and still have lots of force left over to push back. Newton's third law of action–reaction forces will project their center of mass up and forward. As a result, they have a really big stride length because they're projecting their center of mass really far forward with each step. Those lighter, stronger guys with great relative strength have a more acute drive angle—that 40- to 45-degree angle—on the first step or two because they can produce enough force vertically to support their body weight, and the rest of the force is going back. So they have a sharp force vector with a low drive angle as compared to a 320-pound [145 kg] lineman who is strong, but not strong relative to their body weight. For a guy like that, the amount of vertical force it takes for them to support their body weight doesn't leave much force remaining for them to drive back with. So they don't project their center of mass out as well. And, even though they may be a little bit taller, their stride length isn't going to be as good as someone who is say 5' 10" [178 cm], weighs 170 pounds [77 kg], and can deadlift 500 [227]."

This makes relative body strength essential for initial acceleration and greater stride length. In fact, after decades of analyzing athletes at the Parisi Speed School doing 10-yard (9 m) acceleration sprints, we've found that our faster, lighter athletes have a much larger first stride out of the blocks and use fewer strides to get to the 10-yard (9 m) mark. My anecdotal hypothesis regarding this is that, even though they create more braking forces because their foot is landing farther out in front of their center of mass, they have such great relative glute, hamstring, and posterior chain strength and activation that they can overcome it by pulling their center of mass forward over the base of support. They also have more relative elasticity, which means they're more fascia driven. Then, as the center of mass comes forward, a triple extension of the hip extensors, knee extensors, and plantar flexors allows them to push back during the second part of ground contact with each step to create more propulsion during the first couple of strides.

THE 40-YARD GOLD STANDARD

Love it or hate it, the 40-yard dash is the gold standard for acceleration and sprint performance in field and court sports—especially American football. A player's time in the 40 can significantly affect their NFL draft status and college scholarship opportunities. Ironically, the 40-yard dash is not an official track-and-field race. It was originally established as a performance benchmark for American football players because 40 yards is the average distance of a punt. Fun fact: The average hang time for a punt is also approximately four and a half seconds. This means that if a player can run the 40 in four and a half seconds, they can make it from the line of scrimmage to where the ball comes down at about the same time. And that's how you win the $10 million dollars.

In 2016, Ken Clark conducted a research analysis studying the sprint velocity profiles of all 260 athletes who competed at the NFL Combine. The purpose of the study was to evaluate the relationship between maximum velocity and sprint performance and to compare acceleration patterns for fast and slow athletes (Clark 2017). It yielded some noteworthy insights.

"We took all the athletes who completed in the 40-yard dash at the NFL Combine and did some fancy math to come up with a curve that showed how fast each one was going at every yard of their sprint," says Clark. "This allowed us to see what percentage of their top speed they were hitting at every point in the race. And the results were very interesting. For a very long time, classic track-and-field literature and research stated that track-and-field sprinters running a 100-meter dash don't reach peak velocity till 50, 60, or 70 meters into the sprint. So a lot of coaches have it in their minds that runners don't hit peak speed until 60 meters into a race. The old conventional wisdom was that if you're only at 20 meters, you're not really moving that fast. But the analysis we did at the NFL Combine showed that when the race is shorter—in this case, 40 yards versus 100 meters—virtually every single athlete was running at 90 percent of their top speed by the time they were at the 20-yard mark. And this was true for both the guys who were very fast, like the wide receivers, as well as the slower guys, like the linemen. So, for easy numbers, that means if an athlete had a top speed of 10 meters a second, by

Clearly acceleration is paramount in team sports, but research is showing that maximum velocity affects the entire acceleration profile. A useful metric that Clark uses for velocity profiling is called tau, which is a fancy term for the ratio between maximum velocity and initial acceleration. While it's not used in the industry as much as it should be, tau essentially provides a numerical quantification of how well someone accelerates relative to their top speed. By assessing their tau values, a coach can look at a 10-yard dash and know if they are good or bad at the time they were at 20 yards, they were easily at nine meters a second. Even if they were slow—say they had a top speed of eight meters per second—they were easily at seven meters a second by the time they hit the 20-yard mark. It was very consistent from a percentage basis. And this was significant for me as both a researcher and a coach. Because there's this perhaps incorrect conventional wisdom that to do top-speed training, you need to be sprinting for 40 to 60 meters. And my take on it is that if you're doing anything past 20 meters, you're into top-speed mechanics. That's a big deal from a programming standpoint. Because it means that if you're doing 40-yard dashes, you are hitting all the components of speed—including start, transitional acceleration, and top speed [see figure 6.4]."

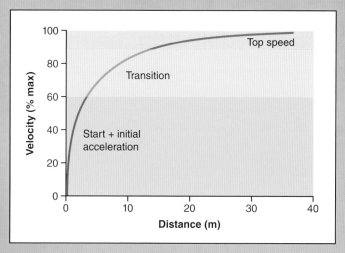

FIGURE 6.4   Ken Clark's study of athletes competing in the 40-yard dash at the NFL Combine revealed that athletes accelerating from a deadstart can reach near-maximum velocity by around 20 meters.

© Kenneth P. Clark. Used with permission.

acceleration in the context of their overall speed capabilities. For example, you could look at a 10-yard dash time that might seem slow, but if it's for an offensive lineman, it might be good compared to their maximum speed. This allows you to do velocity profiling in ways that can help you determine what an athlete needs from a training standpoint. But it's important to note that doing top-speed sprint training and increasing your maximum velocity capabilities may have a direct, measurable impact on acceleration and overall speed.

Strength and Elasticity

Acceleration training is very individualized in terms of the best way to coach an athlete based on their body's natural homeostatic drivers and what they should be doing in the weight room. Before developing a training prescription, you need to look at each athlete and their specific movement drivers. Is the athlete more of a muscle-based rhino or more of a fascia-based cheetah? Obviously, we're training all of the systems all the time, but the questions are: Where do they need more development, and where are their weaknesses? A reasonable strategy is to keep their natural abilities strong while targeting any deficiencies to bring those up. Muscle actions during initial acceleration—from zero through the first three steps—are much more concentric in nature. While there's a little bit of an eccentric phase in steps two and three, the initial muscle actions for acceleration are largely concentric compared to top speed, which relies more on the elastic stretch-shortening cycle of tendons and fascia. So, for example, a muscular-driven athlete who is strong in the weight room and can run a really good start might not have the kind of elasticity they need to achieve great top speed. You have to keep this in mind before prescribing more Romanian deadlifts versus doing more plyometrics. Does the athlete need more strength and shape stability or more elasticity and explosiveness?

Science has proven that a lot of the kinetic energy used for running and jumping is stored in our connective tissues, specifically in the Achilles (Wiesinger et al. 2017). Since the amount, structure, and type of collagen fibers in your fascia tissues and tendons develop based on the load, frequency, and pace of your movements, if you want to be fast, you need to do sprint training more often than not (without jeopardizing recovery times and increasing injury risk). This means doing lots of both acceleration and top-speed work and gradually developing the elasticity of the related tendons and fascia tissues through the power of mechanotransduction. Also, if you're tired of hearing about how important the core is for speed, you should prepare to get eaten by a bear. While research is showing us that relative body strength is the most important feature for maximum acceleration, if you don't have a strong core that can stabilize your center of gravity, create a dense spring of proximal stiffness, and efficiently transfer force, then a lot of that force is going to be wasted. In fact, electromyography (EMG) experiments conducted by Stu McGill analyzing top Olympic sprinters doing acceleration starts showed that their core was already highly activated when they were in the blocks getting ready to blast off. The key to harnessing this pulsing stiffness for improved acceleration and top speed is being able to rhythmically fire and relax it very quickly to let your body move through its motion sequence so it can set up to strike the ground with another pulse of stiffness. This rhythmic stiffening impulse is a trainable skill that the nervous and fascia systems control. It is facilitated through co-contractions of both agonist and antagonist muscle groups all the way up the kinetic chain, as well. The impulse happens not only in the core but also at the distal end of the equation in the foot–ankle complex. Other EMG studies show that there is a similar pulse of co-contraction that happens in the lower leg and foot–ankle complex just before ground contact as the body primes itself to punch the ground (Morin et al. 2015).

Acceleration Training

On an acceleration-training day, training is a three-step strategy. The first step is to progress from the ADW drills listed in chapter 4 to doing two or three acceleration-specific anchor drills that prime the body for acceleration mechanics and tissue activation. The next step is to progress into acceleration-specific application drills done at game speed while maintaining optimal acceleration position and mechanics. The final step is to end the training day by doing acceleration sprints at full intensity because, if you want to be fast, you need to train fast. A few examples of acceleration-specific anchor and application drills are presented here, and you can find more in the training menus in chapter 12. Remember, the essence of a good system is not doing thousands of different drills. It's about taking a few key drills and progressing and regressing them with different loads, angles, and intensities until you master them.

BASIC

WALL DRIVE PLANK

The essence of acceleration, especially in the first two to three strides, is the ability to overcome a static position with dynamic force production, whether you're coming out of the blocks from a track stance or off the line from a football stance. Your core needs to be fully engaged, and your body needs to be angled forward to create maximum drive and acceleration.

When it comes to doing anchor drills for acceleration, the first thing you want to do is get an athlete to feel that 45-degree position. As previously mentioned, the actual angle of the body is going to be different for every person depending on their size, anatomical proportions, and relative body strength. If they're tall, heavy, and not that strong, it's going to be closer to a 50-degree angle. If they're really strong, you may get as low as 42 or 43 degrees. But you want to start out by getting the athlete to feel that position using a foundational drill such as a double-arm wall drive plank, which provides a basic understanding of how to create a mechanical composite across the core and create stiffness in that 45-degree angle position.

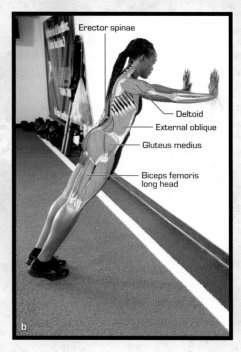

Erector spinae

Deltoid

External oblique

Gluteus medius

Biceps femoris long head

a

b

Primary Muscles Activated

Isometric phase:

- *Wrist (flexion)*: flexor carpi radialis, palmaris longus, flexor carpi ulnaris, flexor digitorum superficialis, flexor digitorum profundus, flexor pollicis longus
- *Shoulder (flexion)*: deltoid anterior fibers, pectoralis major upper fibers, coracobrachialis
- *Trunk (isometric neutral)*: rectus abdominis, internal oblique, external oblique, erector spinae, quadratus lumborum
- *Hip (extension, external rotation)*: gluteus maximus, biceps femoris long head, semitendinosus, semimembranosus (extension); gluteus maximus, gluteus medius posterior fibers, piriformis, gemellus superior and inferior, obturator externus and internus, quadratus femoris (external rotation)
- *Knee (extension)*: rectus femoris, vastus lateralis, vastus medialis, vastus intermedius

1. Stand arm's length away from a wall and put both arms on the wall.
2. Lean into the wall with both arms until your body is at a roughly 45-degree angle with your arms and legs straight (see figure *a*).
3. Let your hips roll forward and find a deep wall-plank position where the spine is in a straight line (see figure *b*).
4. Without lifting your feet, put as much force into the wall as you can by pressing through the ground and wall.
5. Hold the position for 20 to 30 seconds for 2 to 4 sets.

After learning the technique for a double-arm wall drive plank, from there you can go through a series of wall-plank variations, including single-arm wall planks, double-arm and single-leg wall planks, and alternating single-arm and single-leg wall planks.

FEET-EXCHANGE WALL DRIVE

Feet-exchange wall drives help an athlete feel the pulsing twitch of firing their core rhythmically. The goal isn't to do a ton of core exercises; it's about understanding how to fire that crucial twitch of stiffness.

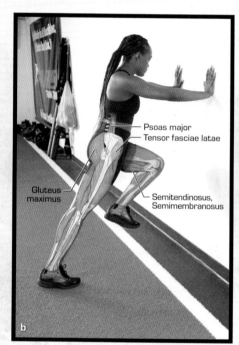

Psoas major
Tensor fasciae latae
Gluteus maximus
Semitendinosus, Semimembranosus

Primary Muscles Activated

Drive phase:

- *Hip (extension)*: gluteus maximus, biceps femoris long head, semitendinosus, semimembranosus
- *Knee (extension)*: rectus femoris, vastus lateralis, vastus medialis, vastus intermedius
- *Ankle (plantarflexion)*: gastrocnemius, soleus

Raise phase:

- *Hip (flexion)*: rectus femoris, iliacus, psoas major, pectineus, tensor fasciae latae
- *Knee (flexion)*: biceps femoris short and long head, semitendinosus, semimembranosus
- *Ankle (dorsiflexion)*: tibialis anterior, extensor hallucis longus, extensor digitorum longus

1. Stand arm's length away from a wall and put both arms on the wall.
2. Lean into the wall with both arms until your body is at a roughly 45-degree angle with your arms and legs straight (see figure *a*).
3. Raise one leg until the thigh is nearly perpendicular to your torso (see figure *b*). The raised shin should be at the same 45-degree angle as the shin in the anchor leg with your foot dorsiflexed (toes pointed up).
4. Drive the raised leg down and back and bring the opposing stance leg up (basically, switch them).
5. Hold the position for a two- to four-second count.
6. Repeat for 4 to 6 reps on each leg.

After doing a few single wall drive foot strikes, move on to doing doubles in a rapid-fire bang-bang rhythm that brings the athlete back to their starting position. Then move on to triples (bang-bang-bang) where the athlete starts and ends on the same foot. Start doing these drills slowly with proper form before increasing speed.

RESISTED RUNS:
SLED DRAG AND SLED PUSH

Resisted runs using sleds are proven to be effective anchor drills for improving acceleration. The goal is to feel inclined movement (at a 45-degree angle) under load, but without moving really fast, so you can develop the specific motor skills for horizontal force production. Loaded acceleration provides an increased amount of time under tension that helps develop neural pathways, engage tissues, and develop fascia along the lines of stress. Additionally, multiple studies looking at both competitive sprinters and team sport athletes from different disciplines found that the optimal load for maximizing acceleration power in resisted sled training is the load that decreases an athlete's maximal running speed by approximately 50 percent (Morin et al. 2017). So, if an athlete's max velocity is approximately 10 meters per second, the optimal weight for a sled drag or push is whatever load slows that athlete down to 5 meters per second (which is, on average, approximately 80 percent of their body weight). Obviously, that load will depend on the athlete's relative body strength.

SLED DRAG

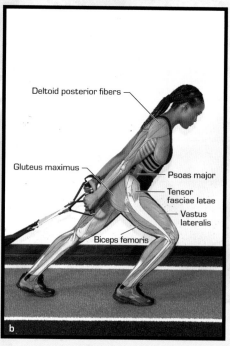

Primary Muscles Activated

Swing phase (front leg in air):
- *Shoulder (isometric extension)*: latissimus dorsi, teres major, triceps brachii long head, pectoralis major lower fibers, deltoid posterior fibers, infraspinatus
- *Hip (flexion)*: rectus femoris, iliacus, psoas major, pectineus, tensor fasciae latae
- *Knee (flexion)*: biceps femoris short and long head, semitendinosus, semimembranosus
- *Ankle (dorsiflexion)*: tibialis anterior, extensor hallucis longus, extensor digitorum longus

Stance phase (front leg hits ground and pushes off):
- *Shoulder (isometric extension)*: latissimus dorsi, teres major, triceps brachii long head, pectoralis major lower fibers, deltoid posterior fibers, infraspinatus
- *Hip (flexion to extension)*: gluteus maximus, biceps femoris long head, semitendinosus, semimembranosus
- *Knee (flexion to extension)*: rectus femoris, vastus lateralis, vastus medialis, vastus intermedius
- *Ankle (dorsiflexion to plantarflexion)*: gastrocnemius, soleus

1. Face away from the weighted sled and attach straps or a suspension system to it. Hold on to the strap or suspension system and stretch your arms out behind you.
2. Walk forward and away from the sled until you feel tension in the strap or suspension system (see figure *a*).
3. Get into the acceleration position, leaning forward at a 45-degree angle and keeping your spine neutral and hips tucked (see figure *b*).
4. March forward slowly, maintaining the acceleration position for 10 to 20 yards (9 to 18 m). Focus on maintaining good form and muscle activation. The goal is to drag 80 to 120 percent of the athlete's body weight on the sled.
5. Repeat for 4 to 6 reps.

SLED PUSH

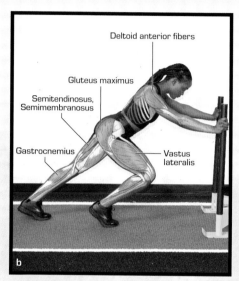

Deltoid anterior fibers

Gluteus maximus

Semitendinosus, Semimembranosus

Gastrocnemius

Vastus lateralis

Primary Muscles Activated

Push phase (foot pushing off ground):

- *Shoulder (isometric flexion)*: deltoid anterior fibers, pectoralis major upper fibers, coracobrachialis
- *Hip (extension)*: gluteus maximus, biceps femoris long head, semitendinosus, semimembranosus
- *Knee (extension)*: rectus femoris, vastus lateralis, vastus medialis, vastus intermedius
- *Ankle (plantarflexion)*: gastrocnemius, soleus

1. Stand facing the weighted sled and grab the sled bars.

2. Lean into the sled, assuming an acceleration position with a 45-degree angle and keeping your spine neutral and hips tucked (see figure *a*).

3. Accelerate quickly for 20 yards (18 m) while keeping your core tight, maintaining a neutral spine, and pushing down and back through the ground as you drive the sled forward (see figure *b*). Focus on proper acceleration mechanics.

4. Repeat for 4 to 6 reps.

MEDICINE BALL BROAD JUMP

A standing broad jump is a simple movement that can be augmented into an anchor drill for acceleration by adding a medicine ball push to link the upper and lower body for increased power production and using a similar dynamic to accelerate from a static start.

Primary Muscles Activated

Explosion phase:

- *Shoulder (horizontal adduction)*: biceps brachii, pectoralis major upper and lower fibers, coracobrachialis, deltoid anterior fibers
- *Elbow (extension)*: triceps brachii all heads, anconeus
- *Hip (extension)*: gluteus maximus, biceps femoris long head, semitendinosus, semimembranosus
- *Knee (extension)*: rectus femoris, vastus lateralis, vastus medialis, vastus intermedius
- *Ankle (plantarflexion)*: gastrocnemius, soleus

1. Stand in a flexed broad jump squat position holding a medicine ball at chest height (see figure *a*).
2. Explode out of the squat position into a forward broad jump while throwing the ball with a forward chest pass at the same time (see figures *b* and *c*). Focus on maximizing force production at a 45-degree angle and engaging the core as you jump forward and throw the medicine ball.
3. Repeat for 10 to 15 yards (9 to 14 m) for 4 to 6 sets.

PUSH-UP START

This exercise features a more horizontal shin angle than most athletic situations call for, which increases the first step's ground-contact time and results in greater force application, especially in horizontal projection. It also requires good isometric postural strength, forceful hip flexion, powerful hip and knee extension, ankle stiffness, and coordinated arm action. The exercise requires a high demand on local and peripheral neural networks, which work best with limited conscious efforts.

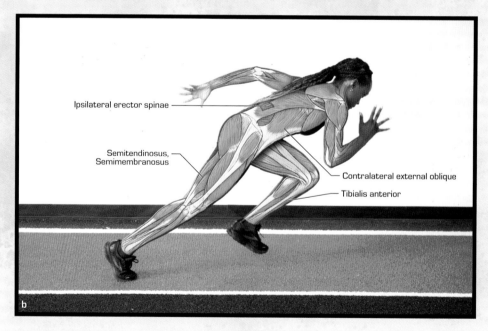

Primary Muscles Activated

Swing phase (front leg in air; contralateral front arm):

- *Shoulder (flexion)*: deltoid anterior fibers, pectoralis major upper fibers, coracobrachialis
- *Elbow (flexion)*: biceps brachii, brachialis, brachioradialis
- *Trunk (rotation)*: ipsilateral erector spinae, contralateral external oblique, ipsilateral internal oblique
- *Hip (flexion)*: rectus femoris, iliacus, psoas major, pectineus, tensor fasciae latae
- *Knee (flexion)*: biceps femoris short and long head, semitendinosus, semimembranosus
- *Ankle (dorsiflexion)*: tibialis anterior, extensor hallucis longus, extensor digitorum longus

Stance phase (front leg hits ground and pushes off; back leg and contralateral back arm shown in figure):

- *Shoulder (extension)*: latissimus dorsi, teres major, triceps brachii long head, pectoralis major lower fibers, deltoid posterior fibers, infraspinatus
- *Elbow (extension)*: triceps brachii all heads, anconeus
- *Trunk (rotation)*: ipsilateral erector spinae, contralateral external oblique, ipsilateral internal oblique
- *Hip (flexion to extension)*: gluteus maximus, biceps femoris long head, semitendinosus, semimembranosus
- *Knee (flexion to extension)*: rectus femoris, vastus lateralis, vastus medialis, vastus intermedius
- *Ankle (dorsiflexion to plantarflexion)*: gastrocnemius, soleus

1. Lie face down in a prone position, placing your hands in a push-up position. Dorsiflex your ankles and pull your toes toward your knees while tucking your chin toward your chest as if holding a baseball (see figure *a*).

2. With a braced core, push up explosively and quickly step forward and sprint as fast as possible (see figure *b*). Set your gaze 2 to 5 yards (about 2 to 5 m) ahead.

3. Repeat 2 to 6 reps of 5-yard, 10-yard, 15-yard, or 20-yard (about 5, 9, 14, or 18 m) maximal efforts with a work-to-rest ratio based on desired energy system development.

ACCELERATION LADDER SPRINT

ADVANCED

Acceleration ladder sprints through stride-specific, spaced ladder rungs (or cones) is a great transition away from anchor drills into application drills because the progressions help you understand the mechanics of stride length and frequency. When you accelerate, you want to maximize your stride length and drive your center of mass as far forward as possible on each stride. But that stride length is dependent on how much horizontal force you can generate. The first phase of acceleration ladder sprints begins with ladder stride lengths that are shorter than what you're capable of producing, which means your step frequency will be higher. As you go through the progression to full-stride length, you gradually switch to a longer ladder that requires progressively longer strides while trying to keep the same stride frequency. This helps develop rhythm and feel for optimal foot placement and drive. While an athlete's stride length will be dictated by their anatomy, power output, surface, and technical mastery, the setup that we use at the Parisi Speed School for acceleration ladder sprints is as follows.

- Paint eight 10- × 1-inch (25 × 3 cm) lines on either end of the track.
- All lines must be measured out and painted from the same starting point to show progression—for example, the beginning of 40 feet (12 m)—according to the measurements in the table that follows.
- If using a three-lane track, follow the measurements for the first three lanes as provided in the table.

	Lane 1	Lane 2	Lane 3	Lane 4
1	2' 2" (66 cm)	2' 5" (74 cm)	2' 7" (79 cm)	2' 10" (86 cm)
2	5' 1" (155 cm)	5' 7" (170 cm)	6' (183 cm)	6' 5" (196 cm)
3	8' 4" (254 cm)	9' 1" (277 cm)	9' 11" (302 cm)	10' 7" (323 cm)
4	12' (366 cm)	13' 1" (399 cm)	14' 4" (437 cm)	15' 6" (472 cm)
5	15' 11" (485 cm)	17' 7" (536 cm)	19' 2" (584 cm)	20' 10" (635 cm)
6	20' 1" (612 cm)	22' 4" (681 cm)	24' 7" (749 cm)	26' 8" (813 cm)
7	24' 6" (747 cm)	27' 5" (836 cm)	30' 3" (922 cm)	33' 1" (1,008 cm)
8	29' 2" (889 cm)	32' 9" (998 cm)	36' 5" (1,110 cm)	40' (1,219 cm)

ADVANCED

Setup for acceleration ladder sprints at Parisi Speed School.

JUMP-BACK ACCELERATION

Jump-back accelerations help an athlete land in a slightly forward-leaning body position where their center of mass is out in front. It also kickstarts the chain-reaction acceleration sequence with a quick, bouncy plyometric response to landing.

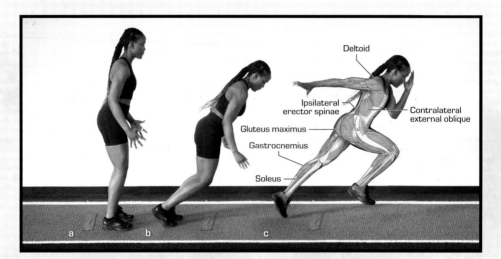

Primary Muscles Activated

Jumping phase (same muscles contracting eccentrically during landing phase):
- *Hip (extension)*: gluteus maximus, biceps femoris long head, semitendinosus, semimembranosus
- *Knee (extension)*: rectus femoris, vastus lateralis, vastus medialis, vastus intermedius
- *Ankle (plantarflexion)*: gastrocnemius, soleus

Swing phase (front leg in air; contralateral front arm):
- *Shoulder (flexion)*: deltoid anterior fibers, pectoralis major upper fibers, coracobrachialis
- *Elbow (flexion)*: biceps brachii, brachialis, brachioradialis
- *Trunk (rotation)*: ipsilateral erector spinae, contralateral external oblique, ipsilateral internal oblique
- *Hip (flexion)*: rectus femoris, iliacus, psoas major, pectineus, tensor fasciae latae
- *Knee (flexion)*: biceps femoris short and long head, semitendinosus, semimembranosus
- *Ankle (dorsiflexion)*: tibialis anterior, extensor hallucis longus, extensor digitorum longus

Stance phase (front leg hits ground and pushes off; back leg and contralateral back arm shown in figure):
- *Shoulder (extension)*: latissimus dorsi, teres major, triceps brachii long head, pectoralis major lower fibers, deltoid posterior fibers, infraspinatus
- *Elbow (extension)*: triceps brachii all heads, anconeus
- *Trunk (rotation)*: ipsilateral erector spinae, contralateral external oblique, ipsilateral internal oblique
- *Hip (flexion to extension)*: gluteus maximus, biceps femoris long head, semitendinosus, semimembranosus
- *Knee (flexion to extension)*: rectus femoris, vastus lateralis, vastus medialis, vastus intermedius
- *Ankle (dorsiflexion to plantarflexion)*: gastrocnemius, soleus

1. Start by standing with your feet together in front of a line (see figure *a*).

2. Jump backward behind the line with both feet while keeping your hips and center of gravity over or slightly in front of the line (see figure *b*).

3. Immediately upon landing, accelerate forward as fast as you can while focusing on proper acceleration mechanics (see figure *c*).

4. Do 10- to 15-yard (9 to 14 m) sprints for 4 to 6 sets.

BALL-DROP ACCELERATION

Ball-drop accelerations use an external visual stimulus to activate the nervous system and trigger intention. This is a fun drill because it gives you a task, and human movement is inherently task driven. The main thing to watch for is that the athlete uses correct form and acceleration mechanics. The challenge with game drills is that proper form often goes out the window, especially for young athletes with minimal training and motor-skill programming.

MODERATE

Gluteus maximus

Biceps femoris

Gastrocnemius

External oblique

a   b

Primary Muscles Activated

Swing phase (front leg in air; contralateral front arm):
- *Shoulder (flexion)*: deltoid anterior fibers, pectoralis major upper fibers, coracobrachialis
- *Elbow (flexion)*: biceps brachii, brachialis, brachioradialis
- *Trunk (rotation)*: ipsilateral erector spinae, contralateral external oblique, ipsilateral internal oblique
- *Hip (flexion)*: rectus femoris, iliacus, psoas major, pectineus, tensor fasciae latae
- *Knee (flexion)*: biceps femoris short and long head, semitendinosus, semimembranosus
- *Ankle (dorsiflexion)*: tibialis anterior, extensor hallucis longus, extensor digitorum longus

Stance phase (front leg hits ground and pushes off; back leg and contralateral back arm in figure):
- *Shoulder (extension)*: latissimus dorsi, teres major, triceps brachii long head, pectoralis major lower fibers, deltoid posterior fibers, infraspinatus
- *Elbow (extension)*: triceps brachii all heads, anconeus
- *Trunk (rotation)*: ipsilateral erector spinae, contralateral external oblique, ipsilateral internal oblique
- *Hip (flexion to extension)*: gluteus maximus, biceps femoris long head, semitendinosus, semimembranosus
- *Knee (flexion to extension)*: rectus femoris, vastus lateralis, vastus medialis, vastus intermedius
- *Ankle (dorsiflexion to plantarflexion)*: gastrocnemius, soleus

MODERATE

1. Start in a low sprint position with a partner standing about 5 yards (about 5 m) away holding a tennis ball high in the air.
2. As soon as the partner drops the ball, sprint forward as it bounces and catch the ball before it hits the ground a second time (see figures *a* and *b*).
3. Repeat for 4 to 6 reps.

When you're starting an acceleration sprint from the split position with one thigh flexed in front of your body, the goal should be to attack down and back toward the ground. You should aim for an initial ground contact that occurs under or behind the center of mass. When that's done successfully, the athlete should be able to keep their center of mass ahead of the stance foot for the majority of the ground contact for the first three critical steps. Ultimately, you want ground contact to happen underneath the center of mass pushing backward with an approximately 45-degree forward lean. Attitude and intention matter. Bears and cash are optional.

MAXIMUM VELOCITY

Sprinting at maximum velocity is the closest we humans get to flying without mechanical or gravitational assistance. And by now, you've hopefully come to understand that it's also a valuable training stimulus regardless of what sport or position you play. As Ken Clark, PhD, and his colleagues have demonstrated in multiple studies (2010, 2019), maximum-velocity capabilities have a direct impact on your entire acceleration profile—even at short distances. Integrating max-velocity sprinting (with the right dosage and form) into your ongoing training program can also act as a vaccine against soft-tissue injuries in the groin and hamstring (Edouard et al. 2019) that athletes commonly incur in field and court sports. From the beginning, we teach new athletes at the Parisi Speed School top-speed mechanics and technique because, in addition to being a vaccine against groin, hamstring, and other soft-tissue injuries, top-speed mechanics and technique are foundational to movement. Many sport movements are a derivative of linear sprinting, so having good sprinting mechanics is important for every athlete. And, as Clark demonstrated with his NFL Combine study mentioned in the previous chapter, having max-velocity capabilities makes a direct impact on game speed, even at short distances. It is also unmatched as a training stimulus. There is simply nothing you can do in the weight room where you apply between two and five times your body weight of force through one limb in a tenth of a second. The question is: How do we help athletes safely turn their speed volume knob up to achieve their full genetic potential? The answer is by teaching them proper form and mechanics from the very beginning, with regular exposure to their top-speed range in low-volume doses that you can progressively ramp up as they develop their relative body strength and master the required technical skills.

DEFINING MAXIMUM EFFORT

Many coaches are hesitant to prescribe max-velocity sprinting as part of their training menu out of fear of the potential injury risk. The fact is that if you teach athletes how to sprint at top speed correctly, it can go a long way toward protecting them from injuries. However, one thing that is often misunderstood is how to safely cue athletes for sprinting. The problem is that if you tell an athlete to go all out and put a 100-percent effort into their sprint, they tend to tighten up too much, which inhibits harmonious neuromuscular firing. Relaxing into a sprint makes it easier for the body to find its optimal rhythm. A better approach is to cue athletes to sprint at about 95 percent so that they stay one very small degree below all-out effort. All the muscles used for sprinting have opposing muscle groups. The idea is to fire each leg into the ground with a pulse of dynamic stiffness in the foot–ankle complex, while the other leg unconsciously flicks back up in front of the body and maximizes the elastic stretch-shortening cycle of the hip flexor so it can harness that kinetic energy before firing it down again. When the hip flexors flex the hip to recover a leg, the opposing muscle group needs to relax enough to allow the windup movement to happen smoothly—just like the upward snap of a yo-yo. Knowing how to rhythmically fire and relax muscles quickly is a learned motor skill whether you're hitting a golf ball, swinging a baseball bat, or playing the drums. Optimal performance in these refined motor skills is achieved when the athlete is feeling mentally relaxed and precise, not when they're grinding their teeth trying to max out.

Elements of Maximum Velocity

Achieving maximum velocity in sprinting is a combination of the amount of mass-specific force you can apply into the ground and the speed and direction at which it's applied. When you're sprinting at full speed, most of the force is projected vertically into the ground and ground-contact times are very short.

Contact Time and Force Application

As Dr. Peter Weyand and his colleagues established in numerous studies (2000, 2010, 2014), one of the key ingredients for human speed is mass-specific force—or the amount of force you can generate relative to your body weight. But the ability to generate a high level of mass-specific force is only part of the maximum velocity equation. Another essential component is ground-contact time and the angle or vector of the force application. Weyand's studies at the SMU Locomotor Lab show that the main thing separating elite-level sprinters from their slower team sport counterparts is how quickly they can punch on and off the ground with high levels of force. In the simplest of terms, to run faster, your ground-contact times need to be shorter and your vertical forces need to be greater. When you're in an upright position sprinting at top speed, the faster you can punch the ground with maximum vertical force, the farther you will propel your mass forward on each stride, and the faster your top speed will be.

The secret to this recipe comes down to a blend of kinetic energy, kinematics, and neural timing—the ability to channel your momentum and vertical force production with optimal running mechanics and rhythmic pulses of super stiffness in the lower leg and core. Clark and Weyand (2014) conducted a study on force plates by analyzing the spring-stance mechanics of both elite sprinters and team sport athletes. Their study revealed that the amount of vertical force they can apply in the very first moment of ground contact is what separates superfast humans from everyone else.

"We looked at the ground forces applied during the first and second half of ground contact and found that sprinters, who are much faster than their team sport counterparts, had significant differences in the first half of their ground contact and specifically in the first quarter of ground contact," says Clark. "There were no real differences between them in the second half of ground contact. In fact, we found that we could look at the force signatures for elite sprinters versus sub-elite sprinters and athletic nonsprinters and—without even knowing who the runner was or how fast they ran—we could tell who the elite sprinters were and who the nonsprinters were just based on the amount of force they applied in the very first moment of ground contact [see figure 7.1]."

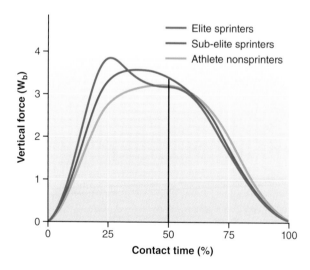

FIGURE 7.1   Force-plate studies show that elite sprinters generate an asymmetrical, vertical waveform with a notably sharp spike of force application at the beginning of ground contact.

Reprinted by permission from K.P. Clark and P.G. Weyand, "Are Running Speeds Maximized with Simple-Spring Stance Mechanics?" *Journal of Applied Physiology* 117 (2014): 604-615.

The asymmetrical, vertical waveform that elite sprinters had generated at the very beginning of ground contact had a notably sharp spike of maximum vertical force application—astoundingly with a peak force of up to five times their body weight—because they had a higher knee lift, faster limb velocity, and a more aggressive ground strike that was stiffer at ground contact. This means they can apply a tremendous amount of vertical force in less than a tenth of a second without leaking much of that energy in the process. By contrast, the slower team sport athletes hit the ground with less knee lift, which resulted in less windup and slower angular limb velocity. They were also less stiff at ground contact. Inevitably, these factors generated a vertical force waveform that looks more like a classic spring-mass model curve (an upside-down U). By having applied much less force at initial strike, the team sport athletes needed longer ground-contact times to produce the necessary vertical impulse. Their lack of distal and proximal stiffness at ground contact resulted in a more passive "catch and rebound" style of force application as opposed to the elite sprinters' more aggressive windup and "punch gravity in the face" mechanics.

"One of the potential mechanisms causing greater vertical force application is the angular velocities of the thigh and leg," explains Clark. "Our recent data collection at West Chester University of Pennsylvania found that there is a direct linear relationship between how fast the limbs rotate and the top speeds that are achieved. A competitive sprinter will have a greater thigh angular velocity than a slower runner. This results in a faster lower-limb velocity at touchdown and—coupled with a stiff ground contact—translates into greater vertical forces and faster speeds."

According to Clark, another important factor is how quickly and smoothly the limbs scissor or switch as the thigh reaches its high point of hip flexion in front of the athlete and then rapidly reverses into hip extension as the opposite limb rapidly reverses into hip flexion.

"Our recent research shows that thigh reversal happens faster and more aggressively in faster sprinters," notes Clark. "So it's not just about getting the range of motion right, but also about how fast you can reverse the limb scissor action once you hit those end ranges of motion of flexion and extension."

Upright Sprinting Mechanics

Transitioning smoothly from the optimal 45-degree angle of initial acceleration through the transition phase into proper, upright sprinting mechanics (approximately strides 8 through 12) is crucial for an athlete to achieve their full potential for maximum velocity. While the movement mechanics for top-speed sprinting are similar to acceleration, there is a significant difference in posture. As previously noted, top-speed sprinting requires stiffness in the core combined with precise pulses of distal stiffness in the lower leg at ground contact for the efficient transfer of force. But this force comes from the thigh's elastic, front-side windup, which the fascia and nervous systems are highly involved with. Having a high rotational-limb velocity combined with good strike mechanics and stiff ground contact results in larger ground forces with shorter contact times and faster speeds. In other words, teaching an athlete how to smoothly transition from the forward-leaning initial acceleration phase into proper, upright sprinting form is key to developing maximum speed. This is especially true for field and court sport athletes who spend much of their time in crouched running positions that allow for rapid change of direction.

"Posture is probably the number one limiting factor to proper top-speed mechanics with the team sport athletes I've worked with," says Clark. "And when I say *posture*, I'm not just talking about the trunk and head position, but also pelvic position. Like a lot of things, there's more than just one cause with these athletes. In my experience, this is often due to how they play their sport and the kinds of positions they're in all the time that cause muscular tightness or shortened muscles, hip flexors that are tight, and hips that aren't as mobile as they need to be. So it's a twofold problem. Number one, they have some physical constraints from not having optimal mobility. And two, not understanding the correct way to move when they get into an upright pattern."

Since this transition phase is such an important concept for coaches and trainers to understand, I reached out to internationally renowned coach Dan Pfaff to get his take on it. Over the course of his career, Pfaff has coached 49 Olympians (including 10 medalists), more than 50 World Championship competitors (nine medalists), and five world-record holders. He's also helped athletes achieve more than 55 national records and served on the coaching staffs of five Olympic Games in five different countries. Pfaff currently serves as the head of jumps and multi-sport training for Altis. His insights are based on decades of experience working with some of the best track-and-field athletes the world has ever produced.

"When it comes to top speed, I think there's been a long-standing bias toward looking at stride length, stride frequency, and outcome measures like what their times are," remarks Pfaff. "Very few people in field and court sports talk about the transition of body parts and body segments throughout the various parts of a run. The vectors that are produced by an athlete during ground contact have a huge influence on an athlete's ability to be in position to apply vertical forces. You can say swing times are equal, but what are the segments doing in a rotary sense, or in a given time frame? There are certain common denominators and landmark positions for top-speed running, and if you're not in those positions, then your ability to apply force is compromised. If you have minimal knee lift, your ability to apply downward force is limited because you're going through a much smaller range of movement in a smaller time frame."

Proper upright sprinting posture enables increased force production, minimized braking forces, and efficient use of the stretch-shortening cycle. While every runner is unique, there are a few postural landmarks that are essential for max-velocity sprinting (see figure 7.2). These include having an upright posture with the head, neck, and shoulders stacked on top of the hips. Another important factor is maintaining a neutral pelvis, which creates a stretch across the hip flexors, minimizes back swing, and enables the rapid return of the thigh to the front side of the body using the elastic stretch-shortening cycle. The knee should come up high enough to be almost level with the hips—at approximately belt-buckle height—with the

Upright posture

Head, neck, and shoulders stacked on top of hips

Knee should be almost level with hips at top of stride

Neutral pelvis

Stance foot strikes under hips slightly in front of center mass

FIGURE 7.2 Optimal upright sprinting posture.

thigh nearly parallel to the ground. The foot should drive down and back into the ground with contact aiming to occur under the hips and slightly in front of the center of mass. The ankle complex should be super stiff on impact so that the force coming from the angular velocity of the limb—the windup—can efficiently transmit into the ground for increasingly higher force application with each step. Ideally, the leg will extend backward just enough to allow for force application as it rebounds upward under the butt and then begins forward movement again.

One of the most common upright sprinting errors is anterior rotation of the pelvis, which causes an overrotation of the entire system, minimizes force production, and increases injury risk. Other common errors include pelvic tilting, excessive backside leg swinging (butt-kicking), not enough front-side lifting, casting the foot too far out in front of the hips (overstriding), striking with the heel first, and collapsing the ankle at ground contact. I'll unpack how to diagnose these movement dysfunctions and help athletes avoid them in the rest of this chapter. I'll also present the fundamentals of max-velocity sprinting mechanics for the upper and lower body.

Pelvic Tilt

Anterior pelvic tilt is one of the main causes of speed-related injuries. When you sprint, your hips oscillate and undulate in a rhythmic fashion, along with the shoulder joint. If your pelvis has an anterior tilt when you're sprinting, it puts unnecessary stress on the hamstrings and causes a chain reaction of other postural imbalances that compromise your ability to generate vertical force and maximum speed. See figure 7.3 for an example of neutral pelvis (*a*) versus anterior tilt (*b*).

There are multiple contributors to anterior pelvic tilt, but generally speaking, it is often caused by muscle imbalances. The musculoskeletal system is designed to work synergistically to stabilize joints and allow the extremities to move with speed and power. More than 20 different muscles attach to the hip, and when some of these muscles get too tight or too weak, it leads to movement dysfunctions across the rest of the kinetic chain. One of the muscle groups that tend to be chronically tight in many people are the hip flexors, specifically the psoas and iliacus. The hip flexors raise the knees when you're sprinting. If you sit for most of the day, your hip flexors are in a shortened position for prolonged periods of

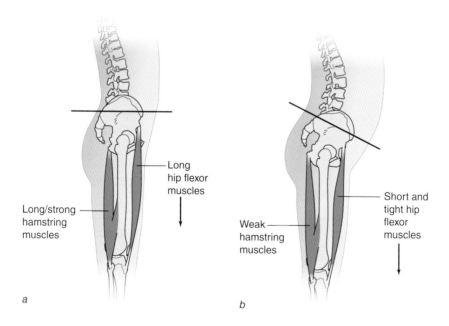

FIGURE 7.3 Anterior pelvis tilt is one of the most common movement dysfunctions in max-velocity sprinting. It leads to a series of other problems that compromise power output and increase injury risk.

time. This can make them weak and tight. When the hip flexors are too tight, they pull the interior pelvis forward into an anterior tilt. Stretching your hip flexors will help the pelvis maintain a neutral position. Maintaining a neutral pelvis also helps prevent hamstring injuries by taking stress and unwanted stretch off the hamstrings during the terminal swing phase of a stride—just before the foot hits the ground.

An anterior tilt of the pelvis will cause you to overextend at the hip and prolong ground-contact time. It also means your posterior recovery mechanics will take longer because the leg is flaring way out behind you as opposed to quickly recovering nice and tight underneath the butt. The hamstring will also be overstretched during the terminal swing phase when it is under the most eccentric load. A key concept to understand is that joint position also determines muscle recruitment patterns. For example, compare the difference between doing a chin-up with your palms facing up (supinated) versus with your palms facing down (pronated). The muscle recruitment patterns throughout the arm and back are very different when you change the wrist and hand positions. Most people can do more reps with their palms in the supinated position. The same holds true for sprinting. Your ankle, knee, and hip joints must be positioned at the proper angles at the right times throughout the entire stride cycle to optimize muscle recruitment and speed and reduce injury risk.

Before sprinting, the Parisi Speed School helps athletes find their neutral hip position by having them stand in place and go through the extreme positions of anterior and posterior tilt. I often describe the hips as a bowl (see figure 7.4). When your hips are in anterior tilt (*a*), it's like you're pouring water out of the front of the bowl. I will have the athlete pour water out of the front of the bowl so they can feel that anterior tilt. Then I'll have them do a posterior tilt (*b*) by telling them to squeeze their butt cheeks together and pour water out of the back of the bowl. Then I tell them to find the neutral middle position (*c*) so they can understand how it feels. Getting athletes to understand their neutral hip position has important benefits. For one, it helps the firing sequence happen more efficiently for increased speed. It also reduces stress on the hamstrings (during sprinting) and injury risk.

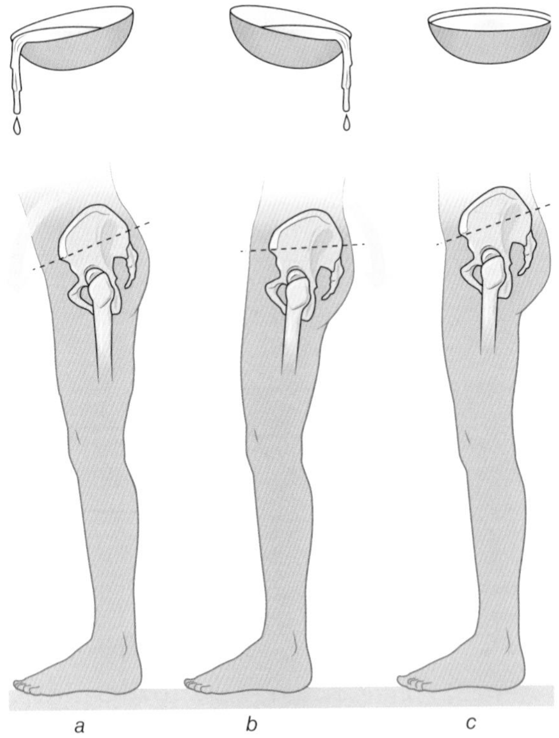

a   b   c

FIGURE 7.4 Visualizing the pelvis as a bowl of water helps athletes conceptualize and feel their neutral hip position.

Another way we like to teach posture is to have athletes lie on the ground with their arms across their chest and their legs straight so they can really understand this concept (see figure 7.5). We ask athletes to identify what's touching the ground (feet, butt, upper back, and head). Then we have the athletes put their hands underneath the small of their back. For most people, there is a space between the lower back and the ground. That amount of space is dependent on the athlete's anatomy, but, for the most part, the thickness of the athlete's flat hand is a good rule of thumb for finding that neutral spine position. If it's overarched, they have too much anterior tilt. If there's no space, they have too much of a posterior tilt.

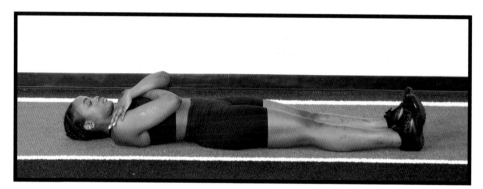

FIGURE 7.5   Lying on the ground with arms across the chest and straight legs helps athletes conceptualize and feel their neutral postural position. The only parts of the body touching the ground in this position should be the heels, buttocks, upper back (thoracic spine), and head. The lower back should be slightly elevated off the ground; typically the distance is about the thickness of the person's flat hand.

After they've determined their neutral postural position, we have the athletes stand up nice and tall and find the same neutral posture they had when they were on the ground. The goal is to get them to focus on having great overall posture. The first step is getting the athletes to understand proper lumbar positioning. From there, we move on to thoracic positioning, the cervical spine, and finally the shoulder girdle. Athletes should think about depressing and retracting the shoulder girdle by bringing their shoulders down and back. Their head should be neutral and the chin tucked in slightly, like they're at attention. It may seem basic, but it's really important for athletes to understand how this position feels, especially kids. Most kids don't even walk with good posture, and now you want them to *run* with good posture? The problem is that if you're running at top speed and you're not aligned, you're increasing your injury risk from faulty movement patterns and misalignment. That's why teaching good posture *first* is essential to top speed. We close our lesson on posture by having the athletes walk up and down the track, up and down the court, or up and down the field for 200 to 400 yards (183 to 366 m), focusing on overall posture. This can be a big game changer because it shows athletes how important proper posture is and allows them to tune in to it.

Hamstring Injury and Risk

Small motor unit recruitment and gluteal activation also play an important role in the general warm-up and ADW routines by protecting the hamstrings on max-velocity days. Athletes generate the majority of their hip extension power for sprinting from the glutes. The hamstrings act as a synergist to the glutes, meaning that they assist the glutes in performing hip extension during the sprinting stride. If the glutes are inhibited in any way, the hamstrings have to pick up the slack. This is called synergistic dominance, meaning if the glutes are not firing first to extend the hip, the hamstrings have to work overtime. The hamstrings are not designed to be the primary hip extensor. They are a synergist in hip extension (see figure 7.6). Many hamstring strain injuries are not caused by a lack of hamstring strength. They happen because the hamstrings are being overworked. Correcting dysfunction in the glutes and improving their recruitment allows the hamstrings to do their job without added stress. This requires training the glutes to be the first muscle group to fire at the initiation of hip extension so they can do the majority of the work.

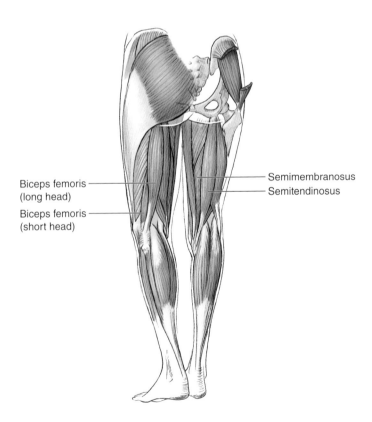

Biceps femoris (long head)

Biceps femoris (short head)

Semimembranosus

Semitendinosus

FIGURE 7.6 The hamstrings, which consist of the biceps femoris, semitendinosus, and semimembranosus, are the primary propulsive muscles used for sprinting.

Since we're on the subject of hamstrings, it's worth noting that they are the most activated muscles throughout most of the sprinting stride cycle. They assist the powerful gluteal muscles in hip extension and help stabilize the knee. They also work in conjunction with the myofascial system as a shock absorber at foot contact. Hamstring injuries usually occur during the terminal swing phase of gait when they are eccentrically controlling the knee extension (extending the lower leg forward and preparing to plant the foot for the next stride). The largest hamstring stretch occurs just before ground contact, and the long head of the biceps femoris is the most frequently injured muscle, accounting for more than 80 percent of all cases (Ekstrand, Hägglund, and Waldén 2011). Contrary to popular belief, having tight hamstrings is not the primary reason people injure them. In fact, hamstring stiffness has been shown to be an attribute of speed rather than an injury mechanism. Every athlete needs some amount of flexibility in their hamstrings depending on their sport and range of motion requirements, but too much flexibility in the hamstrings is just as bad as not having enough.

Upper-Body Mechanics

Proper arm action is a critical part of proper running technique. Synchronizing your arm stroke to move in a mirrored counter-rhythm with the swing cycle of your legs is crucial for achieving maximum velocity. In addition to helping you maintain balance, arm stroke also helps you generate more force into the ground by using the pendulum effect. A longer pendulum swing generates more force. A good analogy for this is if you're swinging a rope with a weight on the end of it, the longer the rope is, the more force it will generate as you swing it. Conversely, if it's a short rope, you will be able to swing it faster, but it will generate less force. The pendulum action of the arms works the same way when you're sprinting. Optimal arm stroke for max-velocity sprinting involves a full range of motion with explosive changes in pendulum length throughout the stride cycle. Extending your arm on the downstroke increases its pendulum length, which, in turn, increases its torque. It also increases the stretch on the hip flexors in the opposite leg, which amplifies force application into the ground. Conversely, flexing your elbow on the upstroke reduces the pendulum length and increases the angular velocity of both the arm and the swing leg on the opposite side as it prepares for the next stride. Closing the elbow on the upstroke produces the athlete's fastest leg turnover. The arms lead the tempo and should be synchronized in counter-rhythm with the legs as the runner increases or maintains speed.

Each arm movement is a one-stroke action that initiates at the shoulder. The hand on the front side of the body should be at or slightly above shoulder height with the elbow flexed at approximately a 75-degree angle (see figure 7.7). From the peak shoulder height, the athlete should strike down and back with their hand. As the hands pass below the hip pockets, the elbow will reach a full extension that allows for slight spinal rotation at the thoracic spine and increases the pendulum force. As the arm swings behind the body, the elbow bends again to approximately 105 degrees. The stretch created on the pectoralis muscle group and the anterior deltoid during this movement will result in a natural elastic return of the arm to the front of the body without the need to consciously pull the arm forward. This is the natural rhythmic symmetry for maximizing extension and ground contact with the opposite leg.

All of that said, at the Parisi Speed School, we get a lot of young athletes who have trouble controlling their arms. One of the things we do is to simply tell them to think about maintaining a 90-degree angle at the elbow joint. And yes, I know I just talked about all the different angular changes that happen during each stride, but I find that it's too much information for most people to process, especially kids. I typically tell them to imagine their arms are in casts and being held at a 90-degree angle. They hold a hammer in each hand. Behind them is a wall, and on every stride, they have to hammer that wall. By hammering backward, their arm will naturally open and create a longer pendulum swing. After hammering the wall, they close their arm and bring that hand forward and back up to their chin. I don't tell athletes at what degree their swing should be. Instead, I just tell them to continue to hammer back.

FIGURE 7.7 Proper arm mechanics that counter opposing leg movement are essential for generating optimal force during max-velocity sprinting.

Another important point of focus is the shoulder girdle complex. If it is not down and back and the scapula is not stabilized, then athletes will leak energy out of their shoulders. While the importance of the core and all the muscles that attach to the hip and spine is often a focal point, it's also important to note that the shoulder has 17 muscles that attach to it. This means the shoulder needs to be stabilized so that arm speed can be dynamic and counterbalance the legs and the sprinting movement of the whole body. It's important to train and stabilize the shoulder girdle so you can fire that limb down and back efficiently. When you fire each arm down and back in a hammering pendulum motion, you want to drive force through the extension of the shoulder and the opposite leg and let the stored elastic energy of the connective tissues assist in bringing each arm forward.

It's worth mentioning that athletes can quickly and easily practice these basic arm action–posture drills while standing in place. Doing so won't limit them from training and will optimize these important postural fundamentals. In fact, practicing these drills in place still allows athletes to work on maintaining hip and elbow positioning, stabilizing the core of the shoulder, and developing top speed through body alignment—all with the added benefit of having a low risk of injury.

Lower-Body Mechanics

When an athlete is sprinting, the cycle of force generation begins as soon as each foot comes off the ground (initial swing phase). This is the beginning of the windup and the punch. One of the main things that plays a significant role in that windup is an athlete's ankle position at toe off. When sprinting at top speed, you want the ankle position to be dorsiflexing immediately at toe off. Active dorsiflexion upon ground contact creates a stretch across the entire posterior chain, which acts as a spring that uses stored elastic energy courtesy of the stretch-shortening cycle. On the other hand, if you stay plantarflexed at toe off, you will not be able to effectively recruit the gastrocnemius muscle, which is a knee flexor, to bring the heel up during recovery. It's going to be spent. This means that the hamstrings have to work overtime to flex the knee, and the hamstrings just got done applying force. If the ankle is plantarflexed, the hamstrings don't get any downtime because now you're also asking them to flex the knee and bring the heel up to the butt. Then the hamstring has to eccentrically contract when the knee swings forward. That's where the firing sequence plays a role in injury. Also, when your foot hits the ground, you want to take advantage of the stored elastic energy in the connective fascia tissues of the Achilles complex—which is essentially free energy—by thinking "toe up" immediately after ground contact. As that leg is recovering with the toe up, the gastrocnemius muscle helps bring the heel back up underneath the butt as you're flexing the hip, helping to minimize ground-contact time. As the hip flexes, you want to think about the knee coming up to belt-buckle height and being nearly parallel with the ground, but you want that movement to happen naturally in a way that not only optimizes the free energy but also enables a powerful front-side windup whip (see figure 7.8 for proper front and back stride mechanics).

Lower shank of swing leg comes up high and tight under butt

Maintain a straight line through shoulder, hip, and knee during force application

Front-side knee comes up to approximately belt-buckle height with thigh near level with ground

Limit hip extension during force application

Active dorsiflexion

Ground contact under or slightly in front of center of gravity

FIGURE 7.8 Proper stride mechanics of the front and back sides are essential for generating optimal force during max-velocity sprinting.

Stride Length

Stride length is an important component in top speed. But there are two different types of stride length that coaches need to understand: actual stride length and effective stride length. Actual stride length is the distance between each foot's ground contact. For example, if you dipped your feet in chalk and sprinted, the distance between the chalk marks would be your actual stride length. By contrast, effective stride length is not where your feet hit the ground. Instead, it's the amount of distance your center of mass travels in space between strides—which is harder to measure—that optimizes the transfer of force. The difference is that you may have a really long stride length, but if you're overstriding (casting out) and your foot is landing way out in front of your center of mass, it's going to create too much of a braking force, which will slow you down. As we discussed in the acceleration chapter, there's an ideal ratio of vertical force and horizontal force, depending on which phase of a sprint you're in. Many athletes, especially younger, weaker athletes, tend to overstride. One technique for combatting this issue and focusing athletes' attention on effective stride length is to combine a coach's eye with slow-motion video of athletes filmed from the side and analyze (1) where their hips are compared to their foot strikes and (2) how far the hips travel in the air from one foot strike to the next. It's really about flight. How far forward can they displace their center of mass on each stride, and how effective are they in recovering that limb to windup for another strike? Sprinting is essentially a sequence of powerful single-leg leaps. So it's all about the ability to put a fast force into the ground quickly and create a powerful series of leaps that push the center of mass forward. That's how you fly.

Cueing for Speed: Maximum Velocity

As previously mentioned, maximum velocity can be broken down into different phases, such as front- and backside mechanics and transition. While coaches can cue individual elements of max-velocity sprinting based on what an athlete needs to work on, the athlete, however, experiences them all as one connected action. Focus on one cue per sprint and try to keep each cue simple and short. Again, there are endless possibilities and technique refinements that can be made. I've listed a few proven max-velocity cues here that I've found effective, but you should experiment with what works for you and your athletes, keeping in mind that every situation is unique.

"Stay focused and tall!"

Imagine a rope is stretched horizontally next to you at head height. Stay focused and tall and keep your head level with the rope as you sprint.

"Hammer back!"

Imagine your forearms are hammers and hammer them back against a wall behind you.

"Spin the globe!"

Imagine you are spinning the globe with your feet as you sprint.

Maximum-Velocity Training

Since the body adapts to the demands of imposed stresses and inputs, the simple rule of exposure means that if you want to be fast, you have to train fast. Drills can facilitate neural priming, help athletes develop muscle memory (motor engrams), improve posture, establish landmark positions, and optimize force production; but they are no replacement for max-velocity sprinting. Linear speed drills help athletes master the technical elements and proper form required for efficient sprinting with reduced injury risk, but exposure to maximum sprinting is what helps develop faster top-end speed capabilities (assuming you have good form and mechanics). On a maximum-velocity training day, the strategy is to progress from the ADW drills explained in chapter 4 to doing two or three linear speed-specific anchor drills that roll into speed-specific application drills and culminate with top-speed sprinting. Here are a few examples of each. You can find more in the training menus in chapter 12.

ARM ACTION

Aligning the body so that it's prepared to run includes paying attention to arm action and helping athletes feel the landmarks they need to hit. Standing in place and working on arm action is a great foundational anchor drill for coordinating the required movement sequence.

1. Start by standing in place with one arm folded forward maintaining a relative 90-degree angle at the elbow and one arm back in a sprinting stance (see figure).
2. On the count of "one," have the athlete scissor their arms one time and hold the position. One arm extends forward, one arm flexes backward. It's okay to be a little loose at the elbow. You want the athlete to think of a 90-degree angle, but allow the arm to go through its natural path and range of motion. For each arm, do a couple of reps for counts of 1-2, 1-2-3, and 1-2-3-4.
3. Lastly, scissor the arms at full continuous effort for about four seconds.

The goal of this anchor drill is to focus on arm positioning, torso posture, working the core of the shoulder, and maintaining hip positioning, all while standing in place. The important part is that it is done with precision. When you're sprinting at maximum velocity these actions happen subconsciously and very fast. It is paramount that athletes practice doing them slowly and accurately first. That's how you translate anchor drills into faster speeds.

LYING LEG RECOVERY

To quickly apply a tremendous amount of force into the ground quickly, it is essential to know what your legs and body are doing during the recovery stage. Lying leg recovery drills help improve recovery mechanics and teach athletes how to efficiently cycle their legs so they can generate more force into the ground without swinging their leg too far behind their body during the recovery phase, which will increase injury risk and slow athletes down. This is a great elastic priming drill that fires the hamstrings and gastrocnemius muscles.

1. Start by lying on one side, on top of a straight line marked on the ground so your body is straight (see figure *a*).
2. Using the top leg, fire the heel up to the butt as fast as you can focusing on "folding the leg" (see figure *b*) and bring your knee up in the same continuous motion (see figure *c*). Pause and hold the knee up for a moment in the flexed and blocked position.
3. Repeat 4 to 6 reps on each side. After doing a few reps on each side, progress to doing this drill while standing in place.

POWER BOUND

Power bounds develop the ability to use the catapult effect of the tendons and fascia system. Powerful extension and flexion from the ankle, knee, hip, core, and shoulder maximize force generation. This exercise triggers the tendons and fascia system to engage in the high-intensity movement of a loaded single-leg bound.

ADVANCED

Primary Muscles Activated

Swing phase (front leg in air; contralateral front arm):

- *Shoulder (flexion)*: deltoid anterior fibers, pectoralis major upper fibers, coracobrachialis
- *Elbow (flexion)*: biceps brachii, brachialis, brachioradialis
- *Trunk (rotation)*: ipsilateral erector spinae, contralateral external oblique, ipsilateral internal oblique
- *Hip (flexion)*: rectus femoris, iliacus, psoas major, pectineus, tensor fasciae latae
- *Knee (flexion)*: biceps femoris short and long head, semitendinosus, semimembranosus
- *Ankle (dorsiflexion)*: tibialis anterior, extensor hallucis longus, extensor digitorum longus

Stance phase (front leg hits ground and pushes off; back leg and contralateral back arm in figure):

- *Shoulder (extension)*: latissimus dorsi, teres major, triceps brachii long head, pectoralis major lower fibers, deltoid posterior fibers, infraspinatus
- *Elbow (extension)*: triceps brachii all heads, anconeus
- *Trunk (rotation)*: ipsilateral erector spinae, contralateral external oblique, ipsilateral internal oblique
- *Hip (flexion to extension)*: gluteus maximus, biceps femoris long head, semitendinosus, semimembranosus
- *Knee (flexion to extension)*: rectus femoris, vastus lateralis, vastus medialis, vastus intermedius
- *Ankle (dorsiflexion to plantarflexion)*: gastrocnemius, soleus

1. Begin with a slow, exaggerated sprint (see figure *a*).
2. Drive one leg backward while exploding the opposite knee out forward and the opposite arm backward (see figure *b*).
3. Upon landing, immediately explode off the ground again into the next stride, driving the opposite arm and leg backward. Repeat the power bounds while striving to cover more horizontal distance on each side. This bounding action is similar to a triple jumper's technique. The goal is to displace the center of mass as forward as possible on each jump.
4. Perform for 20 to 40 yards (18 to 37 m) for 4 to 6 sets.

STRAIGHT-LEG BOUND

A straight-leg bound activates the hamstrings and generates horizontal and vertical driving forces off the ground. Keeping the leg straight and knees locked activates and strengthens the hamstrings by forcing them to do more of the work as opposed to the quads and glutes.

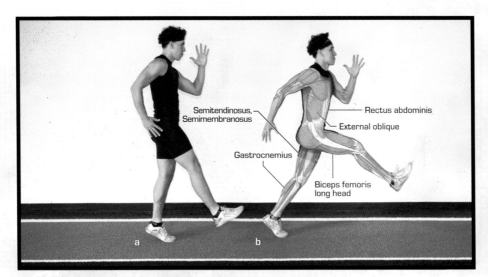

Semitendinosus, Semimembranosus

Gastrocnemius

Rectus abdominis

External oblique

Biceps femoris long head

a   b

Primary Muscles Activated

Swing phase (front leg in air; contralateral front arm):
- *Shoulder (flexion)*: deltoid anterior fibers, pectoralis major upper fibers, coracobrachialis
- *Elbow (flexion)*: biceps brachii, brachialis, brachioradialis
- *Trunk (isometric flexion)*: rectus abdominis, erector spinae, internal oblique, external oblique
- *Hip (flexion)*: rectus femoris, iliacus, psoas major, pectineus, tensor fasciae latae
- *Ankle (dorsiflexion)*: tibialis anterior, extensor hallucis longus, extensor digitorum longus

Stance phase (front leg hits ground and pushes off; back leg and contralateral back arm in figure):
- *Shoulder (extension)*: latissimus dorsi, teres major, triceps brachii long head, pectoralis major lower fibers, deltoid posterior fibers, infraspinatus
- *Elbow (extension)*: triceps brachii all heads, anconeus
- *Trunk (isometric flexion)*: rectus abdominis, erector spinae, internal oblique, external oblique
- *Hip (flexion to extension)*: gluteus maximus, biceps femoris long head, semitendinosus, semimembranosus
- *Ankle (dorsiflexion to plantarflexion)*: gastrocnemius, soleus

---

1. Start by standing tall with both legs firmly locked at the knee joint.

2. Flex and extend the hip in a shuffle-like action while moving forward and slowly increase the intensity of the force production off the ground on each stride (see figures *a-b*). Stay leaning slightly forward with a strong active anterior core while syncing the arms with the legs to maximize force production into the ground. Increase to maximum stride length by increasing force production by accelerating a long (locked) leg into the ground.

3. Do 4 sets of 20 to 40 yards (18 to 37 m).

DRIBBLES: LOW, MEDIUM, AND HIGH

Hip flexion for the front-side windup of the leg is similar to the action of playing with a yo-yo. You fire the leg down with force, but bringing it back up quickly is mostly just an elastic flick of timing. A good drill for helping athletes find the landmarks for this skill is called dribbling or cycling. Dribbles are foundational sprint drills done with a smaller range of motion in either a circular or elliptical pattern based on the athlete's need. Dribbles are great for athletes to learn the proper way to cycle their legs and strike the ground actively and to practice proper posture and head alignment. Dribbling also helps improve hamstring resilience and ankle range of motion with rolling foot contacts. There are three basic levels of dribbling: low (ankle level), medium (shin level), and high (knee level), with multiple variations. Ankle, calf, and knee dribbles can be done at progressively faster speeds to prepare the body for the day's sprinting session.

Primary Muscles Activated

Swing phase (front leg in air; contralateral front arm):
- *Shoulder (flexion)*: deltoid anterior fibers, pectoralis major upper fibers, coracobrachialis
- *Elbow (flexion)*: biceps brachii, brachialis, brachioradialis
- *Hip (flexion)*: rectus femoris, iliacus, psoas major, pectineus, tensor fasciae latae
- *Knee (flexion)*: biceps femoris short and long head, semitendinosus, semimembranosus
- *Ankle (dorsiflexion)*: tibialis anterior, extensor hallucis longus, extensor digitorum longus

Stance phase (front leg hits ground and pushes off; back leg and contralateral back arm in figure):
- *Shoulder (extension)*: latissimus dorsi, teres major, triceps brachii long head, pectoralis major lower fibers, deltoid posterior fibers, infraspinatus
- *Elbow (extension)*: triceps brachii all heads, anconeus
- *Hip (flexion to extension)*: gluteus maximus, biceps femoris long head, semitendinosus, semimembranosus
- *Knee (flexion to extension)*: rectus femoris, vastus lateralis, vastus medialis, vastus intermedius
- *Ankle (dorsiflexion to plantarflexion)*: gastrocnemius, soleus

MODERATE

1. Start in an upright position with eyes looking toward the horizon.

2. For low dribbles, move forward at a fast walking pace by picking up one foot and lifting it over the opposite ankle (see figure *a*). For the other levels, this would be the calf for medium dribbles and the knee for high dribbles—with a focus on horizontal force production.

3. Move the foot in a circular motion around the ankle (again, the calf for medium dribbles and the knee for high dribbles), rather than just up and down. This circular motion can also be done in a more elliptical shape, which allows the knee to open up slightly (see figure *b*).

4. The foot should cycle down and back, making ground contact using either the entire foot or the heel first (depending on the athlete's need). Landing heel first in this drill forces the ankle into dorsiflexion, engages the hamstrings more effectively, and helps align the leg and spine joints for solid ground contact.

5. Roll through the heel and onto the toes before lifting the leg and starting the next repetition.

6. Gradually increase the speed and rhythmic intensity in reps, going from a walk to slightly less than a jog, at distances between 20 and 40 yards (18 and 37 m).

Coaches should confirm that posture, the ground contact of the foot or heel, rhythm, and head position are all dialed in before moving on to sprinting. If there are issues, they should be addressed before doing any full-intensity sprints. Also, it's important that this drill is done with a full-foot, heel–toe ground contact because you want to make sure you're activating the posterior chain, getting the glutes involved, and activating the sequence correctly. Rolling through the foot contact from back to front helps ensure the connective tissues and hydraulic mechanisms are dispersing force.

LOWER-LIMB FAST CLAW

This exercise requires high levels of neural control and coordination but helps athletes program the proper motor engrams for sprinting.

Primary Muscles Activated

Down phase (moving limbs):

- *Shoulder (extension)*: latissimus dorsi, teres major, triceps brachii long head, pectoralis major lower fibers, deltoid posterior fibers, infraspinatus
- *Elbow (extension)*: triceps brachii all heads, anconeus
- *Hip (extension)*: gluteus maximus, biceps femoris long head, semitendinosus, semimembranosus
- *Knee (extension)*: rectus femoris, vastus lateralis, vastus medialis, vastus intermedius
- *Ankle (dorsiflexion)*: tibialis anterior, extensor hallucis longus, extensor digitorum longus

Up phase (moving limbs):

- *Shoulder (flexion)*: deltoid anterior fibers, pectoralis major upper fibers, coracobrachialis
- *Elbow (flexion)*: biceps brachii, brachialis, brachioradialis
- *Hip (flexion)*: rectus femoris, iliacus, psoas major, pectineus, tensor fasciae latae
- *Knee (flexion)*: biceps femoris short and long head, semitendinosus, semimembranosus
- *Ankle (dorsiflexion)*: tibialis anterior, extensor hallucis longus, extensor digitorum longus

1. Stand next to a wall and extend the wall-side arm, pressing your hand against the wall to provide your body support. Stand tall on the inside leg with your weight on the ball of the foot and squeeze the glute throughout the exercise. When you're first learning this exercise, place your outside hand on your hip. After you become proficient at doing the lower-limb fast claw, add arm action with the outside arm.

2. Raise the outside leg to 90 degrees hip flexion with the knee flexed so that the foot is vertically in line with the knee (see figure a). Focus on having maximal intention to hold dorsiflexion throughout the drill.

3. Drive the foot down and slightly forward. As the foot descends past the upper two-thirds of the shin, pull back as if clawing at the ground (see figure b). Ground contact should be made lightly with the ball of the foot.

4. After ground contact, the upper and lower leg should fold and return the thigh and shin to the starting position.

5. Repeat 6 reps for 1 to 3 sets on each side.

BASIC

MODERATE

IN-AND-OUT SPRINT

The in-and-out sprint, also known as the floating sprint, teaches athletes how to stay relaxed at high speeds and shift gears while sprinting. For this drill, you need several cones—one placed at the starting line and the others placed every 10 meters, beginning at the 20-meter mark. Have the athlete sprint at alternating levels of effort between each cone. To increase intensity, you can place the sprint cones 15 or 20 meters apart (while keeping the float distances at every 10 meters).

Stand at the start line in a ready position and sprint as fast as you can to the 20-meter mark, the first in section. Hold a floating rhythm with relaxed arm mechanics where you neither intentionally decelerate nor accelerate (think of it as coasting) between the 20- and 30-meter cones, the first out section. Sprint as fast as you can between the 30- and 40-meter cones—the second in section—and then hold a floating rhythm between the 40- and 50-meter cones, the second out section (see figure). Continue alternating max speed with floating until you hit the 60-meter mark and then slowly decelerate for a final 30 meters. Recover between reps with a slow walk back. Do 3 sets with a rest break between.

The goal is twofold: (1) making the out sections relaxed without causing deceleration and (2) making at least a 90-percent effort in the in sections without fatigue turning into lactic acid buildup. It's a speed session, not an endurance session.

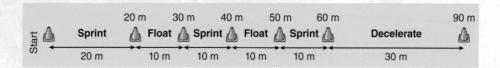

OVERHEAD STICK DRILL

The overhead stick drill emphasizes postural positioning of the hip in combination with the trunk. This helps to improve ground-reaction forces by stacking the hips and trunk in vertical alignment. It also trains the trunk to resist excessive rotation that creates energy leaks. This allows the shoulders to apply greater arm action forces in the sagittal plane, which effectively transfers forces through the fascia to the hips where it can be applied to increase ground-reaction forces.

BASIC

1. Start by standing tall with a stick held overhead, elbows locked out, trying to pull the stick apart. Use a grip wider than shoulder width; an experienced athlete can begin to narrow the grip to increase the challenge.
2. Maintaining a tall posture with hips forward, begin running like you would for a build-up run.
3. Make sure to hold the stick parallel to the ground, avoiding both side-to-side movement and lateral rotation of the stick.
4. Do 4 to 6 sets for 20 to 40 yards (18 to 37 m).

WICKET

The wicket is a valuable max-velocity application drill that should be in every coach's toolbox. Wickets help athletes (and coaches) naturally identify and solve many of the common postural dysfunctions that inhibit top-speed mechanics. Originally developed by elite NCAA sprint and hurdle coach Vince Anderson, wickets provide an obstacle course using miniature "banana hurdles" (or cones) set up with a progressive spacing pattern that gives athletes a task and forces them to respond by self-organizing their upright sprinting posture and movements. Two of the most common top-speed sprinting errors that athletes make after initial acceleration are overstriding too far in front of their center of mass by casting their lower leg out (which results in excessive braking impulses) and excessively back-swinging (butt-kicking, etc.). Wickets help athletes learn how to maintain a tall posture and neutral pelvis with good front-side mechanics and knee lift. It also helps them learn to drive force downward, strike with their feet under their center of mass, and push their hips forward on each stride (see figure).

The key to setting up wicket drills is dialing in the wicket spacing—which has multiple variables that depend on the athlete and surface, among other things. I'll provide some basic guidelines here for conceptual purposes, but each coach will want to play around with different spacing formulas based on the individual athlete they are working with. The target spacing for wickets will depend on the athlete's maximum effective stride length, with the spaces increasing from start to finish as the athlete's speed increases. Initial settings are also determined by skill level, training age, and surface. A good approach is to start with a target baseline for spacing and adjust accordingly after watching how the athlete performs at that spacing. Here are some general guidelines:

- A good general target for initial spacing is 6 feet (just under 2 m) for males and 5 feet (1.5 m) for females.
- Start with 6 acceleration steps prior to the wicket zones and then set up between 10 and 21 wickets with progressive spacing.
- Ideally, the athlete should land in the middle of zone I (between wickets 1 and 2). Using this first zone as the baseline, mark the 6 run-in acceleration steps with chalk, low cones, or yard (or meter) sticks. These acceleration steps should be counted and marked backward, starting from the middle of the first wicket zone, reducing each acceleration step 3 inches (about 8 cm), and going backward to the starting wicket. Athletes should hit each mark of the acceleration run-in while ensuring each foot strikes under each corresponding hip. This will put them in the optimal spot to hit the center of the first wicket zone. Use the following spacing parameters:
  » *Zone II (wickets 2 and 3)*: identical to zone I
  » *Zone III (wickets 3 and 4)*: an additional 2 inches (5 cm)
  » *Zones IV through VI (wickets 4 and 5, 5 and 6, 6 and 7)*: an additional 2 inches (5 cm)
  » *Zones VII and beyond*: for every group of three wicket zones, an additional 2 inches (5 cm)

A number of creative progressions and variations can be used, including finishing the wicket section with a 20- to 30-meter sprint to reinforce the muscle memory. You can also have the athlete hold a dowel or PVC pipe over their head to feel what the proper upright sprinting position is. This is where the art of coaching comes into play.

MAX-VELOCITY SPRINT

There is no stimulus that compares to all-out, max-velocity sprinting. Targeted drills can help you get stronger and develop proper form, but without regular exposure to full-throttle sprinting, your top-speed gains will be minimal. At some point, you have to fly—and you need to do it regularly to develop the necessary neurological and tissue adaptations for top speed. The good news is that cranking the throttle up to full gas is one of the most exhilarating feelings in the human experience. The key is developing proper technique first in order to minimize injury risk and optimize speed.

As I already mentioned, athletes must practice high intensity on a consistent basis. Coaches who dose athletes sporadically with high-intensity sprinting are just inviting injury. According to Dan Pfaff, a good strategy is to microdose athletes with top-speed work a few times per week by adding it into other training sessions—meaning in smaller bouts and, ideally, when athletes are warmed up but not fatigued. This allows athletes to hit maximal intensity on a regular basis without becoming overly fatigued in any given session. That said, the Parisi Speed School also aims for at least one dedicated max-velocity training session per week. Here are some guidelines for max-velocity sprint training.

- Sprinting sessions should be done at or above 95-percent effort with ample rest sessions between sprints to avoid turning sprinting sessions into endurance-training sessions. Having athletes walk back to the starting line after each effort helps build in natural rest cycles.

- As Ken Clark points out, upright sprinting mechanics are relevant at distances as short as 20 meters, which means that max-velocity training for team sport athletes should be done at distances of at least 30 to 60 meters.

- Microdosing means using the smallest amount of high-quality work necessary to drive adaptations on a consistent basis. This dosage is highly individualized based on the athlete. Again, it's where the art of coaching comes into play.

- The key to upright sprinting is delivering a series of powerful ground strikes with a super-stiff foot–ankle complex. The ground strikes should come from above with a smooth elastic whip of windup and land just under the hips without yielding. Gravity is the most powerful force in the universe, so think of gravity as you punching it in the face over and over again. Those punches should be violently aggressive and accurate. To use one of Ken Clark's cues: "Cock the hammer and strike the nail."

- When upright sprinting, athletes should run tall with their head aligned over neutral hips, shoulders back and down, and chest up and proud. The thigh should be nearly parallel with the ground as it reaches the top terminus of the front side. The hands should be relaxed and open with arm movements that swing from the face past the butt.

- The nervous system and all human movement are task driven. To get the best sprinting performance out of athletes, I find it is useful to have them race against a clock or each other (assuming they are of similar skill level—if not, you can have the faster runner begin at a starting line that is farther back).

ADVANCED

Rest is one of the most important and least respected ingredients in top-speed development. Sprinting is metabolically and neurologically intense. When athletes reach a point of fatigue, they get sloppy and fall back into movement dysfunctions, or "viruses," as Dan Pfaff calls them, which increase injury risk and diminish their refinements in technique. Also, the body's energy and fascia systems need time to reboot and refresh. This makes incorporating rest cycles into your exercise bouts just as important as engineering strategic rest-and-recovery cycles between bouts. When it comes to incorporating rest cycles into a max-velocity workout, a good benchmark is to aim for 30 to 60 seconds of rest for every 10 meters of sprinting. For example, a 40-meter sprint should be followed by at least two to four minutes of rest (or longer)—ideally accompanied by some low-intensity movement that keeps tissues warm and fluids pumping through the fascia, lymph, and circulatory systems. And, lastly, I really can't overstate the importance of ample downtime between sessions combined with a lifestyle of healthy movement, eating, and sleeping habits. Strategically engineered cycles of rest and recovery between training bouts and competition can yield significant speed benefits because they give the elastic connective tissues and other systems valuable time for remodeling and development. Mechanotransduction is a slow process, and fascia takes longer to develop than muscle. This is one of the cruel ironies of speed development: Getting faster takes time. Weeks of intense work turn into months of refining rhythm and focus. And then, out of the blue, one day you wake up and realize you can fly.

DECELERATION

Speed development is a world of many paradoxes. Among the most counterintuitive of them is that the ability to decelerate is key to speed and quickness. When most people talk about speed training, they primarily think about improving acceleration, max velocity, and overall running mechanics. But being able to quickly apply the brakes and safely control your momentum and center of gravity are essential to the high-speed cuts, darts, and changes of direction (CODs) involved in most field and court sports. If you put two race cars on a track with equally skilled drivers and identical engines and suspension systems, but one car has significantly better brakes, the car with the better brakes will be the easy winner every time. This is because the driver will be able to enter and exit the corners with greater precision and higher speeds. The same principle applies to sports. Stopping speed is just as important as sprinting speed.

Neuromuscular Coordination and Eccentric Strength

Proper deceleration technique and a strong foundation of eccentric strength play huge roles in injury resilience. On average, there are more than 100,000 ACL injuries every year in the United States (Musahl and Karlsson 2019). Studies show that more than 80 percent of ACL injuries occur during loaded noncontact movements—for example, landing from a jump or suddenly decelerating while running (Shimokochi and Shultz 2008). I believe that, in many cases, these athletes either didn't have the neuromuscular coordination to facilitate a smooth, controlled deceleration, or they lacked a sufficient amount of eccentric strength to stabilize the knee joint and core. As I mentioned in the opening chapter, the gravitational braking forces a decelerating athlete experiences can be up to twice their body weight. This means that eccentric strength and anterior chain strength play huge roles in safe deceleration. And deceleration—just like acceleration and max velocity—is a skill that can be trained and improved in any athlete.

While deceleration training may seem like a novel concept to some coaches, it has been a foundation of the Parisi Speed School methodology since the very beginning. In fact, we were one of the originators of a focused approach to deceleration training back in 1999. At that time, Martin Rooney, now the founder and CEO of Training for Warriors and a best-selling author, joined us early in his career as a physical therapist. Rooney spearheaded much of the original research and drill development we used to create a series of best-selling videos on the subject. As a professional physical therapist who was focused on helping high-level athletes recover from soft-tissue injuries (many of them ACL injuries), Rooney understood how eccentric strength and the ability to control momentum on all three planes are critical to performance and injury prevention. Furthermore, they are foundational skills for multidirectional speed and agility. Before you train athletes to improve their speeds for changing direction (cutting, darting, reversing) and agility skills (reacting quickly to external stimuli), it is essential that they have a solid base of eccentric strength and can execute proper deceleration techniques. Otherwise, you're putting them at risk for injury. That's why doing deceleration drills is a good way to begin a multidirectional training day. By microdosing athletes with anchor and application drills for deceleration *before* getting into COD and agility work, you will help athletes develop better neuromuscular awareness of their body position, posture, and motor vocabulary. Having a deep level of internal, proprioceptive awareness and reaction speed are essential to optimal performance with reduced injury risk.

When it comes to form, one of the most common deceleration errors we see in kids who come through the Parisi Speed School is that they decelerate with too high of a center of gravity that is too far behind their support base and they land flat-footed. This causes them to be very unbalanced. Their knee comes in straight because their legs are straight—which is a recipe for noncontact ACL disaster if there's a divot or variation of hardness in the running surface.

Controlled deceleration requires lowering your center of gravity and getting your feet in front of it so you can quickly gain control over your momentum and distribute the ground-contact force across your body's entire shock-absorption system (see figure 8.1). The arms help maintain your center of balance by countering the braking forces created by flexion in the hip, knees, and ankles. The feet should make ground contact on the forward part of the foot with the ankle plantarflexed. In fact, video analysis of Boden and colleagues' study (2009) revealed that subjects who experienced ACL ruptures had landed either flat-footed or on their hindfoot at initial ground contact. On the contrary, control subjects who avoided rupturing their ACL while doing a similar activity landed on their forefoot with more plantarflexion. This is partly because the gastrocnemius–soleus

FIGURE 8.1   The key to deceleration is lowering your center of gravity and getting your feet in front of it so you can quickly gain control over your momentum.

complex and tendons of the lower leg play a significant role in absorbing ground-reaction forces. Making initial ground contact on the forefoot with a plantarflexed ankle enables the lower leg to more effectively absorb and distribute the forces before they get to the knee. In most competitive situations, deceleration is immediately followed by an explosive movement in a different direction. This means you want to harness that kinetic energy in your elastic tissues by loading it into the ground. Doing so allows you to use this kinetic energy to dynamically recoil during the stretch-shortening cycle. That's how better deceleration correlates to quicker CODs and faster game speeds.

Eccentric-Strength Training for Deceleration

A solid foundation of eccentric strength is the first component of good brakes. This means deceleration training starts in the weight room. When most athletes go into the gym, they often have the mentality that they're working to develop their engines and increase their horsepower. As a result, they focus a lot on concentric muscle contractions. But muscles and the myofascial system function in three ways: (1) concentrically to facilitate explosive acceleration, (2) isometrically to provide stability, and (3) eccentrically to enable deceleration. When a field or court athlete suddenly stops, pivots around an opponent, and reaccelerates in a different direction, they eccentrically decelerate, isometrically stabilize to pivot, and concentrically explode as they reaccelerate again. This means all three types of muscle contractions are used in virtually all athletic movement patterns, and therefore, it is essential to take a balanced approach to strength training that focuses on all three types of muscle contractions. Loading tissues with loaded sagittal plane movements, such as squats and deadlifts, helps strengthen muscles, ligaments, and tendons. But athletes often focus too much on producing the concentric force needed to lift the load going up and not enough on the eccentric control of the load going down.

The paradox is that by training your tissues to control loads eccentrically, you can develop more injury-resilient tissues while also helping them absorb force in a way that ultimately makes you faster. And that's where the lowering phase of a lift becomes significant. In the weight room, you want to pay close attention to the eccentric lowering phase of a lift and do it slowly with maximum control rather than rushing through it to bang out the next rep. This allows you to increase time under tension and get the most eccentric benefit out of the lift. A good protocol is to spend three seconds lowering the weight, pausing for one second at the bottom, and then exploding concentrically upward again for the next lift. Slowing things down and really tuning in to what's happening will help facilitate greater neurological recruitment, enhance technical aptitude, and increase muscle recruitment—all of which translate to better efficiency of movement and control.

The fibers of the gluteus maximus travel down and away from the iliac crest and sacrum to the femur and the IT band. Then, working together with the quads, hamstrings, and core, the muscles of the hip complex form a significant part of the body's braking system (see figure 8.2). It works to control force through a combination of hip flexion, adduction, and internal rotation as each leg hits the ground. Eccentric strength in these integrated structures is crucial for hip, knee, and ankle stability while running, stopping, landing, and changing directions. Eccentric exercises (like Nordic hamstring curls) have been shown to add sarcomeres in a series and increase muscle strength when the muscles are extended at length, giving the myofascial system a better ability to resist the high forces experienced during deceleration.

Controlled Multiplane Deceleration

Before you have an athlete do COD movements that inherently involve positions of instability, it's essential that the athlete can demonstrate the ability to precisely control their momentum and decelerate in a controlled fashion on all three planes of motion. Deceleration in the sagittal plane is easiest because your body can more efficiently use the larger braking muscles of the hip and knee, such as the glutes and quads. But competitive game movements typically involve a multidimensional mix of sagittal, frontal, and transverse planes where deceleration is often immediately followed by an explosive movement in a different direction. If we teach the body how to load into the ground multidimensionally using proper deceleration technique, that kinetic energy can be stored briefly in the tendons, muscles, and fascia with a short moment of stretch and then used for a rapid recoil that provides an athletic advantage for quick change of direction

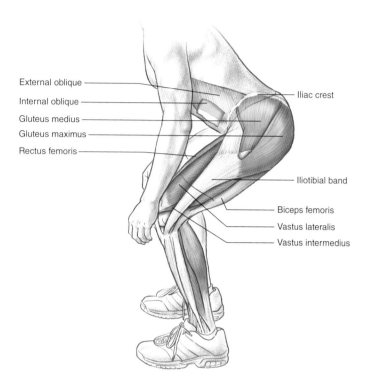

External oblique

Internal oblique

Gluteus medius

Gluteus maximus

Rectus femoris

Iliac crest

Iliotibial band

Biceps femoris

Vastus lateralis

Vastus intermedius

FIGURE 8.2   The quads, hamstrings, core, and muscles of the hip complex are the foundation of the body's braking system.

with minimal metabolic costs. Developing a multidimensional shape stability and the capacity to control momentum on all three planes is essential for improving both multidirectional game speed and injury resilience. Loaded-movement drills and exercises using submaximal loads, such as a medicine ball, kettlebell, or ViPR PRO, are highly beneficial for developing multiplanar deceleration control and shape stability. I rang up Michol Dalcourt, founder of the Institute of Motion and developer of the ViPR PRO, to get his perspective on how coaches can help athletes improve their three-dimensional deceleration capabilities using loaded-movement drills and exercises. Dalcourt had this to say.

"Deceleration is all about reaction. The system gets acted upon by the outside forces of momentum, gravity, and ground reaction. So when we consider the concept of deceleration training, it's a good idea to look at the nervous system first because the nervous system needs to sense what's going on and then make the best motor decision in the moment. It has to quickly figure out where your knee is going, where your ankle is going, and where your body mass is going relative to your foot. Then it has to slow all of that down and convert that energy. The nervous system's ability to have that level of acuity is a learned skill that is more neurologically advanced. So you really want to expose an athlete—particularly a multidirectional athlete—to that kind of sensory information in a three-dimensional environment."

This signifies that, in addition to training the musculoskeletal system to develop eccentric strength, you also need to develop the motor engrams (i.e., muscle memory) to respond to variable inputs with unconscious precision. This unconscious refinement of coordination is called automaticity, which is the ability to perform an action or sequence of actions unconsciously, with speed and accuracy, while consciously engaging in other brain functions like spotting an open teammate in the passing lane or telling a joke as you juggle torches on a unicycle. Achieving automaticity of a refined motor skill comes from extensive practice and repetition. A simple example of this is learning how to play the piano. At first, you focus on learning the musical notes, which are discrete individual inputs. It takes time. The music is soulless and clunky. After enough practice, though, you stop looking at the notes and start playing the music with nuance and emotion. Eventually you can play entire compositions effortlessly while having a conversation or improvising lyrics.

Learning the skill of deceleration happens in the same way. To achieve automaticity, you need to program the required motor engrams for the desired skill to fire reactively and automatically using the gamma loop of the somatic nervous system (SNS). As discussed in chapter 2, the SNS consists of sensory (afferent) nerves and motor (efferent) nerves that are located within the muscle spindles themselves. Afferent nerves relay incoming sensations to the central nervous system (CNS), while efferent nerves send out muscle-contraction commands in response. These nerves respond to changes in muscle length (based on the amount and speed of stretch), which are then adjusted for by fusimotor neurons. The gamma loop is a communication pathway between the spinal cord and the peripheral muscles that expedites reaction time in response to external stimuli before the conscious brain even gets involved. For example, if you're sprinting across a field and step in a divot, by the time that signal gets to your higher brain so you can respond by preventing yourself from rolling your ankle, it's already too late.

Instead, the gamma loop makes it possible for the signal to go from the peripheral sensory tissues of the ankle to the spinal cord and back again in a rapid-fire reflex arc of proprioception and reaction. But recent research is indicating that the fascia system and its multitude of proprioceptors also play a significant role in this phenomenon. According to studies conducted by Robert Schleip (2017), there are up to 10 times more proprioceptors in fascia tissue than muscle tissue, and there is growing evidence that the proprioceptors of the knee can send signals directly to the hip, and the hip can communicate right back to the knee using the whole-body fascial net. In other words, the signal doesn't even need to go to the spinal cord. This is important because we are now learning that, in addition to providing shape stability and mechanical support, the fascia system is also a critical sensory organ that provides a network of sensation information that communicates directly with the nervous system (along with other systems) to quickly right the ship in response to stimulus. So fascia tissue that is more trained, optimized, and healthy results in it being better at aiding the nervous system in precise, high-performance movements. The idea behind deceleration training of the nervous system is to teach the body to unconsciously gather massive amounts of information from whole-body proprioceptors—including those in the fascia tissue as well as the joint proprioceptors and other mechanoreceptors across the body—so your body can respond in an automatic yet highly coordinated way.

"When we three-dimensionalize [sic] deceleration training, it's not just because it's a new fad," explains Dalcourt. "It's because we want to expose the body's systems to a variety of inputs in the right way, with the right dosage, so it can respond and adapt over time. Then, as it gradually adapts, we can add more complicated inputs with targeted regressions and progressions that prompt it to continue responding and adapting until it supercompensates. If we can do that in the right dosage, then that individual will eventually become very unbreakable, relatively speaking. Because we've challenged them to be able to thrive in environments where there's a reaction, there's a change of direction, there's a cut and a drive. When you're playing a sport, your cognition is outside your body. It's on the play. We want to fortify the body so that when it hits the ground, it harnesses that ground-reaction force as a kinetic pulse to store energy in the body and then use it for conversion. Training this way accomplishes two things. It's going to decrease injury risk. And it's going to optimize the biological properties of the tissue. Because there's a benefit to these tissues when we teach them how to load into the ground."

Dalcourt advocates using a four-step process for three-dimensional deceleration training that progresses from working with just body weight on the sagittal plane to working with submaximal loads on multiple planes.

"We start by working with body weight in a linear way. Once there's a capacity built there, we continue working with body weight in a more multiplanar environment, which we call unloaded multiplanar training. From there, we advance to linear, load-based deceleration training, doing things like loaded squats and basic depth-deceleration exercises where you're just going from a tall position into a squat position with a load and you work on applying the brakes as you come down. So you can really learn to own that momentum control. You can also do what we call 'prepositioning the load,' where you hold a ViPR PRO or any other mass to one side of your body with both hands. Everything else is pretty symmetrical, and you're looking straight ahead, but both your arms are holding a load on one side of your body. You start off on your tiptoes and then drop into the ground and try to catch yourself as quickly as you can. It's still a linear movement in terms of what your knees, hips, and shoulders are doing, but the mass is asymmetrically loading the tissues more on one side than on the other. Basically, you're starting to triangulate the stress inputs at this point.

"From there, we work on loaded multiplanar deceleration training where we're moving into the ground with a load and trying to put the brakes on in different vectors and different directions. The sum total of all of this organization—going from working with body weight in a linear environment to working with body weight in a multiplanar environment to adding load in a linear environment and then working with loads in a multiplanar environment—is that this four-step process is going to gradually fortify the tissues. We're putting lines of force through the fascial net as we're decelerating, which means those lines of force are going to be magnified. That will prompt the fascia to deform and depolarize along those lines of stress and remodel collagen, elastin, and other protein fibers within the extracellular matrix in response to fortify the body based on the magnitude and direction of those loads. As the body responds to these inputs and remodels over time using the process of mechanotransduction, it will lead to tissue adaptations in a very multidirectional way. Essentially, we're using the magnitude and direction of loads in a predictive training environment to tell the structures where and how to remodel. So when it comes to an unpredictive environment like sport, the athlete will have a broader capacity to automatically respond the right way to the forces of momentum, gravity, and ground reaction."

Deceleration Training

For deceleration training, the Parisi strategy is to start off with fundamental anchor drills targeted at maintaining proper body position (just like max-velocity training). The goal is to help athletes build on everything you've learned about posture in the previous chapter—including proper upright posture with neutral hips as well as in the lumbar and thoracic spine and shoulder girdle. These same postural principles also apply to deceleration and agility training. Granted, when you perform deceleration and CODs in a competitive situation, you are inevitably going to twist and come out of ideal posture, putting your spine in more vulnerable positions. That's part of the risk we take when playing sports. But when we're training in a controlled environment, we want to maintain good spinal posture. You are going to come out of these optimal neutral positions in competition, but you want to come out of them because the sport requires you to.

When you think about posture, you want to get down into an athletic "linebacker stance" where the knees are bent, the butt is back, the weight is on the balls of your feet, the spine is neutral, and the shoulders are retracted down and back with a strong elevated chest. We want athletes to really understand and master that stance. One of the elements of this position that often goes unseen is the shoulder girdle and the position of the shoulders. A lot of times athletes are not thinking about their shoulders. They're not contracting their rhomboids, posterior delts, or lats. They're not actively pulling their shoulders back. But this is really important for helping maintain spinal alignment and force production because when you're out of alignment, your ability to control and generate force is going to be limited. Again, movements like picking off a pass or maneuvering a soccer ball around an opponent will make you twist, and that's when things are going to change. But when you're training, you want to activate the key muscle groups and help the body understand where the optimal athletic ready stance is.

Then we present deceleration application drills to help athletes develop neuromuscular coordination and practice controlling their momentum in these more gamelike conditions. These drills include side shuffles, box drops, and acceleration and deceleration runs, among others (which can be found in the menus in chapter 12). These are great drills to work in at the beginning of a multidirectional training day since deceleration is the first step in COD movements.

SNAP DOWN

The first deceleration anchor drill we typically teach at the Parisi Speed School is called a snap down. The snap down reinforces proper positioning and helps athletes understand deceleration mechanics.

Primary Muscles Activated

Down phase:
- *Shoulder (extension)*: latissimus dorsi, teres major, triceps brachii long head, pectoralis major lower fibers, deltoid posterior fibers, infraspinatus
- *Hip (flexion)*: gluteus maximus, biceps femoris long head, semitendinosus, semimembranosus
- *Knee (flexion)*: biceps femoris short and long head, semitendinosus, semimembranosus
- *Ankle (dorsiflexion)*: gastrocnemius, soleus

1. Stand really tall on the balls of your feet and raise both hands over your head (see figure *a*).
2. Snap (accelerate) the torso and arms down into an athletic linebacker position by flexing at the hip, knee, and ankle and then decelerate and hold that position (see figure *b*). The shoulders should be over the knees with the knees over the ankles. Maintain a neutral spine with the shoulders retracted.
3. Repeat for 6 to 8 reps.

VERTICAL JUMP

After snap downs, we progress to vertical jumps. Vertical jumping drills are common in most training routines, but all too often coaches don't focus enough on the importance of landing in a smooth, athletic way that optimizes the absorption of force. With vertical jump and deceleration training, you really want to focus on eccentric loading and controlling the landing. The key is learning how to absorb the force and load it into the ground.

Deltoid anterior fibers

Pectoralis major upper fibers

Rectus femoris

Vastus intermedius

Vastus lateralis

a   b

Primary Muscles Activated

Jump phase:

- *Shoulder (flexion)*: deltoid anterior fibers, pectoralis major upper fibers, coracobrachialis
- *Hip (extension)*: gluteus maximus, biceps femoris long head, semitendinosus, semimembranosus
- *Knee (extension)*: rectus femoris, vastus lateralis, vastus medialis, vastus intermedius
- *Ankle (plantarflexion)*: gastrocnemius, soleus

1. Start in the snapped-down (athletic linebacker) position—bent at the hips, knees, and ankles with arms flexed backward. Your shoulders should be over the knees with your weight equally distributed throughout your feet (see figure *a*).

2. Explode upward into a vertical jump, driving down through the entire foot and then launching off the balls of your feet while extending at the hips, knees, and ankles and swinging your arms overhead (see figure *b*).

3. Once airborne, focus on landing softly and athletically on your forefoot with your ankle plantarflexed like a cat as you absorb the force by bending at the hips, knees, and ankles. The chest should be over the knees, and the butt is down and back. Focus on controlling your momentum. The more athletic you are, the higher you can jump, and the more force will be transmitted through your body, which means there will be more force that you need to absorb. The goal is to absorb that force in a light, athletic way with control (as opposed to just crashing down).

4. Repeat for 6 to 8 reps.

PUSH LUNGE

A more advanced drill in our deceleration training is push lunges where a coach or partner pushes the athlete from behind or the side (depending on the lunge) as they do a forward or side lunge. Obviously, the amount of push needs to be appropriately gauged by the coach to ensure athlete safety, but the goal is to provide an added amount of force the athlete must overcome with eccentric control. This is an advanced anchor drill that helps athletes develop a feel for the strength required for controlled deceleration.

MODERATE

Primary Muscles Activated

Swing phase:

- *Shoulder (top hand, diagonal adduction)*: pectoralis major upper fibers, pectoralis major lower fibers, coracobrachialis, deltoid anterior fibers
- *Shoulder (bottom hand, diagonal abduction)*: deltoid posterior fibers, infraspinatus, teres minor
- *Trunk (rotation)*: ipsilateral erector spinae, contralateral external oblique, ipsilateral internal oblique
- *Hip (extension)*: gluteus maximus, biceps femoris long head, semitendinosus, semimembranosus
- *Knee (extension)*: rectus femoris, vastus lateralis, vastus medialis, vastus intermedius
- *Ankle (plantarflexion)*: gastrocnemius, soleus

Landing phase:

- *Hip (flexion)*: gluteus maximus, biceps femoris long head, semitendinosus, semimembranosus
- *Knee (flexion)*: rectus femoris, vastus lateralis, vastus medialis, vastus intermedius
- *Ankle (dorsiflexion)*: gastrocnemius, soleus

1. Start in a squat position holding a ViPR PRO or similar loading device using a shovel grip (see figure *a*).

2. Quickly and forcefully explode the ViPR PRO over your shoulder as you jump and rotate 90 degrees into a split-stance side lunge (see figure *b*). Move the ViPR PRO as if you're forcefully throwing dirt over your shoulder with the shovel motion and in an upward direction as if to punch a hole in the sky.

3. Control the load as you absorb the force into the ground without spinal flexion and then walk back to the starting position.

4. Repeat for 6 to 8 reps on each side.

For increased challenge, use a heavier load or hold the starting and stopping positions longer. You can also hold the load overhead and swing it down to one side (alternating sides).

CROW HOP

Crow hops are a one-legged version of a squat jump that challenges an athlete's ability to balance and co-contract muscles to create pulses of stiffness in the lower leg, hip, and core while absorbing the force on the deceleration phase of the jump. The crow hop is also an advanced anchor drill that starts blending into application drills. It helps develop the deceleration, stability, and control necessary for rapid COD movements in a game situation. Watch the athlete closely upon landing. Do they have control? Is their ankle stiff? Are they smooth and stable? Are they landing flat-footed? Are their knees valgus? Address any issues you've identified before proceeding; otherwise, you'll put the athlete at an increased risk of injury during play.

ADVANCED

Primary Muscles Activated

Jump phase:

- *Shoulder (flexion)*: deltoid anterior fibers, pectoralis major upper fibers, coracobrachialis
- *Hip (extension)*: gluteus maximus, biceps femoris long head, semitendinosus, semimembranosus
- *Knee (extension)*: rectus femoris, vastus lateralis, vastus medialis, vastus intermedius
- *Ankle (plantarflexion)*: gastrocnemius, soleus

1. Start in an athletic quarter squat with hands in front of you and balance on one leg (see figure *a*).
2. Jump up vertically as high and forcefully as you can and land with stable, balanced control on the same leg (see figure *b*).
3. Repeat for 6 to 8 reps on each side.

MODERATE

SIDE SHUFFLE

Side shuffle (and forward shuffle) drills help athletes understand momentum control during COD movements. Work this drill for approximately 15 yards (14 m) in each direction without crossing your feet. Remember to keep your weight on the front part of your feet.

Primary Muscles Activated

Step leg (leg that steps first):
- *Hip (abduction)*: gluteus medius, tensor fasciae latae, gluteus maximus upper fibers, gluteus minimus
- *Hip (isometric flexion)*: gluteus maximus, gluteus medius posterior fibers, piriformis, gemellus superior and inferior, obturator externus and internus, quadratus femoris
- *Knee (isometric flexion)*: rectus femoris, vastus lateralis, vastus medialis, vastus intermedius
- *Ankle (isometric dorsiflexion, swing phase; isometric plantarflexion, stance phase)*: tibialis anterior, extensor hallucis longus, extensor digitorum longus (dorsiflexion); gastrocnemius, soleus (plantarflexion)

Trail leg (leg that steps second and follows):
- *Hip (adduction)*: pectineus, adductor brevis, adductor longus, adductor magnus, gracilis
- *Hip (isometric flexion)*: gluteus maximus, gluteus medius posterior fibers, piriformis, gemellus superior and inferior, obturator externus and internus, quadratus femoris
- *Knee (isometric flexion)*: rectus femoris, vastus lateralis, vastus medialis, vastus intermedius
- *Ankle (eversion, push phase; isometric dorsiflexion, swing phase; isometric plantarflexion, stance phase)*: peroneus longus, peroneus brevis, extensor digitorum longus (eversion); tibialis anterior, extensor hallucis longus, extensor digitorum longus (dorsiflexion); gastrocnemius, soleus (plantarflexion)

1. Start by holding an athletic quarter squat with hands in front of you in a deceleration, or landing, position (see figure *a*). Hold this position for an extended moment to get a strong sense for how it feels.

2. Shuffle sideways at a walking pace while maintaining good body position and then slowly increase speed and intensity (see figure *b*).

3. Plant both feet at the end, keeping your weight on the inside (support) leg, and then shuffle back to the starting spot.

4. Repeat for 6 to 8 reps for 10 to 20 yards (9 to 18 m) going sideways in both directions.

One of the most common mistakes athletes make when side shuffling is putting their weight on their outside foot (as opposed to the inside support leg), which isn't as efficient and can lead to a chance of injury. This drill can and should also be done moving forward and backward. The principles are the same. Accelerate forward approximately 15 yards (14 m); decelerate to a stop; hold the crouched position for two claps; then backpedal to the starting position and hold again. It is important for athletes to come to a complete stop every time because it provides a great training input. The more they practice decelerating and coming to a complete stop, the better they're going to be at doing it on the athletic field under pressure.

DEPTH DROP

Depth drops, also known as altitude landings, are similar to vertical jumps, but depth drops focus exclusively on the landing and deceleration part. They help athletes understand how to absorb force by raising their center of gravity and having them drop down from that position. It is a more advanced drill that requires a solid foundation of strength and skill to do safely. Make sure your athlete is competent enough to control their landings smoothly first.

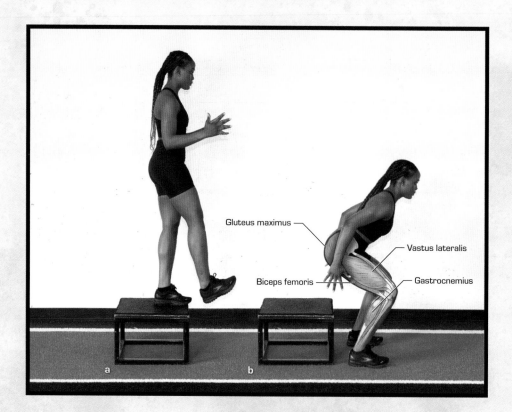

Primary Muscles Activated

Landing phase:
- *Hip (flexion)*: gluteus maximus, biceps femoris long head, semitendinosus, semimembranosus
- *Knee (flexion)*: rectus femoris, vastus lateralis, vastus medialis, vastus intermedius
- *Ankle (dorsiflexion)*: gastrocnemius, soleus

1. Start by standing on a box or raised surface that is around knee height or lower, depending on the athlete's training history and skill level.
2. Step out and off the box; do not jump down or out (see figure *a*).
3. Land in the deceleration position with the joints slightly bent and properly aligned (shoulders over knees, knees over ankles) while athletically absorbing the force of the drop throughout the entire body (see figure *b*). You should exhibit good control and strength in your hips and core as you land.
4. Hold the landing position for a few beats. Do 4 to 6 reps for 2 to 4 sets.

Box height can be progressively increased based on athlete skill and control. Obviously, heightening the box makes the drill more challenging. Another valuable progression is to practice landing in a split-stance position. Just be sure to do the same number of drops on both sides to balance the force inputs.

A lot of athletes focus on building up their engine in the weight room and sprinting on the field, doing resistance runs, hill runs, and so on, but it's just as important to develop the critical braking, suspension, and steering systems at the same time. These are all finely tuned instruments that demand just as much focus and attention as the engine. If you put a turbocharged Maserati engine in a 20-year-old Camry with lousy brakes and suspension and drive it fast on a curvy road or suddenly try to stop at high speed, you're (literally) going to run into problems. You can significantly reduce injury risk by helping athletes build a solid base of eccentric strength in the early stages of their training life and develop the muscle memory to automatically engage proper body positioning for deceleration through repetition and microdosing. Learning to fly safely means knowing how to land gracefully.

MULTIDIRECTIONAL SPEED

You know what's better than flying? Outmaneuvering your opponent like a jet pilot in a dogfight. Beating them in the micro-moments when it counts—where superiority is measured in fractions of inches and seconds. In these moments, the focus is not about how fast you can run a 40 but rather how fast you can hit the brakes, change directions, create space, and capitalize on opportunities. This kind of multidirectional game speed requires ultrafast reflexes, the ability to control your momentum with tremendous precision, and a high level of mastery over the basics of linear speed. While acceleration and maximum velocity are expressions of linear speed in its purest form, multidirectional speed is the most advanced and nuanced. This is why training for it is almost as hard as executing it under pressure for the game-winning buzzer-beater. Being strong and fast doesn't guarantee that you can transfer those physical capacities into the kind of real-time, split-second changes of direction that give you a competitive advantage.

Forms of Multidirectional Speed

Before getting into how to train for multidirectional speed, I want to define the concept in its various forms—since they are often confused. As mentioned in chapter 1, multidirectional speed is technically divided into three subcategories commonly referred to as the following:

1. Change of direction (COD)
2. Agility
3. Maneuverability

COD is a rapid, *preplanned* change of direction or velocity that is intentional and planned and often associated with the offensive side of the ball—like a point guard driving toward the basket and then suddenly cutting or stepping back to create space between them and their defender so they can take a shot or fire a pass. It involves executing neurological motor programs (motor engrams) for movements that can be rehearsed as part of a closed-loop or constraint-based approach to training (e.g., simulated plays, cone drills, pattern sprints). COD skill development is highly dependent on the required movement demands of each specific sport and position.

Agility is a rapid change of direction or velocity in *response* to external stimuli. It is associated with both the offensive and defensive sides of the ball. Not only is it unplanned, reactive, and cognitive but also requires the ability to rapidly read visual and audio cues so the athlete can respond with appropriate countermovements. Think of a highly skilled fighter evading a punch that misses them by a whisker and then using that momentary opening to land a strike on their opponent. Great agility takes a highly tuned neurological and fascia system combined with refined visual scanning, pattern recognition, decision making, and reaction speed. And the reality is that some athletes are just more gifted at it than others. The number of real-time neurological factors and situational variables involved in expressing agility makes it much more challenging to train and assess—which is why I dedicated the next chapter to cover it (entire books have been written on the subject). The main thing to keep in mind is that solid COD skills are an essential prerequisite for good agility.

Maneuverability is the ability to manage the angular momentum of your body at discrete angles—like a baseball player sprinting around the curvilinear path of bases. It involves managing your center of gravity at high speed while applying slight shifts in body angle and lean, movement tempo, and trajectory so you can safely and effectively apply ground force in awkward positions. Good maneuverability requires foot, ankle, and hip stability with robust connective tissues around the joints. It should come as no surprise that it also requires an extremely strong core.

This chapter focuses on training athletes for better COD and maneuverability, while the next chapter expands on how these skills contribute to reactive agility.

Movement Vocabulary

In simple terms, multidirectional speed is a high-level expression of momentum control. If you want to be good at it, you need to master the basic motor vocabularies of acceleration, deceleration, and lateral movement. It's very much like learning a new language. You start out by memorizing words, basic grammar rules, and common phrases. Then you practice them over and over until you are able to have a conversation, but you are still thinking and processing translations as you speak. Then, after more practice, you become fluent enough to naturally fall into random conversations with interesting native-speaking strangers. If you want to have a conversation with them that's engaging, open ended, and expansive using slang, sarcasm, and contextual nuance, you first need to be competent in the basics of the language. Training your muscle memory and building the physical capacity to express good movement literacy in linear speed are essential prerequisites to adding the increased complexity of multidirectional speed in meaningful ways. When you have highly competent movement literacy in the basics of acceleration, deceleration, and lateral movement, you can execute faster changes in direction with less risk for injury. I mention this because there has been some debate in our industry around the effectiveness of constraint-based, closed chain drills (e.g., shuffle drills, ladder drills, cone drills) versus open chain, gamelike activities for training—with some coaches dismissing closed chain drills as being largely irrelevant for multidirectional speed and agility.

My take on this subject is that the pendulum of popular opinion is constantly swinging from one extreme to the other and that both training approaches have their role in a well-rounded speed program. Constraint-based drills help athletes target and develop the motor programs for unconsciously executing foundational movements with proper form, translating to more effective expressions of force application, faster speeds, and reduced injury risk. Open chain drills help athletes develop creative adaptability, fluency of application (when, where, and how to change direction), and the heightened situational awareness and neurological programming needed for great reactive agility.

Of course, the first step in any training program is to help athletes develop the physical capacity to meet the demands of their specific sport and position. This includes optimizing their strength-to-weight ratio with resistance training—for men, the ability to squat twice their body weight and for women, 1.8 times their weight—ensuring they have the right combination of flexibility and stiffness for their movement needs, increasing their aerobic thresholds, and so on. As physical capacity is developed, you want to reinforce and expand their movement vocabulary while targeting any deficiencies or imbalances they have with constraint-based drills. That way you can determine their capacity and level of fluency and prescribe training accordingly. As capacity and capability are advanced, you can begin challenging them in gamelike situations with unexpected variables that require them to adapt to the moment.

At the Parisi Speed School, we think of this process as training like a martial artist. A fighter needs to practice the basic movements of punching and kicking over and over until they are pristine, but they also need to spar with other fighters with different styles so they can practice applying those skills to a wide range of practical situations. But it all starts with refining the basic skills of movement, like practicing a kata. The goal is to build capacity and capability with constraint-based drills in a predictable training environment so that when they get to an unpredictable game environment, they can respond with the best strategy in the moment.

Movement Strategies

When it comes to training multidirectional speed, one of the problems with doing exclusively open chain, gamelike drills is that athletes will naturally use the familiar movement strategies that they're comfortable with, which reinforces the things they're already good at and the things they're not so good at. One of the important goals of training is to challenge athletes in ways that help them become more balanced, adaptable, and resilient. Obviously, you want to help an athlete keep their strengths strong, but it's a coach's responsibility to help athletes be the best they can be by strengthening their weaknesses, balancing their systems, and giving them a broader vocabulary of movement strategies to use based on demand. Every athlete has unique movement biases based on their anthropometrics, tissue compositions (whether they're more fascia driven or muscle driven), training history, injury history, and sport—among other things.

The challenge is that if you don't help them develop a wider movement vocabulary using constraint-based drills that force them to develop different strategies outside of their comfort zone, you limit their ability to adapt to the unexpected. If they're double-teamed, find themselves off balance because an opponent is pulling on their jersey, or need to keep a foot on the ground as they turn to catch a pass in the end zone, but they've never practiced the movement skills to adapt to that situation, they will be limited in their ability to execute that movement and more likely to get injured.

A good example of movement bias can be found in a study conducted by biomechanics researcher Dr. Andy Franklyn-Miller and colleagues (2017) looking at whole-body kinematic and kinetic data of multidirectional field athletes doing several repetitions of a preplanned 110-degree cutting maneuver at maximum effort. The study identified three distinct movement strategies among the athletes in the test group—where 40 percent were knee dominant (meaning the knee joint was doing most of the work), 45 percent were hip dominant, and 15 percent were ankle dominant. This resulted in longer ground-contact times and greater ground forces being transferred up the kinetic chain to the other joints.

These data have numerous implications. For example, if an athlete is biased to certain movement strategies during planned CODs and they aren't challenged with alternative strategies in practice that expand their movement vocabulary, they will be limited in their options when things don't go to plan during competition. This can make them less effective from a performance standpoint and more susceptible to injury. Also, if their movement strategy is inherently flawed (e.g., they flex too much at the ankle and not enough at the knee and hip), they are one unplanned step away from an injury. The challenge is that, without an experienced coach's eye or a mountain of kinematic and kinetic data, it can be difficult to identify your athlete's movement biases in different situations and levels of exhaustion.

Additionally, there's no way to know what situations they will encounter in competition. This is why constraint-based drills are valuable—you can use them to expose your athletes to a wide range of scenarios with different loading patterns and movement demands in a somewhat controlled environment. Therefore, when they find themselves in an unexpected "movement conversation" on the field or the court, their nervous system and muscle memory will have alternate responses they can adapt because they've experienced them in training. You can also use constraint-based drills to identify and balance specific movement dysfunctions. All of which is to say a well-rounded approach to successful multidirectional training uses a progression of both closed chain and open chain approaches to help athletes safely unlock their full potential for competitive COD and agility.

Reactive Strength

One of the most powerful features a multidirectional athlete can possess is a high level of reactive strength that amplifies the stretch-shortening cycle (SSC) in their ankle complex and lower leg. During a fast SSC, the muscles go through a rapid eccentric contraction followed by a concentric contraction that stores elastic energy in the associated connective tissue and tendons—loading them like a rubber band—to efficiently deliver force. With a fast SSC, ground-contact times are less than 250 milliseconds. Reactive strength is essentially defined as an athlete's ability to exploit this rapid eccentric-concentric coupling for greater force production and shorter ground-contact time. It also has mechanical and neuromuscular components that are highly trainable.

The mechanical side of this equation comes down to the quality, density, and direction of the collagen fibers in the connective tissues of the ankle complex. When your foot hits the ground, the Achilles tendon stretches like a rubber band. The stiffer that rubber band is, the more elastic energy it can store, and the faster it can release it—just like a stiff spring. Conversely, if the ankle complex is compliant at ground contact, it will leak energy and result in longer ground-contact times with slower speeds. Since force is generated through the kinetic chain from the ground up, a compliant ankle will also result in reduced power transfer at the knee and hip joints. This makes ankle stiffness one of the most important elements of multidirectional speed. Plyometric deceleration drills, such as crow hops, depth drops, and bounding drills, can all help increase ankle stiffness and elastic storage capacity in the Achilles tendon.

The neuromuscular component of reactive speed is connected to the activation and contraction of the triceps surae—the two-headed pair of muscles consisting of the gastrocnemius and the soleus that form a major part of the calf (see figure 9.1). This comes back to the importance of preliminarily tensioning the system

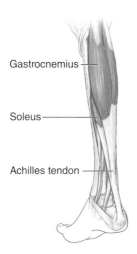

Gastrocnemius

Soleus

Achilles tendon

FIGURE 9.1 Reactive strength relies on a high level of stiffness in the myofascial tissues and tendons of the calf and ankle complex.

with pulses of co-contractions strategically timed to take the slack out of the muscles and allow the tendons to store and release more elastic energy at ground contact. A 2017 ultrasound study analyzing the effects of long-term plyometric training on reactive strength showed that the participating athletes (1) activated the muscles of their lower legs right *before* ground contact and (2) fired them in a pulsing co-contraction of both agonist and antagonist muscles that contributed to greater ankle stiffness on landing (Hirayama 2017).

Additionally, improved neuromuscular control of the timing and magnitude of these contractions was shown to produce better performance in depth jumps even when there was no improvement in maximal strength. Basically, the evidence suggests that intention matters, and the nervous and fascia systems run the show. These are neuromuscular attributes that can be improved with training. When you work on drills targeted at programming an athlete's neuromuscular system for better reaction speeds in a predictable training environment, properly timed preliminary activation and co-contraction of the muscles can happen more automatically in competition. Keep in mind that increasing tendon and ankle stiffness as well as programming the neuromuscular system for optimal timing and intensity of contractions develop better reactive strength.

MANEUVERABILITY AND CURVILINEAR RUNNING

Somewhere between COD and agility is the land of maneuverability and curvilinear, or curved, running. Underappreciated and understudied, curvilinear running, as shown in figure 9.2, requires the ability to generate ground force while loading the body in asymmetrical ways that are very different from linear running. It takes center-of-gravity management to a whole new level.

FIGURE 9.2 Curvilinear running requires athletes to generate ground force and control their center of gravity while running at discrete angles.

One of the main differences in curvilinear running is that the body leans slightly inward (as opposed to the upright max-velocity position). Since your center of gravity is more influenced by centripetal force, you need to produce more mediolateral ground-reaction force to maintain balance. The take-home point is that curved running is an acquired skill with body positions, force vectors, joint angles, and torso articulations that are different from linear speed and COD. If you doubt that maneuverability and curvilinear running are relevant to field and court sports, watch any NFL game and wait for the moment when a sprinting offensive player with the ball magically bends and leans as they run on a curved path to evade the reach of a flying defender. While many coaches tend to overlook it, training athletes to specifically handle the centripetal forces of running on a curved path is hugely beneficial. Curved running loads up the tissues in multidimensional ways that can give them a broader set of movement options. It also requires good pelvic gimbal and torso control. The science of prescribing curved sprinting for field and court athletes is still young, but it's clear that preparing athletes for the different forces and vectors it imposes does matter. This can be done by microdosing COD training programs with cone drills—for example, serpentine runs that require athletes to run longer curvilinear paths through figure-eight and S-shaped patterns or working on objective-based drills that simulate swerving to avoid an opponent.

According to GPS data from a study of elite male youth soccer players, the average angle of a curvilinear sprint when running faster than six meters per second (14 miles per hour) was around five degrees, with extremes around 30 degrees (Fitzpatrick, Linsley, and Musham 2019). This suggests that a good training strategy is to incorporate (1) curved-running drills with small angles of between 5 to 10 degrees, (2) linear-speed drills, (3) COD drills, and (4) for athletes who are more advanced, "worst-case scenario" drills that are more challenging by targeting an aggressive 30-degree curve.

An athlete's reactive strength can be assessed using the reactive strength index (RSI), which is commonly measured by having them perform a drop jump on and off of a force plate or contact mat. It can also be measured using a wearable velocity measurement device like the PUSH Band. To conduct an RSI test, the athlete drops from a height and immediately performs a maximal-effort vertical jump upon landing. Their RSI is calculated by dividing how high they jump by their ground-contact time. It is essentially a measurement of the athlete's ability to generate an impulse. An athlete's RSI can be improved by either increasing jump height or decreasing ground-contact time. In addition to being a valuable diagnostic tool for prescribing and monitoring training outcomes, it is also useful for determining the optimal height for doing depth drops from both a performance-enhancement and injury-risk perspective. If an athlete maintains or improves their RSI with an increase in drop height (and their contact times are below 250 milliseconds), the athlete's reactive strength is sufficient for that intensity of depth jump. If the RSI decreases or their ground-contact times are over 250 milliseconds, the drop height will create excessive loads on their myofascial system.

On that note, it's important that athletes develop their capacity for absorbing eccentric loads before advancing to developing their reactive speed capabilities. This is because, while eccentric strength and neuromuscular timing can be improved relatively quickly, fascia tissue and tendons remodel slowly. The objective is to maintain a good balance between contact times and flight times to ensure athletes are being challenged with an appropriate load that provides enough stimulus to drive tissue adaptation. Of course, not every facility has force plates or velocity bands, but an experienced coach can still identify critical benchmarks for assessing reactive speed. One of the things to look for is whether the athlete stays mostly on the balls of their feet at ground contact, which dictates how much force must be absorbed by the other joints up the kinetic chain. The ankle complex should resemble a stiff, dynamic spring with powerful recoil, and there should be just enough flexion at the hips and knees to produce an explosive reaction.

Foundational Strength

The training strategies for multidirectional athletes depend heavily on the specific demands of their sport, position, and competitive scenarios. An athlete who uses rotational throwing, such as a baseball shortstop, has very different movement demands than those of a soccer goalie or basketball forward. But all of them start with the need for good linear speed mechanics. I've established that sufficient foundational strength in relation to your body weight is a major component of acceleration and max velocity. However, it's even more important for multidirectional speed. The mechanics of COD can be separated into three distinct phases:

1. Planting (transition), when the muscles primarily contract isometrically
2. Braking (deceleration), when the muscles primarily contract eccentrically
3. Reacceleration (conversion), when the muscles primarily contract concentrically

During the planting phase between braking and propulsion, an athlete's velocity is essentially reduced to zero, but they still need to control tremendous amounts of gravitational force and momentum that expose the joints to sudden moments of extremely high sheer force. This means multidirectional athletes need good preparatory mechanics and considerable isometric strength to avoid injury. Most noncontact ACL injuries come from planting and cutting movements executed during a rapid COD. It's worth noting that ACL injury moments happen very quickly—between 17 and 50 milliseconds after impact—which suggests that the injury is likely rooted in what happens in the movement moment just before impact—during the preparatory step or flight phase. As I mentioned earlier, I believe that, in most cases, athletes in these situations often have either inadequate core strength or poor neuromuscular control, or a combination of both. Studies show that adverse preparatory movements can lead to what is known as dynamic valgus knee: the combination of internal hip rotation and abduction along with knee flexion at impact, where the knee lands medial to the hip and foot, causing the ground-reaction force to further tax an already tensioned ACL. Video analysis indicates that this high-risk position is often related to how an athlete tilts their pelvis or fails to control their core combined with preliminary activation of the leg muscles (Olsen et al. 2004). This is why practicing fundamental COD movements, such as side steps, crossover runs, and cutting patterns that involve an acute anticipation moment before the cut, are important for multidirectional training. These drills help athletes develop the muscle memory and neuromuscular control for proper technique and execution in the stress of competition. This is one of the reasons why, at the Parisi Speed School, we focus on emphasizing the braking phase of our COD drills by holding the crouched, loaded stance for two claps at the end of every deceleration. It exposes the activated tissues to increased eccentric and isometric loading (time under tension) and helps program the neurological system with proper form.

When it comes to COD technique, athletes should maintain a low athletic position with a slight amount of flexion in the hips, knees, and ankles. Joint angles should be bent just enough to enable optimal force transmission and fast reacceleration. Maintaining this low position during cutting, sidestepping, pivoting, and other COD maneuvers while also controlling the force of momentum requires solid isometric strength. If you lack isometric strength, you will constantly be fighting your own momentum as it pushes you one direction while you try to go in another. This is why developing whole-body, isometric shape stability using loaded movements and other techniques is important for multidirectional speed. Momentum control and the ability to simultaneously manage both your center of gravity and the transfer of ground-reaction force are key to COD performance and injury resilience.

Cueing for Speed: Change of Direction

Rapid changes of direction typically require athletes to use a compound series of actions and movements to outmaneuver opponents and create space. To execute them well, athletes need a refined movement vocabulary and well-developed muscle memory (motor engrams). Common COD movements are the side shuffle and the cut, and they are often combined. For athletes, though, it's all one connected action. Focus on one cue per rep and try to keep each cue simple and short.

As you approach your opponent, start to lower your body. Imagine you are running in an A-frame attic and stay low as you prepare to cut to one side or the other.

Imagine a string is tied to your ankles. To side shuffle, push sideways with the outside foot and pull with the inside foot, keeping your feet low to the ground without breaking the string. After side shuffling, accelerate forward (cut) explosively and break the string as you cut.

Imagine a bungee cord is attached to your knee and pulling it up and across your body. Allow your knee to come up fast and high. Then reverse the action by forcefully driving the leg back down fast and hard—try to break the bungee cord.

Multidirectional Speed Training

As previously stated, deceleration is a foundational component of both COD and agility, so part of any multidirectional training day is usually spent working on deceleration anchor and application drills listed in the previous chapter and the menus in chapter 12. As we turn our focus to target COD-specific anchor drills, we coaches begin incorporating exercises that help athletes develop their center-of-gravity management skills, timing, and balance in ways that help them tune their neuromuscular system and improve the stiffness in their lower legs and ankle complex. These include stationary speed skaters, bounds (vertical and lateral), and resistance side shuffles and side runs.

After that, we progress toward more open chain, gamelike application drills with few (if any) constraints. The first priority is to help athletes develop their preparatory movement, anticipation, and timing skills. This is where patterned cone drills, mini-hurdle drills, and ladder runs are valuable training stimuli. The creative variables for pattern drills are endless but, as previously stated, the COD patterns you run as a baseball infielder are going to be different than the patterns you run as a defensive lineman or soccer forward. This is art-of-coaching territory. Common COD cone drills include the classic 5-10-5s (pro-agility shuttles), L runs, and combination runs. The goal in patterned runs is to challenge athletes with constraint-based COD maneuvers that involve preplanned multiplanar direction changes relevant to their sport or position.

CENTER-OF-GRAVITY MANAGEMENT

The first thing to think about when it comes to enhancing your ability to change direction quickly is understanding how to control your center of gravity in relation to your momentum, your movement intention, and the ground-reaction force. No matter what direction you're going, you need to get your center of gravity in front of your base of support so you can push instead of pull. A good way to think about this is, if your car ran out of gas a block from the gas station, you would likely push that car to the station, not pull it. This is because you instinctively know you can generate more force in that position. You would lower your center of gravity to get it in front of your base of support—your legs—and push the car using your entire body (you would also likely ask passing strangers to help you—and they would get in the same position). Understanding where your center of gravity is in relation to your base of support no matter which direction you are moving is critical for optimizing your COD abilities in ways that also optimize reactive agility. This drill help athletes understand this principle.

1. With a stopwatch hanging around your neck to your navel, spread your feet wide and crouch into an athletic linebacker stance so you have a broad base of support. When you're standing upright, your center of gravity is at your navel, represented by the stopwatch hanging around your neck (see figure *a*).
2. Lean to one side so your center of gravity ends up slightly in front and to the outside of a single-leg base of support—your stance foot (see figure *b*).
3. Return to the athletic linebacker stance and repeat on the other side.

BASIC

STATIONARY SPEED SKATER

When developing COD skills, we want to build an athlete's motor vocabulary around managing their center of gravity. The stationary speed skater helps athletes learn how to shift their weight from one leg to the other with control. The goal of this exchange is to change the base of support quickly so the athlete can feel where that is in relation to their center of gravity. When done correctly, the base of support should always be directly under (or close to directly under) the center of gravity.

Primary Muscles Activated

Push-off phase (flexed leg; contralateral arm):

- *Shoulder (extension)*: latissimus dorsi, teres major, triceps brachii long head, pectoralis major lower fibers, deltoid posterior fibers, infraspinatus
- *Shoulder girdle (adduction)*: trapezius middle fibers, trapezius lower fibers, rhomboids
- *Elbow (extension)*: triceps brachii all heads, anconeus
- *Hip (extension, abduction)*: gluteus maximus, biceps femoris long head, semitendinosus, semimembranosus (extension); gluteus medius, tensor fasciae latae, gluteus maximus upper fibers, gluteus minimus (abduction)
- *Knee (extension)*: rectus femoris, vastus lateralis, vastus medialis, vastus intermedius
- *Ankle (plantarflexion)*: gastrocnemius, soleus

Push-off phase (extended leg; contralateral arm):

- *Shoulder (flexion)*: deltoid anterior fibers, pectoralis major upper fibers, coracobrachialis
- *Shoulder girdle (abduction)*: serratus anterior, pectoralis minor
- *Elbow (flexion)*: biceps brachii, brachialis, brachioradialis
- *Hip (flexion, adduction)*: rectus femoris, iliacus, psoas major, pectineus, tensor fasciae latae (flexion); pectineus, adductor brevis, adductor longus, adductor magnus, gracilis (adduction)
- *Knee (flexion)*: biceps femoris short and long head, semitendinosus, semimembranosus
- *Ankle (dorsiflexion)*: tibialis anterior, extensor hallucis longus, extensor digitorum longus

1. Start in an athletic position on one leg, bending at the ankle, knee, and hip while keeping your spine and head neutral with your shoulders back and retracted.

2. Extend the opposite leg laterally on the frontal plane so it's fairly straight with very little weight on it (see figure *a*).

3. Exchange feet and replace the base of support as quickly as possible without raising the height of your hips (see figure *b*).

4. Repeat for 12 to 16 reps.

LATERAL JUMP

Lateral movement drills are an essential part of multidirectional training because we spend so much time working on linear speed in the sagittal plane, but multidirectional athletes need to learn to master the lateral ground-reaction forces that are fundamental to COD movements. Frontal plane drills such as the double-leg lateral jump not only improve strength, stability, and coordination but also help reduce injury risk by improving overall hip, knee, and ankle stability. Lateral movement drills also help athletes develop more balanced strength in lower-body muscles, including the hip abductors and adductors, while loading the tissues in ways that can help stiffen the ankle complex and lower legs. This is a moderate drill that requires a solid base of foundational strength and coordination. Before doing lateral jumps, athletes should progress from center-of-gravity management and stationary speed skater and be able to easily handle jumping forward to backward and side to side over low barriers (like mini hurdles). It's also important to focus on having a controlled, catlike landing to get the most eccentric benefit out of the drill and help program the neuromuscular system.

Primary Muscles Activated

Jump phase:

- *Hip (extension)*: gluteus maximus, biceps femoris long head, semitendinosus, semimembranosus
- *Hip (abduction, outer leg)*: gluteus medius, tensor fasciae latae, gluteus maximus upper fibers, gluteus minimus
- *Hip (adduction, inner leg)*: pectineus, adductor brevis, adductor longus, adductor magnus, gracilis
- *Knee (extension)*: rectus femoris, vastus lateralis, vastus medialis, vastus intermedius
- *Ankle (plantarflexion)*: gastrocnemius, soleus

1. Start in the athletic quarter-squat position—bent at the hips, knees, and ankles (see figure *a*). Your shoulders should be over the knees with your weight equally distributed throughout your feet.

2. Jump laterally and explosively off both feet as far as possible while focusing on a controlled landing without twisting sideways or having any sideways motion in the knees (see figure *b*).

3. Immediately upon landing, jump back laterally as fast as possible (see figure *c*).

4. Repeat continuously for 12 to 16 total reps, or 6 to 8 reps on each leg, for 2 to 3 sets.

SPEED SKATER BOUND

The dynamic speed skater bound is a whole-body movement that emphasizes the glutes and the posterior fascia chain. Due to the extreme hip flexion and stretch put on the glute complex in this bent position, the initial concentric contraction challenges the body's fascia slings more than traditional exercises. It is an expression of power and lateral momentum control that relies on neural activity, proprioception, balance, and timing. In addition to firing the glutes, this drill also targets the legs' lateral abductors in a very explosive way. Another important aspect of this exercise is that you always want the center of gravity to be in front of the direction of the jump. For example, if you're jumping to the right, your center of gravity should be leading that jump to the right. By shifting your center of gravity to the right just before the jump, or as the jump is occurring, you will be able to generate more power. This teaches athletes that the more they can get that center of gravity in front of that leg (and the lower they can get), the more horizontal force they will be able to produce; and the tougher the exercise gets, the higher the training effect will be.

Tensor fasciae latae

Rectus femoris

a   b   c

Primary Muscles Activated

Jump phase (leg jumping off of):

- *Hip (extension, abduction)*: gluteus maximus, biceps femoris long head, semitendinosus, semimembranosus (extension); gluteus medius, tensor fasciae latae, gluteus maximus upper fibers, gluteus minimus (abduction)
- *Knee (extension)*: rectus femoris, vastus lateralis, vastus medialis, vastus intermedius
- *Ankle (plantarflexion, eversion)*: gastrocnemius, soleus (plantarflexion); peroneus longus, peroneus brevis, extensor digitorum longus (eversion)

1. Stand on one leg flexed at the hip and knee with the opposite hand down in front of the stance leg (see figure *a*).
2. Explosively jump laterally as fast as possible (see figure *b*). Focus on having a full extension of the hip and knee of the jumping leg while jumping laterally.
3. Land and balance on the opposite leg (see figure *c*).
4. Immediately upon landing, jump back laterally to the other leg as fast as possible.
5. Repeat continuously for 4 to 6 reps.

Start working on this drill using a slightly more vertical position to get the athlete acclimated to the movement. Then have the athlete progressively lower their center of gravity as they become more advanced.

RESISTED LATERAL SHUFFLE

The lateral shuffle is a critical COD skill and one of the most common movement phrases in virtually all COD settings—regardless of sport. It's also a skill where the attention to detail in training is often neglected. Some coaches might not even think of shuffling as a skill, per se. But watch any multidirectional field or court sport game and you will see that there are some athletes who can do it really smooth and fast, and others who simply don't do it as well. The key to developing the skill of lateral shuffling is to practice often with clean form. This is why we have our athletes start this exercise by just walking through the movement in a low athletic position really slowly for 10 yards (9 m) and back for 30, 60, and then 90 seconds at a time, just feeling that movement sequence while focusing on their breathing, neutral spine position, and retracted shoulder positioning. From there we progress the exercise by gradually increasing the speed and intensity—eventually throttling it up to approximately 85-percent intensity. One of the best ways to help athletes slow things down and better engage their tissues, joints, and neurology is to have them do lateral shuffling drills with some form of resistance by using weighted vests or resistance bands attached to a fixed point or being held by a partner. These vertical and horizontal loads help to vary the stimulus while addressing any weakness or deficiency in the movement. It is important to start slow. Rushing can ingrain faulty movement patterns and reinforce improper technique. By moving slow under load with pristine technique, you help develop a more efficient movement signature.

External oblique

Vastus lateralis

a   b

Primary Muscles Activated

Drive phase (pushing leg):

- *Shoulder (adduction)*: latissimus dorsi, pectoralis major lower fibers, teres major, subscapularis, coracobrachialis
- *Shoulder girdle (adduction, depression)*: trapezius middle fibers, trapezius lower fibers, rhomboids (adduction); pectoralis minor, trapezius lower fibers (depression)
- *Trunk (isometric lateral flexion)*: erector spinae, quadratus lumborum, external oblique, internal oblique
- *Hip (abduction, extension)*: gluteus medius, tensor fasciae latae, gluteus maximus upper fibers, gluteus minimus (abduction); gluteus maximus, biceps femoris long head, semitendinosus, semimembranosus (extension)
- *Knee (extension)*: rectus femoris, vastus lateralis, vastus medialis, vastus intermedius
- *Ankle (plantarflexion, eversion)*: gastrocnemius, soleus (plantarflexion); peroneus longus, peroneus brevis, extensor digitorum longus, peroneus tertius (eversion)

1. Attach an elastic resistance band to a fixed, secure point (or have a partner hold it). Attach the resistance band to a secure belt around your waist (see figure *a*).

2. Shuffle sideways against the resistance while maintaining a low body position. Keep your weight on both feet and drive off the inside (support) leg while pulling with the outside side (see figure *b*). Work against the resistance on the way out and add speed with the assistance on the way back while focusing on decelerating at the end of the return.

3. Keep both feet pointed straight ahead in line with the hips and shoulders. Maintain a level head the whole time while moving laterally. The feet should stay low to the ground. Proper shoulder positioning is one of the key details that is often neglected in the lateral shuffle. The scapulae should be pulling down and retracting while the lats contract to create a lifter's wedge. It's really important that athletes are strong up top, firing their core, and keeping their feet pointed forward. You also want to focus on pushing off the entire foot. The weight should be shifted toward the front, but the entire foot should make contact with the ground.

4. Repeat this exercise equally in both directions, gradually increasing speeds with each rep. Repeat 2 reps for 1 to 3 sets on each side.

SIDE-RUN HOCKEY STOP

During the side-run hockey stop, both shins should be parallel and pointing in the direction of intended movement. This exercise requires high levels of neural control and coordination in the tibialis posterior, fibularis longus and brevis, intrinsic foot muscles, adductors, abductors, and gluteus medius and maximus.

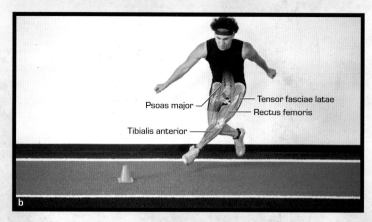

Primary Muscles Activated

Drive phase (pushing leg on ground):

- *Hip (abduction, extension)*: gluteus medius, tensor fasciae latae, gluteus maximus upper fibers, gluteus minimus (abduction); gluteus maximus, biceps femoris long head, semitendinosus, semimembranosus (extension)
- *Knee (extension)*: rectus femoris, vastus lateralis, vastus medialis, vastus intermedius
- *Ankle (plantarflexion, eversion)*: gastrocnemius, soleus (plantarflexion); fibularis longus, fibularis brevis, extensor digitorum longus (eversion)

Swing phase (initial drive leg in air):

- *Hip (adduction, flexion)*: pectineus, adductor brevis, adductor longus, adductor magnus, gracilis (adduction); rectus femoris, iliacus, psoas major, pectineus, tensor fasciae latae (flexion)
- *Knee (flexion)*: biceps femoris short and long head, semitendinosus, semimembranosus
- *Ankle (dorsiflexion, inversion)*: tibialis anterior, extensor hallucis longus, extensor digitorum longus (dorsiflexion); tibialis posterior, tibialis anterior, flexor digitorum longus, flexor hallucis longus (inversion)

1. Start in a loaded position on the balls of your feet, standing over the center of a line or cone, with another line or cone 5 yards (approximately 5 m) to the right, left, or both. Bend elbows at 90 degrees with the arms parallel and held out slightly forward. Accelerate toward the line or cone.

2. Shift your body weight in the direction of travel. When your center of mass is outside the base of support, the force you generate will move your body in that direction.

3. Take two acceleration steps laterally without turning your hips, trunk, or feet in the direction you are going (see figures *a* and *b*). The third and fourth ground contact (hockey stop) requires an opposite shift in foot placement to decelerate and stop (see figure *c*).

4. Repeat 2 reps for 2 to 4 sets on each side.

CROSSOVER RUN

The two primary types of cutting maneuvers in COD movements are sidestep cutting and cross-step cutting. Sidestep cutting involves moving your center of gravity in the opposite direction of the planted foot, while cross-step cutting is performed in the direction of the planted foot. Cross-stepping is a more unnatural movement than sidestep cutting because the opposite leg has to cross over the planted foot. While sidestep cutting is a quicker movement, cross-step cutting has been shown to decrease loads on the knee. Ultimately, you want to give athletes the widest movement vocabulary possible so they have multiple options for responding to the demands of the moment. This is why it's important to practice doing crossover runs in the same way we practice sidestepping—by moving slowly and focusing on form first and then gradually increasing speed and explosiveness. Crossover runs help improve lateral strength, foot speed, and coordination. The high-knee carioca is a derivative of the crossover run. The crossover run is an active skill used in field and court sports while the high-knee carioca is a drill to help warm up and refine lateral movement patterns. This exercise can be done using a speed ladder to help athletes focus on precise foot placement, timing, and center-of-gravity management.

Psoas major

Vastus lateralis

Tensor fasciae latae

Adductor longus

a   b

Primary Muscles Activated

Swing phase (front leg in air):

- *Hip (flexion to adduction and extension)*: rectus femoris, iliacus, psoas major, pectineus, tensor fasciae latae (flexion); pectineus, adductor brevis, adductor longus, adductor magnus, gracilis (adduction); gluteus maximus, biceps femoris long head, semitendinosus, semimembranosus (extension)
- *Knee (flexion to extension)*: biceps femoris short and long head, semitendinosus, semimembranosus (flexion); rectus femoris, vastus lateralis, vastus medialis, vastus intermedius (extension)
- *Ankle (dorsiflexion)*: tibialis anterior, extensor hallucis longus, extensor digitorum longus

Stance phase (front leg on ground):

- *Hip (flexion to abduction and extension)*: gluteus maximus, biceps femoris long head, semitendinosus, semimembranosus (flexion eccentric, extension concentric); gluteus medius, tensor fasciae latae, gluteus maximus upper fibers, gluteus minimus (abduction)
- *Knee (flexion)*: rectus femoris, vastus lateralis, vastus medialis, vastus intermedius
- *Ankle (dorsiflexion)*: gastrocnemius, soleus

Swing phase (back leg):

- *Hip (abduction, extension)*: gluteus medius, tensor fasciae latae, gluteus maximus upper fibers, gluteus minimus (abduction); gluteus maximus, biceps femoris long head, semitendinosus, semimembranosus (extension)
- *Knee (extension)*: rectus femoris, vastus lateralis, vastus medialis, vastus intermedius
- *Ankle (dorsiflexion)*: tibialis anterior, extensor hallucis longus, extensor digitorum longus

Stance phase (back leg):

- *Hip (flexion)*: gluteus maximus, biceps femoris long head, semitendinosus, semimembranosus
- *Knee (flexion)*: rectus femoris, vastus lateralis, vastus medialis, vastus intermedius
- *Ankle (dorsiflexion)*: gastrocnemius, soleus

1. Start in the athletic quarter-squat position—bent at the hips, knees, and ankles (see figure *a*). Your shoulders should be over the knees with your weight equally distributed throughout your feet. Your feet should be pointed straight ahead throughout the entire exercise.

2. Accelerate sideways 10 to 20 yards (9 to 18 m), using a dynamic cross-over step while maintaining good body position and driving off your inside (support) leg (see figure *b*). Quickly stick the next crossover step into the ground while maintaining a square forward body position with the feet and hips. Try to keep a low center of gravity with your knees and hips bent. It's also important to keep from swinging the crossing foot too far out in front of your center of gravity.

3. Repeat this exercise equally in both directions, gradually increasing speed with each rep.

ADVANCED

X RUN

X runs help develop COD skills at different angles. It's great for practicing quick transitions and faster reaction speeds.

To perform X runs, set up an area by placing four cones in the shape of a square, each 10 yards (approximately 9 m) apart (see figure) and have the athlete do the following:

1. Start at the first cone and accelerate to cone 2.

2. Shuffle laterally to cone 3.

3. Pivot 45 degrees and crossover run backward to cone 4.

4. Turn and sprint back to cone 1.

5. Once the athlete arrives back at the first cone, do it again in the opposite direction. Repeat for 2 to 4 reps.

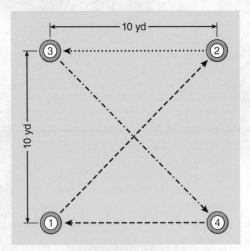

W RUN

The W run helps develop forward-to-backward acceleration and direction changes in tight spaces. This drill can also be performed side to side using the same cone layout by combining diagonal sprints and lateral shuffles.

To perform W runs, set up an area by placing seven cones each 5 yards (approximately 5 m) apart in a zigzag pattern (see figure) and have the athlete do the following:

1. Start at the first cone and accelerate to cone 2.
2. Backpedal at a 45-degree angle to cone 3.
3. Sprint to cone 4.
4. Repeat until you reach cone 7.
5. Do it again in the opposite direction (from cone 7 back to cone 1). Repeat for 2 to 4 reps.

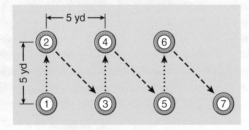

COMBINATION RUN

ADVANCED

Combination, or combo, runs combine the full menu of basic COD movements on the sagittal and frontal planes. Athletes should transfer between cones as quickly as possible while keeping their center of gravity low.

To perform combo runs, set up an area by placing two cones 5 yards (approximately 5 m) apart and have the athlete do the following:

1. Start at cone 1 and do a crossover run to cone 2, planting the outside foot on arrival.
2. Sidestep shuffle back to cone 1, planting the outside foot on arrival.
3. Rotate 45 degrees and sprint back to cone 2, decelerating to a stop on arrival.
4. Backpedal to cone 1.
5. Repeat for 8 to 12 reps.

Joe Judge, now the head coach of the New York Giants, worked for years under Bill Belichick and Nick Saban—two of the all-time greatest coaches in the NFL and college football, respectively—garnering numerous Super Bowl wins and BCS national championships. When Judge was asked what made these coaches so great, I recall he explained that their greatness comes from the fact that they focus on mastering the basic fundamentals at every level. It's not some sort of secret sauce. The reality is, they worked hard and paid attention to getting the details right. This is why the most important part of practicing COD exercises and drills is paying close attention to details of body position, form, and execution. After you build the physical capacity for speed, you need to program the nervous system to control it with ultrahigh levels of precision. And the best neurological results are achieved working with fresh, well-rested athletes. This means that COD and agility training should not be done after a big weight-training day or game day. If your athletes look tired, unsure of their movements, or clumsy—stop the training session. It's time for recovery. Optimizing multidirectional speed is about building a diverse and fluent movement vocabulary; enhancing the elastic recoil properties, stiffness, and shape stability of the connective tissues; and programming the motor engrams with the sequences for instant execution under stress. And all of that starts with dialing in the basics of high-quality movement. That's how you unlock the next level of agility and reaction so you can fly like a fighter jet.

AGILITY

While agility requires well-honed COD and maneuverability skills, they are not the same thing—though they are often confused with each other. If you want to understand the difference between COD and agility, all you have to do is play a live-action, multiplayer video game online. If you're not already familiar with the game and controller interface, you'll likely start out in a training module so you can learn how to move around while punching, shooting, and throwing things. This is the constraint-based, closed chain COD part. You need to figure out what the buttons, triggers, and toggles do and what the specific sequences are for doing different things.

You have to learn the physics of the environment and practice the movements until they become second nature. You are building your virtual motor vocabulary in a digital space with a limited number of variables. Eventually you will beat the training levels and feel pretty confident in your skills. You'll upgrade your avatar to make them look cooler. Then you'll decide you're ready to get real and play online against live opponents where you will immediately get owned and humiliated, probably by a kid who is less than half your age. You may have developed good COD skills playing against the artificial intelligence of the game in the training environment, but the kid owning you online has better reactive agility in real time. And that's the difference. They have developed a highly refined ability to quickly read whatever situation they're in and process a near-endless number of variables regarding timing, position, and intent so they can tactically respond with pinpoint accuracy in nanoseconds. As a skill, agility is cognitive, reactive, creative, and spontaneous. It combines situational awareness with anticipation, strategic decision making, foot–hand–eye coordination, whip-fast reaction speed, and precise timing—all of which make agility highly neurological in nature.

This neurological facet is also why reactive agility favors the young. And while you may be thinking video games are not sports, consider that studies have shown 20 minutes of competitive online gaming can increase a player's physical agility and balance in postgaming benchmark tests (Su et al. 2015). Results from MRI studies also suggest that playing live-action video games can enhance probabilistic learning and improve visual cognitive abilities, including visual short-term memory, rapid visual categorization, and cognitive processing speed—especially in situations characterized by high levels of uncertainty (Schenk, Lech, and Suchan 2017). It's true that video games are not athletic sports, but gamifying your athletic drills to generate an unpredictable environment where athletes must quickly identify and respond to unexpected stimuli is a great way to help athletes improve their reactive agility.

Some coaches will say that the ability to read and react in competitive situations is not a skill that can be taught; athletes either have it or they don't. I respectfully disagree. You may not be able to give every athlete the same superhuman ability to read and react as Steph Curry, Roger Federer, or Nate Diaz have, but you can certainly improve their mechanics, give them a diverse vocabulary of COD movements, help them develop healthy fascia tissue with optimized proprioception and elastic storage, and train them to keep their head up and eyes open. You can also improve their visual scanning and reaction speeds by challenging athletes with competitive, gamelike drills and objectives that force them to analyze their environment, anticipate timing, and respond tactically.

Agility combines every aspect of speed development I've covered in this book—including optimal strength-to-weight ratios, super stiffness in the core and distal joints, acceleration, deceleration, and COD—and adds an ethereal sixth element: cognitive reaction speed. It is easily the most complex subject I've tried to tackle here. All of that said, I like to keep things simple. My perspective is that if I teach you some drills, you will understand how to do them. But if I teach you the principles behind those drills, you can use that knowledge to build your own sport-relevant approach to prescribing them. It's the coaching equivalent of giving you a fish versus teaching you to fish. One results in a meal. The other results in a lifetime of meals.

Agility and the Fascia System

By now you've likely figured out that I'm a huge advocate for understanding how important and underappreciated the fascia system is in athletic movement, but its role in optimizing agility cannot be overstated. In addition to contributing significantly to explosive COD moments, joint stability, and core strength, research is showing us that it is also rich with nerve receptors that detect pressure, pain, temperature, and movement throughout the entire human body. As previously mentioned in chapter 4, there are between 8 to 10 times more nerve endings in fascia tissues and tendons than in red muscle fibers, with higher densities of nerve endings in the fascia tissues and joints of our extremities (hands and feet). The number of sensors and nerve endings in the fascia tissue surrounding your muscles far exceeds the number inside the muscles.

Additionally, it has been shown that our sense of spatial awareness comes from nerve endings, receptors, and sensors in the fascia tissues that surround our internal organs. These nerve endings, receptors, and sensors continuously communicate information about the position and location of the internal organs to the brain—including their motion, temperature, and biochemical composition. Based on these findings, the fascia system is now considered a major sensory organ with a direct link to the functions of the nervous system. It can therefore be assumed that human movement is, in part, a reaction to our internal sense of motion—which is initiated through the nervous and fascial systems—rather than solely triggered by muscular activity.

For example, as we discussed in chapter 8, research indicates that proprioceptors in the knee can send signals directly to the hip using the body's integrated fascial network, and the hip can communicate directly back to the knee before the signal reaches the spine (Schleip 2017). A good metaphor for this can be found in the way researchers believe large groups of flocking birds, such as starlings, can move in unison as a single organism to confuse predators. These birds often fly in large groups at speeds in excess of 40 miles (64 km) per hour with only a body-length of space between them, but the entire group can make astoundingly sharp turns and dives in unison as a single entity (Potts 1984). Imagine being a fighter pilot performing unrehearsed evasive maneuvers in formation with a group of 100 other jet pilots, all separated by the length of a wingspan while simultaneously calculating for constant variations in speed, gravity, and turbulence. This is essentially what your fascia and nervous systems are doing when you are cutting and darting in response to a competitor's movements. If the flock waited for one bird to initiate action, it would take too long for that signal to spread throughout the entire group so that every bird could move in unison.

What researchers have found is that birds flying in dense flocks don't follow a leader or even their immediate neighbors. They read and anticipate sudden changes in the greater flock's direction of motion. Once a change in direction begins somewhere in the flock—say in response to an attacking falcon—that change-of-direction impulse spreads throughout the entire flock in what's called a maneuver wave, happening at speeds that are three times faster than would be possible if the birds were just reacting to a leader or their immediate wingmates. This internal cuing dynamic is called the "chorus line effect," and it implies that flocking birds are like a chorus line of dancers who sense the wave of an approaching kick coming down the line and anticipate what to do based on the unique timing and speed of the moment. This has huge implications for agility when we pair this information with the fact that all human movement comes from a kinetic chain reaction triggered by the functional drivers of mass, momentum, gravity, and ground-reaction force. If there is an imbalance or weakness in the kinetic chain (chorus line) due to an injury, joint immobility, or tissue restriction, it will affect the other links up the kinetic chain and force them to compensate. In other words, having a healthy, well-balanced fascia system is essential for achieving optimal reactive agility.

As a result, it's recommended that you start agility-focused training days (and game days) with a short fascia-tissue preparation session that includes warming the tissues and improving their fluid dynamics by rolling out the structures that get the most activity in your respective sport or position, and doing some self-myofascial release to find trigger points and improve fluid flow (all of which are covered in chapter 3). Additionally—just like COD, acceleration, and max-velocity training— to get the best results, agility work should be done only when athletes are well rested and fresh. It's a neurologically focused, reactive speed session, not a conditioning session.

Agility and Flow State

Agility—the ability to spontaneously read, react, and execute—is tightly connected to our sense of timing and spatial awareness. Athletes who express this trait at a high level commonly refer to the experience as being "in the zone." They are intrinsically connected to the world around them and their position within it on deep levels. Some people refer to this connection as the sixth sense. Famed Hungarian-American psychologist Mihaly Csikszentmihalyi describes this experience as being in a state of "flow."

"When a person is in flow state, time disappears," says Csikszentmihalyi (pronounced "cheeks send me high"). "Every action, movement, and thought inevitably follows from the previous one, like playing jazz. Your whole being is involved, and you're using your skills to the utmost."

Analyzing case studies involving a wide range of athletes, musicians, and artists, Csikszentmihalyi established nine dimensions of flow state: challenge-skill balance, action-awareness merging, clear goals, unambiguous feedback, concentration on task, sense of control, loss of self-consciousness, time transformation, and autotelic experience (Nakamura and Csikszentmihalyi 2002).

Of the nine dimensions of flow state, challenge-skill balance is tremendously relevant from an agility-training standpoint. Challenge-skill balance is believing you have the skills to meet what you perceive as challenges. Therefore, if you perceive a challenge to be greater than your skill level, you will likely become stressed and anxious and perform poorly. This is one of the reasons why closed chain skill development involving multiple scenarios is an important part of agility training. The athlete needs to feel confident that their skills are well matched to the challenges they will face in competition so that they have the freedom of mind to improvise. The action-awareness merging dimension is similar in that it involves feeling at one with the activity being performed. It is an expression of automaticity: Having deeply ingrained neurological sequences (motor engrams) allows you to subconsciously execute maneuvers while paying full attention to what's happening around you and anticipating opponents' and teammates' actions (reading). The dimensions of concentration on task (where there are no other outside thoughts) and time transformation (where the experience of time disappears or slows) are two of the clearest indications of being in flow state. At the risk of sounding too esoteric for a speed coach, the basic gist is that flow state comes from being completely present in the moment and having the skills to meet the challenge.

When asked what made Michael Jordan—one of the most agility-gifted athletes in the history of sports—so great, Mark Vancil, author of the book *Rare Air: Michael on Michael* (1993), replied in the ESPN documentary *The Last Dance*: "His gift was not that he could jump high, run fast, or shoot a basketball. His gift was that he was completely present in the moment. That was the separator." Jordan was a master of flow, in part because he practiced incessantly and mastered the basics of the game until they became second nature, until he was unfalteringly confident he had the skills to match any challenge or defender, until he could melt into the moment and become one with the ball. *That*'s how you enter the world of flow.

Agility and the OODA Loop

When it comes to reactive agility, speed alone does not ensure victory. What matters most is timing and strategic decision making, which require the ability to rapidly read multiple variables and tactically respond at the most advantageous moment. This cycle is best characterized by what is known as the OODA (observe-orient-decide-act) loop (see figure 10.1). Defined simply, the OODA loop is a four-step, strategic decision-making cycle that continuously repeats and adapts,

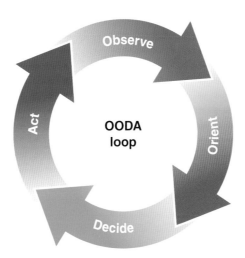

FIGURE 10.1 The OODA (observe-orient-decide-act) loop is a tactical decision-making model for rapid observation and response.

drawing from the evolving flow of events and information. The OODA loop was initially developed by Colonel John Boyd, a U.S. Air Force pilot who fought in the Korean War, where he earned the nickname "40-Second Boyd" for his ability to win dogfights against opponents (who were often flying arguably superior MiG-15 fighter jets) in under 40 seconds. The OODA loop cycle begins with (1) making an observation, which leads to (2) orienting yourself to possible options, (3) deciding on an action, and then (4) executing the action, at which point, you observe the action's results and begin the cycle again. Rapidly executing the OODA loop enhances agility to help you defeat an opponent with superior power or speed.

In the observe stage, you are gathering visual and other sensory information. This information includes your opponents' movements and body positions. It also involves sensory information coming from physical contact with your opponent or your own teammate; the anticipation of contact behind you; or your perception of changes in light and shadow, sound, and air movement—all of which are types of proprioceptive awareness. A key distinction Colonel Boyd made is that this observational information is always incomplete and must continually be reassessed.

During the orientation phase, you position yourself within the context of the unfolding situation. In competitive athletic settings, this means positioning your body advantageously and preloading your tissues for reactive action based on your opponent's position and your anticipation of where they are going. All of this depends on the quality and content of the information you gathered during the observe phase. Since this information is incomplete by nature, you may need to quickly reorient as you continue to observe unfolding events.

In the decision stage, you must select the best decision option for the moment and then commit to that action. The more potential options you have, the longer this step takes, but rushing to the conclusion is a recipe for failure. Likewise, if the information gathered during the observe cycle is imperfect or your physical orientation to the movement decision is flawed, rapid decision speed will only accelerate your mistake. Also, it's important to remember that these are not isolated sequential steps. Observation is an evolving awareness of continually changing circumstances and incomplete information, and your orientation to that information will inevitably evolve as you receive new data. Likewise, the decide and act steps are connected to this ongoing feedback loop, with some actions occurring simultaneously or in a required sequence.

During the act stage, you release the action potential of your central and peripheral nervous systems. Actions should be done with total commitment and, hopefully, optimal form. Think of a boxer making the decision to deliver a jab. You don't throw a half-punch. You strike with all the force you can deliver. This means the outcome of the action depends greatly on the quality of your movement and execution, which is why perfecting form and mechanics in a predictable training environment is crucial to success in unpredictable situations where you are operating on instinct and muscle memory. Consequently, it's essential that athletes practice tactical agility training at max volume in order to refine and improve their reactive capabilities and develop a robust and flexible movement vocabulary so they can instinctively apply the optimal maneuver for any situation.

Fundamentally speaking, the OODA loop is something we all unconsciously do all the time. That said, Colonel Boyd's explanations of it were extremely nuanced, detailed, and complex. Since military strategy is highly classified, many of Boyd's concepts were only presented orally during hours-long briefings, and many were intentionally left unpublished. The upside is that this left these concepts open to wider interpretation in athletic training, martial arts, and business. One of the more subtle yet powerful strands of his framework is the idea of using variable cadence and tempo to disrupt the rhythm of your opponent's OODA loop. In music, tempo is the rate and speed of a song's rhythm, counted in beats. In field and court sports, these beats could be footsteps, ball passes, and other actions. In fighting arts, they could be strikes and blocks (e.g., a one–two punch). If you've studied music, you are aware of the half-beat. Your music teacher likely counted it out as "one-*and*-two-*and*-three-*and*-four," where the "and" represents the half-beat. In a one–two boxing combo, for example, the half-beat is the moment after the first jab (one) lands, but before the cross-jab (two) is thrown. This half-beat is a micro-moment when you are vulnerable to having an opponent disrupt the tempo of your decision–action cycle. And this is why timing and rhythm are so important in competitive agility. Your speed of observation, decision making, and execution all matter—but they are all trumped by strategic timing. Using an opponent's OODA loop against them means countertiming your decisions and actions in ways that break their rhythm and allow you to exploit the disruption. Think of a basketball guard driving crosscourt who must evade a taller or faster defender. Instead of driving straight toward the basket, which is unlikely to succeed, they'll make an off-timed series of cuts, fakes, or both. Simultaneously, the basketball guard will change the cadence of their timing by slowing down and then speeding up, or vice versa, in order to disrupt their opponent's OODA loop, prompting the opponent to make a mistake that gives the guard an opportunity to take control of the situation. In this framework, the goal is not to cycle through the OODA loop as fast as possible; instead, it is a way to exploit the rhythm of your opponent's half-beats so you can take control.

Cueing for Speed: Agility

Reactive agility is challenging to cue because competitive situations are fluid and agility movements are rapid and subtle. They are unplanned by nature. That said, one of the main rules for defenders is to keep your opponent in front of you by keeping your hips square to theirs and watching their hips or the number on their jersey to anticipate their direction of travel.

"Keep them in your headlights!"

Imagine you have headlights on each hip. Keep your headlights aimed at your opponent's hips as they change direction in front of you.

Agility Training

As we shift gears from COD training into agility training, the intention is to create a more unpredictable environment, using external stimuli that athletes must quickly respond to using anchor drills. One way to do that is to blend classic COD drills with variability and the unknown. This can be done using a coach's voice command, whistle, hand raise, or other audio and visual cues. The specific drills and cues you choose should be based on the targeted sport and position. You can also load agility drills to increase tissue adaptations and help athletes develop better muscle memory by slowing things down a notch and increasing workload.

When it comes to agility application drills, there are multiple ways to create an objective-based, reactive training environment; for example, using numbered cones with either verbal commands or interactive touch-sensor lights like the BlazePod (see figure 10.2)—which triggers the body's natural response to flashy lights and provides the added tactile element of touch. Coaches can set up programmed pattern drills using light-up cones that turn off when you tap them. While there are a number of other reactive training tools that have similar functions, the BlazePod platform also connects to a smartphone app for setting up different sport-based sequences with multiple cones and giving you instant performance-tracking data, which provide measurable feedback that helps motivate athletes. I mention it because it's one of the few tools available that is specifically designed to train and measure open chain, cognitive reaction speed. A similar DIY setup can be created using numbered cones with voice commands and a stopwatch. The key to getting athletes to perform at a high level of intensity is to use a stopwatch and make it competitive. Our experience is that athletes won't truly push themselves without having the performance feedback of a stopwatch or tracking app. This type of game-based training also helps develop other dimensions of flow including clear goals, unambiguous feedback, and concentration on task.

FIGURE 10.2 BlazePods provide a responsive training objective that requires athletes to react to the unknown.

COMMAND COMBO DRILLS

When transitioning from COD training to agility training, we work on many of the basic movement vocabulary drills—including side shuffles, crossover runs, forward and backward acceleration sprints, and forward and backward deceleration sprints—but we add the stimulus of a coach's signal to make the drills reactive. Just like when we're doing COD drills, athletes should master the mechanics of each drill by starting off very slowly at a walking speed before ramping up to full speed. After focusing on each movement individually, we transition to combining the movements on command, with the coach either barking out the movement or pointing in the direction they want the athletes to go.

For example, you can do a side shuffle into a side run, into a backpedal, into a forward acceleration, into another side run, into a W pattern—emphasizing the deceleration component with each direction change. The coach gives a hand signal, left or right, and yells out what they want the athlete to do—pointing in a direction and yelling: "Side shuffle . . . decel!" Then pointing back and yelling "Backpedal . . . decel!" "Accelerate . . . decel!" And so on. This approach blends both closed and open chain movements in constraint-based and semiplanned ways while also being reactive and unknown. It also helps athletes focus on keeping their heads up and paying attention to their movement and environment and not just what's immediately in front of them. This approach allows you to methodically combine and reinforce the core movements that are essential to building a strong COD vocabulary. In addition, you're adding an element of the unknown that requires athletes to transition between these different movements while also keeping their eyes up so they can pay attention to the situation and react to external cues.

Alternating between COD training and agility training in this way creates a blended continuum for the athlete to progress from conscious competence to unconscious competence. When an athlete is focused on external stimuli and forced to quickly choose the best movements to apply in response to those stimuli, it gives the coach an opportunity to identify their limitations in terms of tissue thresholds at specific angles, on specific planes, and during specific movement transitions. Do they pause too long between deceleration and acceleration transitions? Do they have dysfunctions in the drive phase? Are they weak in the core? Are their hips disassociated from their trunk? Using this information, you can create resistance-training prescriptions that target the desired coordination or tissue thresholds that need attention before getting back into application drills. For example, as a backpedaling athlete transitions to a linear sprint in the same direction on the same line, they need to maintain sagittal plane stability while transitioning 180 degrees in the transverse plane and accelerating through the frontal plane in the steps between the backpedal and linear-sprint phases.

Coaches can use these transition moments to identify potential dysfunctions. For example, an athlete begins the rotational transition by pushing through their stance leg with proper knee extension, hip extension, and external hip rotation. You notice, however, that they lose postural integrity in their trunk and spine. It could be due to an inability of the adductor complex to respond appropriately with the pelvic floor to the demands of the movement. In this case, you would target those tissues by prescribing more resisted exercises that focus on the transverse plane transition. That is where the athlete can practice the specific drive and rotational sequences of that movement under load in order to develop the related tissues and motor engram coordination. Alternating between resisted COD transitions and unloaded COD movement applications in both preplanned and open chain reactive situations allows athletes to progressively advance from the conscious competence of mastering a skill to the refined unconscious competence required for better, real-time agility. Loading COD drills with variable-resistance tools (like medicine balls, weighted vests, aqua bags [see figure 10.3], or elastic bands) also helps them build up the shape stability of their internal connective tissues and increase their movement-specific tissue thresholds.

FIGURE 10.3   Aqua bags add variable resistance that helps develop more robust whole-body shape stability.

DROP STEP DRILLS

The drop step is a fundamental COD maneuver in many field and court sports and essential to a well-rounded movement vocabulary. In American football, the drop step is commonly used by defensive backs when playing man-to-man. The defensive back typically starts in a stationary position at the beginning of the play, facing their opponent and waiting for them to make a move. The defensive back may begin with a slight backpedal while the offensive player is running toward them. When the offensive player commits to one side or the other, the defensive player must drop step in that direction by opening and swiveling their hips so they can turn their body and transition into a crossover run. If the offensive player cuts to the opposite side to try and outmaneuver them, the defensive back must swivel their hips 180 degrees to the opposite side so they can track their opponent without slowing down. The longer the defensive player can stay in transition, the better chance they have of being able to lock down the receiver.

Consequently, the ability to drop step quickly and maintain a transitionary orientation for as long as possible before committing to a linear direction is so important that college football coaches award athletic scholarships based on an athlete's ability to do it well. Keeping a low center of gravity in this situation is crucial to being able to generate enough force to rotate your body quickly. For the defensive player to react swiftly they must be bent at the ankles, knees, and hips. And this is where constraint-based COD training comes in. The question is: How much tissue threshold have you built into the ankle to be able to run laterally?

Additionally, the quadratus lumborum and the internal and external obliques play a huge role in facilitating a dynamic and powerful drop-step rotation through isometric contraction. If you disassociate your hips from your upper body, it will create energy leaks that translate to slower speeds and increased injury risk. The hips, rib cage, and shoulders are all linked together. And the degree of turn is really important. Ideally, you want to initiate by planting the lead foot at around three o'clock without overturning the hips or overcommitting. If you overturn where you plant the foot, the hips are going to follow. And when the offensive opponent makes an inside break, you're finished. If the offensive player is running a deep route, at some point, you have to commit and run with them. But you need to manage your orientation and center of gravity until you really know where they are going. This is all part of the observe–orient stages of an OODA loop.

Likewise, in basketball, the drop step is typically used as an offensive post move where the offensive player uses the defender's body against them. In a basketball setting, an offensive player initiates a drop step while keeping their back to the basket and their defensive opponent. Holding the ball up strong under their chin, the offensive player opens their hips and drop steps around the defender—rotating almost 180 degrees around the defender on the most strategically advantageous side—as they pound the ball off the floor, square up to the backboard, and go up strong with both hands or step back and shoot a fadeaway. If you watch an experienced player do this maneuver, you will notice they lean their upper back slightly into their opponent's body while they're holding the ball. This is part of the offensive player's observe–orient phase, when they increase the amount of information they're getting from their opponent through physical contact. Doing this allows them to feel where their opponent is in space, what direction they're pushing back in, and with how much force (intent) they are applying. This tactile information helps them orient and make a decision about the most advantageous action: In other words, should they fake a drop step in one direction first to draw their opponent off-center or make a hard and fast drop step that exploits their opponent's weak side? Again, constraint-based COD training helps athletes tune their neuromuscular systems to make these movements second nature so that when they make the decision to act, it will happen faster with a higher likelihood of success. Once it's a solid part of their movement vocabulary, you can turn it into an agility drill by having athletes drop step on a visual or audio command in both directions to make it unpredictable and reactive.

When doing drop steps, athletes should focus on stabilizing their core—so their ribs are locked to their pelvis and shoulders—and everything should rotate together. In addition to making it reactive, this drill can be practiced loaded to help fortify the tissues along different vectors.

Primary Muscles Activated

Backward rotation (stance and swing legs):

- *Hip (external rotation, abduction)*: gluteus maximus, gluteus medius posterior fibers, piriformis, gemellus superior and inferior, obturator externus and internus, quadratus femoris (external rotation); gluteus medius, tensor fasciae latae, gluteus maximus upper fibers, gluteus minimus (abduction)

Forward rotation (stance and swing legs):

- *Hip (internal rotation, adduction)*: gracilis, semitendinosus, semimembranosus, gluteus medius anterior fibers (internal rotation); pectineus, adductor brevis, adductor longus, adductor magnus, gracilis (adduction)

1. Start in an athletic position with the feet aligned and slightly bent at the hips, knees, and ankles, while bracing the core (see figure *a*).

2. Rotate to one side quickly by pivoting off the front foot and abducting the opposite leg backward. Be sure to rotate the hips, rib cage, and shoulders all as one unit (see figures *b* and *c*).

3. Return each rep to the starting position with the feet aligned before performing the next rep. Increase the speed of movement as the athlete masters the technique. An important part of this movement is controlling the deceleration phase of the drop step and then reaccelerating back to the starting position.

4. Do 10 drop steps on each side for a total of 20 steps with 2 to 3 sets.

GAMIFICATION DRILLS

Games like cat and mouse or tag are another great way to train agility because they are objective driven and prompt athletes to apply creative responses to unpredictable situations. Tag games can be set up in a variety of ways based on sport or discipline. One simple game that can be done in most any facility is the end-zone drill, where you set up a pair of cones that represent the goal line of a football field. One athlete is positioned at the edge of the end zone next to one of the cones. The other athlete starts out on the five-yard line and, on the coach's cue, must reach the end zone for a touchdown without getting tagged by the other athlete. Then you move the starting point to the 10-yard line, then the 20, and so on. At Parisi Speed School, we have the athletes switch roles at every distance interval so they each get a turn on offense and defense.

CURVILINEAR AGILITY DRILLS

There are multiple ways to execute COD movements in real-time game situations. You might transition suddenly from linear sprinting into a shuffle, a back-pedal, or a side step. But, often, instead of sidestepping or crossover running, athletes will end up running curvilinearly to evade their opponent. This is one of the multidirectional vocabulary movements many coaches often overlook. As previously mentioned in chapter 9, curvilinear running involves different body positions, force vectors, joint angles, and torso articulations. In agility settings, these maneuvers often happen as an instinctively spontaneous reaction to an opponent's movements when the athlete tries to reach their forward objective. It is therefore important to train athletes for better reactive agility in odd, curvilinear-running positions by exposing their tissues, joints, and nervous system to different centripetal forces in dynamic, gamelike settings.

One of the ways we do this is to play games of tag in a curvilinear space using two big tires or a series of cones set up in a figure-eight pattern that naturally induce curved-running patterns in response to an opponent's movements. In this situation, we'll often start with one person lined up a few yards in front of the person who is "it" and have them start on a coach's cue.

OPEN CHAIN GAME DRILLS

Of course, one of the challenges of training in an open chain game environment is that athletes—especially kids—will often throw their mechanics out the window and get sloppy, which is not behavior you want to reinforce. This is why it's important to progress to unpredictable open chain game drills only after you've spent a considerable amount of time reinforcing good movement behaviors using closed chain drills—and then alternate back and forth between the two. That said, one of the advantages of game drills is that coaches can use these learning moments to identify where athletes have weaknesses or ineffective movement biases that should be addressed using targeted, constraint-based training.

Since agility is cognitive and neurological in nature, practically any reactive game or activity can help athletes develop better situational awareness, timing, anticipation, strategic planning, and neurological firing speed. This includes playing things like dodgeball, handball, hot potato, and, yes, even video games—especially video games that reinforce game theory and decision-making strategies like *Madden* or *NBA 2K*. Strategy matters and when it's game time, knowing *when* to drop step is just as important as knowing *how*. That's how you win a dogfight with a fighter jet.

11

SYSTEM-SPECIFIC RECOVERY

What do Tom Brady, LeBron James, Serena Williams, and Roger Federer all have in common? Math says they should all be retired by now. Yet they are all still playing at the very top level of their respective sports. How? They are all extremely intentional about their recovery programs. This is one of the most underestimated paradoxes of speed training. In the never-ending pursuit of faster, higher, and stronger, many athletes and coaches forget about the crucial importance of rest, recover, and rebuild. The reality is that if you want to unlock your body's full performance capabilities while reducing your injury risk—especially as you age—it's essential you give rest and recovery the same level of attention you give sets, drills, and competition.

To put this in perspective, LeBron James famously spends more than US$1.5 million a year on his training, diet, and recovery program, including a personal chef, a team of bodywork specialists, and most of the modern recovery technology known to humans. And while you may not be able to drop seven figures on your recovery routine, understanding the scientifically validated principles behind the most effective techniques can provide just as valuable a return on investment as James's. The challenge is that covering these topics in depth could easily turn into an entire book all its own, but a book focused on the anatomy of speed would be incomplete without at least touching on them. So, with that said, we'll cover the basic principles in this chapter to help you understand the importance of incorporating intentional recovery strategies into your training program and what the key ingredients are for getting the most benefit out of them. Just keep in mind there's a lot to know, and new research is coming out every year that continually improves our understanding.

In-Bout Recovery

The first thing to note is that when we talk about performance recovery (as opposed to injury recovery), most people tend to think about what can be done to accelerate healing, reduce pain, and rebuild tissues between bouts of training and competition. While adequate recovery between bouts is important to improving speed and injury resilience, what often gets overlooked is the importance of including recovery protocols *within* workout bouts—between reps and sets.

"Traditionally, with speed or power training, athletes will repeat a series of high-intensity sprints or lifts or whatever without thinking much about the need for recovery between those reps," says Michol Dalcourt, founder of the Institute of Motion. "But the question we need to ask is: Why are we doing these reps? If we're doing these reps for generalized conditioning, well, that's fine. But if we're working on developing speed and power, then the intention needs to be high, which means we're revving the engine high. And when we rev the engine like that over a series of efforts, we are depleting the body's systems. So those high-intensity efforts need to be balanced with recovery measures that help you reconstitute those systems during the training bout so you can continue to perform at a high level."

When it comes to in-bout recovery, there are three key strategies that need to be addressed: metabolic recovery, neural recovery, and fluid recovery. Understanding how the body's systems are depleted during high-intensity efforts and what can be done to restore them during a training session is essential for improving long-term performance and reducing injury risk.

Metabolic Recovery

As mentioned in chapter 2, the body generates the metabolic fuel required for muscle contractions (ATP) using three different energy systems: the ATP-PC system, the lactic acid system, and the aerobic system. The ATP-PC system provides the most immediate energy source because it is fueled by phosphocreatine (PC), which is a high-energy chemical compound stored directly within the muscle cells, making it immediately available for short, high-intensity efforts. The catch is that this anaerobic fuel injection system gives your muscles only about 10 to 15 seconds of high-octane energy before the lactic acid system kicks in to continue providing you with the energy needed for up to two more minutes of high-intensity output before you become anaerobically fatigued and start breathing hard because you need oxygen. At this point, your body switches from the anaerobic energy system to the aerobic energy system, and your training starts to become a conditioning session. This makes the ATP-PC system a critical component of acceleration and speed (as opposed to endurance). One of the great features of the ATP-PC system is that PC can be quickly resynthesized by the cells, and there are no fatigue-causing by-products created in the chemical reaction. This means that incorporating a relatively short period of recovery into your training bouts between efforts allows you to refresh this system and prepare your body for another short burst of intense output.

Typically, your maximum capacity for an all-out effort at or above 90 percent is about 20 to 30 seconds. After that, the ATP-PC system is depleted, and you will start dipping into your lactic acid system to keep the engine revving (refer back to figure 2.5 in chapter 2). How much of each of these two anaerobic energy systems you use depends on the intensity and duration of the effort involved, but they will both need to be replenished before you can do another all-out effort.

For high-intensity efforts above 90 percent, a good work-to-rest ratio for metabolic recovery is between 1:10 and 1:20 (e.g., 10 seconds of maximum effort should be followed by at least one to three minutes of low-activity rest). At a minimum—for more moderate work levels—you should apply a ratio of 1:4. To put this in perspective, elite sprinters will commonly walk around the track for as much as five minutes or more before attempting another max-effort sprint. While this might seem like an eternity in coaching or competition minutes, metabolic recovery is not a chemical process that can be rushed. You can't eat, drink, or foam roll your way back to a topped-off ATP-PC fuel tank. While a periodized training program can eventually improve your capacity for workload and shorten your recovery times, there are biological speed limits for the chemical reactions of metabolic recovery. That said, metabolic (and neural) recovery cycles should include some very low-intensity movement, such as walking. In addition to alleviating fatigue and allowing your anaerobic energy systems to replenish, low-intensity movements help your body stay warm and flush out some of the metabolites that accumulate during high-intensity efforts.

Neural Recovery

Neural recovery also involves replenishing your body's chemistry reserves, but, in this case, instead of topping off your energy pools, it's about topping off your neurotransmitter pools. Movements that involve high levels of complexity and intensity require an unfathomable number of chemical reactions happening in a precise sequence at precise volumes and ultraprecise rhythms. As previously mentioned, one of the many paradoxes of speed is that it's less about quickly turning muscles on than it is about being able to quickly turn them off. The ability to fire superfast pulses of distal and proximal stiffness is what makes elite sprinters (as well as jazz drummers, world-class fighters, and professional golfers) elite. True speed comes from the ability to rhythmically turn the system off quickly—that's how you achieve a fast punch, kick, or throw. From a biomechanical standpoint, a signaling network in the nervous system initiates muscle contractions and creates action potentials using a cascade of chemical reactions (sodium potassium and acetylcholine) in the synaptic cleft—the junction between the nerve and the muscle. When acetylcholine fills this gap, it fires an action potential that causes the muscle fibers to contract.

In simple terms, the more of these gaps that flood with acetylcholine, the more forceful the muscles will contract relative to their capabilities. After the muscle fibers contract, an enzyme called acetylcholinesterase breaks down the acetylcholine and turns the muscle off by eating up the acetylcholine—like Pac-Man.

Of course, when I oversimplify a complex neurological process like this, it sounds like it takes a lot of time. The reality is that these chemical reactions happen in a rapid-fire series of transmissions across your body in the space of milliseconds. And when you're moving with high levels of intention and force, these chemicals get depleted. Even though you may not be doing something for a long period of time, when you do it with full intensity, your neurological chemistry for nerve conduction is being spent because you're opening those valves all the way up. And when you do that multiple times within an exercise bout, your nervous system gets tired. This means your reserves of acetylcholine and acetylcholinesterase need to be replenished if you want your nervous system to be operating at full capacity for the next effort.

According to Dalcourt, a good work-to-rest ratio for neurological recovery is approximately 1:6. For example, if you have an athlete do a series of three hang-clean reps with full intention over the course of 30 seconds, the athlete should take around three to five minutes to neurologically recover by walking around the gym, breathing deeply, and chalking their hands before trying again. Also, you don't want them to do things that tax their nervous system. The goal is to let those neurologic chemicals replenish without letting the tissues get cold.

Fluid Recovery

While the need to integrate metabolic and neural recovery cycles within training sessions is fairly well known, one strategy that is often overlooked is in-bout fluid recovery. In this case, fluid recovery isn't about staying hydrated (which is obviously important); it's about facilitating fluid recovery in the localized tissues. When you do something intensely—whether it's sprinting for 40 yards (37 m) or throwing a fastball over and over—limb velocity is high, muscle contraction rates are high, and your mental intention is high. This violent contraction of muscles causes a change in the osmotic pressure gradients of your fascia, muscles, and other tissues. Basically, when you flex your muscles really fast over and over, you push water and other fluids—including blood, lymph, and interstitial fluid—away from those structures. Over the course of an extended training bout (above 30 minutes), those tissues will start reaching a dehydrated state. This is especially significant for the connective fascia tissue. As discussed in chapter 3, fascia tissue is more dynamic and resistant to compression when the extracellular matrix has more bound water in it (when H_2O molecules bind to sugar receptors in the tissue). But, if the fascia tissue is squeezed intensely over and over again, those H_2O molecules get pushed away. This reduces the fascia tissue's capacity to resist deformation and tears, which both reduces performance and increases injury risk. High-velocity contractions also make it harder for blood to get in, thereby limiting the amount of oxygen being delivered to the muscles and inhibiting the muscles' ability to contract. All of this means that including fluid recovery techniques in training bouts that last longer than 30 minutes is essential for maximizing returns.

According to Dalcourt, a good work-to-rest ratio for in-bout fluid recovery during longer workouts is approximately 3:1 (i.e., for every 30 minutes of work, you would need 10 minutes of fluid recovery). "With metabolic and neural recovery, you want to avoid revving the engine beyond a low idle because you don't want to use up the energy stores or neural chemistry," says Dalcourt. "But, with fluid recovery, you want to do some foam rolling, you want to use compression garments, and you want to do some rub-and-scrub or massage techniques that push fluid back into where it was pushed out. Those fluids were pushed out by pressure gradients and osmotic flow. So the idea is to push them back into that area by reversing the pressure gradients. That can be achieved through things like self-myofascial release, foam rolling, compression garments, and vibration guns."

Load Management

It's arguable that the NBA and NHL have the most rigorous and competitive schedules of any professional sports league. Their intensive eight-month, 82-game regular seasons require grueling travel, frequent time zone changes, and constant sleep disruption, all of which are punctuated by intensely physical competition in front of thousands of hyped-up fans. Therefore, closely monitoring the intensity of player workloads so coaches and teams can strategically engineer their rest and recovery routines is essential to reducing injury and ensuring that athletes can play at a high level night after night. The mildly controversial (and somewhat misleading) NBA term for this process is called *load management*—the practice of using biometric and other data to monitor player workloads and rest ratios in order to determine when athletes are bumping up against their individual load capacity. It includes monitoring actual game minutes played in addition to how much players exert themselves during practice, skill training, and active dynamic warm-ups as well as their postgame recovery routines, sleep metrics, and injury issues. And the person in charge of quickly organizing all of these data on a daily basis so teams can make actionable decisions based on this information is Paul Robbins, EVP of Sports Performance for Kinexon and Owner of Cardio2Tech LLC. Paul is an internationally recognized expert on metabolic testing, workload tracking, and training optimization. In addition to overseeing load management in the NBA and USTA, he also helps oversee the wearable tech division for Kinexon and serves as a sports performance and recovery coach at Scottsdale Sports Medicine Institute. He has also served as a consultant for many new start-ups. Consequently, he has studied virtually every performance tracking and recovery gadget on the market, conducting evidence-based research that helps him separate the game changers from the marketing hype. That's why I reached out to him to get his take on workload monitoring, recovery, and the most effective recovery modalities.

"The main things we look at for the NBA are individual player loads, intensities, and high-effort accelerations," says Robbins. "The actual game is only a part of each player's day, but you also need to look at what else is going on the rest of their day. How much did they travel? How well did they sleep? What did they eat? Are they dealing with an injury? Every player is different, so there is no one plan that fits all. Load capacity and recovery are very specific to the individual."

Heart Rate Monitoring

While Paul Robbins has an arsenal of technology at his disposal for monitoring player workloads and readiness, one of the most basic metrics any coach or athlete can use to create a baseline is heart rate monitoring. But there is a lot of misunderstanding on the relevance and application of heart rate monitoring, so I asked Paul to clear it up for us.

"A lot of people try to make the heart rate more than it is," says Robbins. "Heart rate is a useful guide, and it's a great number to start with, if that's what you want to use, but it's just a guide. In order for it to be truly useful, you need to have some type of cross-reference for it, like wattage, or speed, or distance covered. For example, let's say you ran X distance at Y speed today, and your heart rate got up to 160. If you run that same distance a few days later, and your heart rate only gets to 155 at the same speed, that's good because you're covering the same amount of distance, generating the same power, and doing the same amount of work, but your heart rate didn't go up as fast. But an even more important thing to look at is how fast that heart rate goes up and comes back down relative to the workload. Those are the basic things you need to understand when it comes to heart rate, and you need to have a reference for how much work they do. Since I mostly work with competitive team sport athletes, I like to look at their active heart rate recovery. This comes back to workload. If they're covering a certain distance at a certain speed, you want to have them do some form of active recovery like walking around so you can see how much and how fast it comes down, as opposed to just having them sit. There are lots of different charts out there that will tell you you're doing great if your heart rate drops 15 or 20 beats or whatever in a minute. But you have to understand what type of recovery activity they're doing. Is it seated or walking or what? More importantly, you need those data to be individualized for the athlete. Some athletes have better cardiovascular strength, so it takes them longer to get their heart rate up. So you want to know what their peaks are, and then you want to know what their recovery rates are. And you do this by watching them over time, not by looking at some generalized chart and saying, 'You should be dropping 15 beats, or 30 beats.' It's more important to watch them over time and see how they are reacting to their training."

The next question I had was this: How can coaches use a simple metric such as heart rate as a guide for determining optimal in-bout recovery times between reps?

"Well, to understand that, you need to have a reference for what the athlete's top end is, which is based on a number of things including their cardiovascular strength and genetics and so on," says Robbins. "When I'm doing tests with most of my athletes, I'm trying to find what their peak heart rate is. To be clear, I'm not talking about their max heart rate. Because at the end of your max, you're probably going to go to a knee and be done. You're not going to go to your max for multiple sprints or intervals. You just can't. What you're really training is that peak range, which is around 90 to 95 percent. That's where you want [your heart rate] to be [so it is] able to go up and come back down and go back up multiple times. So most of my tests are trying to find that peak 90- to 95-percent range that you're going to do multiple times in a workout. That's the zone where you want to know what your power output is and what your recovery times are so you can come back down from that zone and know when you can push another interval and get to that top level again.

"I like to use a Wattbike for this because it gives me the average wattage over a three-minute period of time—where you're trying to hold the highest wattage you possibly can for three minutes. Three minutes is a very long interval for anyone other than endurance athletes. It certainly isn't easy, but it's a great test that will get you to that peak heart rate number. I like three minutes because, again, the population I deal with, they're not going to do a 15-minute ramping up protocol on a treadmill or bike. They'll give up after eight or nine minutes because they just don't bike that long. But I can get them to focus for three minutes. And this is something I've discovered with testing. It has to be short and focused or I don't get good results.

"You also want to look at their anaerobic threshold if you're really trying to dial things in. But that's a whole other subject, and most people are not going to go out and do $\dot{V}O_2$[max] tests to find their anaerobic threshold. But once you have that peak number, a good estimate for anaerobic threshold is about 15 to 20 percent below it. This helps you understand what energy systems you're tapping into. Heart rate is a guide, but time is going to give you a way to understand the energy systems being used. If you can only sustain it for three to four seconds, that's definitely the upper end of the anaerobic system. If you can go for an hour, then it's aerobic. I also have a treadmill test I've been developing that I have a chart built around, and I have an NBA team running it for their athletes right now helping me to adjust it. Basically, I have the athlete walk for three minutes and then run 10 miles an hour for 30 seconds. And what we're looking at is how fast their heart rate slope goes up and comes back down [see figure 11.1]. It doesn't give me their peak heart rate so much as it gives me their estimated $\dot{V}O_2$max based on how fast their heart rate goes up and comes back down. So there's a variety of different things you can do on treadmills and bikes. If you're trying to get peak heart rate, you want to do it for roughly three minutes. If you just want to get their estimated $\dot{V}O_2$max, you can do that in roughly 30 seconds by looking at the heart rate slope."

Distilling all of this math down to the basics, the general target you want to aim for when using heart rate as a guide is to do peak intervals at around 90 to 95 percent, while anaerobic threshold training should be done at around 80 to 85 percent. For in-session recovery, you want to get back down to under 65 percent of whatever your peak number is before doing another interval. For example, if your peak heart rate is around 180, you want to get your heart rate down to at least 120 before doing another interval in order to get the most out it. The main thing to keep in mind is that these figures are different for every individual athlete, and they're going to change over time based on fitness levels and other variables.

Speed	HR increase / Watts	10 ml/kg	15 ml/kg	20 ml/kg	25 ml/kg	30 ml/kg	33 ml/kg	36 ml/kg	39 ml/kg	42 ml/kg	45 ml/kg	48 ml/kg	51 ml/kg	54 ml/kg	57 ml/kg	60 ml/kg	63 ml/kg
	180	35	33	32	30	29	28	27	26	25	24	24	23	22	22	21	21
	190	36	35	33	31	30	29	28	27	26	25	24	24	24	23	22	21
	200	38	36	34	33	31	30	29	28	27	26	25	24	24	23	23	22
	210	39	37	35	34	32	31	30	29	28	27	26	25	25	24	23	23
	220	41	38	37	35	33	32	31	30	29	28	27	26	25	25	24	23
	230	42	40	38	36	35	33	32	31	30	29	28	27	26	25	25	24
	240	43	41	39	37	36	34	33	32	31	30	29	28	27	26	26	25
	250	45	42	40	38	37	35	34	33	31	30	29	29	28	27	26	26
	260	46	44	42	40	38	36	35	34	32	31	30	29	28	28	27	26
	270	48	45	43	41	39	37	36	34	33	32	31	30	29	28	28	27
	280	49	46	44	42	40	38	37	35	34	33	32	31	30	29	28	28
	290	50	48	45	43	41	39	38	36	35	34	33	32	31	30	29	28
	300	52	49	46	44	42	40	39	37	36	35	34	33	32	31	30	29
	310	53	50	48	45	43	42	40	38	37	36	34	33	32	31	31	30
6	320	55	52	49	47	44	43	41	39	38	37	35	34	33	32	31	30
	330	56	53	50	48	46	44	42	40	39	37	36	35	34	33	32	31
7	340	57	54	51	49	47	45	43	41	40	38	37	36	35	34	33	32
	350	59	56	53	50	48	46	44	42	41	39	38	37	36	34	33	33
8	360	60	57	54	51	49	47	45	43	41	40	39	37	36	35	34	33
	370	62	58	55	52	50	48	46	44	42	41	40	38	37	36	35	34
9	380	63	59	56	54	51	49	47	45	43	42	40	39	38	37	36	35
	390	64	61	58	55	52	50	48	46	44	43	41	40	39	37	36	35
10	400	66	62	59	56	53	51	49	47	45	44	42	41	39	38	37	36
	410	67	63	60	57	54	52	50	48	46	44	43	41	40	39	38	37
11	420	69	65	61	58	56	53	51	49	47	45	44	42	41	40	39	37
	430	70	66	63	59	57	54	52	50	48	46	45	43	42	40	39	38
12	440	71	67	64	61	58	55	53	51	49	47	45	44	43	41	40	39

FIGURE 11.1 $\dot{V}O_2$max is a measurement of aerobic endurance and cardiovascular fitness that represents the maximum amount of oxygen you can use during exercise. Paul Robbins developed this chart in collaboration with a group of professional sport team coaches and Woodway. It shows speed in the first column and watts of energy output in the second column, both cross-referenced with heart rate increase in the top row. For example, if you're running at 10 miles per hour (16 km) for 30 seconds, and your heart rate goes up 25 beats per minute, then your estimated $\dot{V}O_2$max is 56.

© Paul Robbins

Sleep and Recovery

You know what else LeBron James, Serena Williams, and Roger Federer (and Usain Bolt) all have in common? They've all said on record that they need between 10 and 12 hours of sleep a night to perform at their highest level. Sleep is one of the most important biological functions in life, and its role in athletic performance, mental acuity, and metabolic recovery can't be overstated. It's not hyperbole to say that sleep has the single biggest impact on recovery and performance of any aspect of your life, including diet. If you doubt this assertion, consider the fact that you will spend approximately one-third of your life sleeping (which adds up to around 25 years of snoozing over the course of the average American life span). There's a reason that sleep deprivation is considered an illegal form of torture by the Geneva Conventions. The biological processes that occur during sleep are essential for cellular restoration, energy replenishment, tissue healing, neural activity, cognition, memory, sexual activity, and . . . yeah, basically everything involved with being human. This means that you can add being unconscious for extended periods of time to the long list of paradoxes that make you faster. Of course, I'm oversimplifying things in the interest of not spending this entire chapter putting you to sleep (the puns write themselves over here), but let's cover the important bases as they relate to training and recovery. The first and most obvious thing to keep in mind is that sleep cycles vary for each person based on a wide range of factors. While the average adult can function just fine on between six and eight hours of sleep—relative to their age, stress levels, and the presence of small children—high-performance athletes need more hours of quality sleep between bouts of training and competition to fully restore their systems because they expend more energy and challenge their systems more.

Circadian Rhythm

The internal biological clock that dictates the functions of all the cells, tissues, and organs in your body is known as your circadian rhythm. This master clock for your circadian rhythm, which is located in your brain's hypothalamus, controls a network of peripheral clocks in locations across your body such as your heart, lungs, kidneys, and other organs by using hormonal and neurological signals. Together, these clocks create your body's circadian system, which controls sleep, metabolism, hormone release, alertness, blood pressure, cognitive functions, and reproductive systems. One of the most interesting things about our internal circadian rhythms is that they are based on our daily exposure to the most fundamental timekeeper in the universe—sunlight. The natural light of the sun stimulates our systems for alertness and activity, while the darkness of night primes our need for sleep, recovery, and repair. Therefore, maintaining consistent rhythms in your daily habits and getting regular exposure to natural light are key to your ability to recover quickly and perform at high levels. When your routines are disrupted by travel, compulsive nighttime screen use, or late-night drinking sessions with friends, the natural circadian rhythms of your body are reset to either speed up or slow down. Not surprisingly, humans are creatures of habit. Your body likes to know what's happening, and when, so that it's prepared for the metabolic and energy demands. If you've ever traveled cross-country (or internationally) to give an important presentation or compete in a game the following day, you understand the negative impacts jet lag can have on your performance. This is one of the reasons the NBA schedule is so taxing. Most games happen in the evening at around 7:00 p.m. local time. But, if you've just flown from your hometown in Philadelphia to compete against the Lakers in Los Angeles, that game is starting at 10:00 p.m. on your circadian clock, and you won't get anywhere near a bed until well after midnight. Keep jumping time zones and competing like this for three to four days a week and your body's circadian rhythms will be more confused than a cat in a room full of laser pointers, and your athletic performance and overall health will inevitably suffer. Establishing a regular daily routine with good sleep hygiene that optimizes your body's natural response to light and dark can help your circadian rhythms stay in sync. In other words, it requires going to bed at the same time every night, getting daily exposure to natural light (especially in the morning), eating meals at around the same time every day, and creating a nightly decompression routine that helps calm your body and mind—this includes tapering off the amount of light you're exposed to in the evening, especially the blue light emitted by digital devices.

Sleep Cycles

Over the course of a typical night's sleep, the average person will go through four to six sleep cycles that undulate in rhythmic sequence and shift in duration as sleepers progress through the night. Each sleep cycle comprises four stages that are defined by the frequency changes of your brain waves. Your first sleep cycle is typically the shortest, ranging from 70 to 100 minutes, while the later sleep cycles are between 90 and 120 minutes (see figure 11.2). The four sleep stages you go through in each cycle can be separated into two subcategories: one for REM sleep and three for non-REM sleep. Researchers describe this as your sleep architecture. Both REM and non-REM sleep influence your ability to recover and perform at a high level.

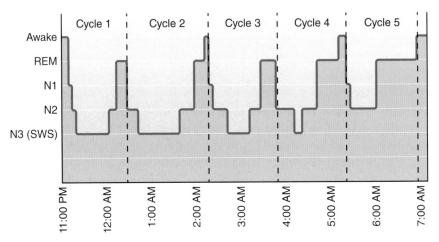

FIGURE 11.2 The average person goes through four to six sleep cycles a night. Each cycle consists of four stages (REM, N1, N2, N3 [SWS]), with the duration of each stage changing depending on which cycle the person is in.

The initial dozing-off stage (N1) normally lasts around one to five minutes, after which your body enters a passive non-REM state (N2) characterized by muscle relaxation, a drop in core temperature, slowed breathing, and reduced heart rate. Eye movement stops, and your brain activity shifts into low gear with short bursts of activity that help keep you from being woken up by external stimuli. During your first sleep cycle of the night, the N2 stage will last about 10 to 25 minutes and then become longer during your later sleep cycles. The average person spends about half their total sleep time in N2. The third stage of deep sleep (N3)—known as short-wave sleep (SWS) or delta sleep for its slower frequency, high-amplitude EEG waves (delta waves)—is arguably the most important stage of sleep when it comes to recovery. Delta sleep stages last for around 20 to 40 minutes. During delta sleep, your body releases pulses of human growth hormone (HGH) and other hormones that promote cellular repair and regeneration. If there is an interruption in this phase, the hormone release stops abruptly. In addition to allowing your body to repair tissues and replenish metabolic stores, recent research suggests that delta sleep changes the fluid pressure in your brain, allowing cerebrospinal fluid to flood the fluid-filled cavities that transmit information across the brain tissues and flush out the toxins built up during your waking hours. Sleep experts believe that the delta stage is critical to recovery and healing. It also has a significant influence on the immune system. Most delta sleep occurs during the first two sleep cycles. As you continue sleeping, your N3 stages get shorter and you spend more time in N2 and REM sleep as you approach morning. You also spend less time in delta sleep as you get older.

REM sleep is a unique state where your body experiences a temporary paralysis of the muscles, called atonia, but your brain activity kicks back up to levels that are similar to when you are awake. As the name suggests, your eyes move quickly in different directions; your heart rate and blood pressure increase; you experience shallow, irregular breathing; and you continue to receive information from your senses like touch, sound, and smell. REM sleep is the most important phase of sleep for learning and memory function because this is when your brain is processing and consolidating information for storage in long-term memory. While the first REM cycle may last only a few minutes, later stages can last up to an hour.

Failure to get enough of both deep sleep and REM sleep has been shown to have profoundly negative impacts on athletic performance, mood, energy levels, and healing. Research indicates that sleep deprivation increases the levels of the stress hormone cortisol while decreasing production of the glycogen and carbohydrate fuel sources that your energy systems use. On the flip side, getting surplus amounts of quality sleep has been shown to significantly improve speed and performance. A study of Stanford University basketball players showed that players who added an average of two extra hours to their nightly sleep routines had a 5-percent increase in speed, faster reflexes, and a 9-percent improvement in free throw accuracy. They also reported having more energy and reduced fatigue (Mah et al. 2011). All of this is my long-winded way of saying that focusing on good sleep hygiene is the single most important thing you can do to improve performance and reduce injury outside of training and competition.

It should therefore come as no surprise that when I asked Paul Robbins—a guy who has tested practically every fitness tracking device available on the most highly trained humans in the world—what he thought the most useful of these gadgets was, he responded without hesitation by singling out a sleep tracking and heart rate monitoring device called the Ōura Ring.

"Look, I'm a consultant for my clients. What I care about is getting good data and getting results," says Robbins. "I don't get paid by any of these companies or accept any kind of endorsement deals from them, but they all send me their products to test. Some of them make the cut. Honestly, most of them end up in the graveyard of my storage closet. But the device that I use the most and has probably had the biggest impact is the Ōura Ring. I mainly look at it to understand how well I slept at night—how much REM and deep sleep I'm getting—and how well my body is recovering based on my heart rate variability and resting heart rate. Looking at those three things in the morning allows me to quickly understand how hard I can push that day. The problem with a lot of the products on the market is that they only look at short windows of data during the night and they don't show you the whole picture. Some of their recovery scores involve so many metrics you don't know which one really affected you."

Heart Rate Variability

While heart rate variability (HRV) is a metric related to your heart rate, it's actually a measurement of your autonomic nervous system, which has two branches—parasympathetic and sympathetic. These two branches control your body's involuntary functions. The parasympathetic, or rest-and-digest, branch manages processes such as digestion and hair growth and causes a decrease in heart rate. The sympathetic, or fight-or-flight, branch controls your body's response to factors such as stress and exercise and increases your heart rate. Heart rate variability happens because these two branches are simultaneously competing with each other as they send signals to your heart. When your nervous system is balanced, your parasympathetic branch tells the heart to beat slower while the sympathetic branch tells it to beat faster. This polarity of signals causes a variable fluctuation in your heart rate. For example, if your heart is beating at a rate of 60 beats per minute, it isn't beating once every second like a metronome. There might be 0.9 seconds between two beats and then 1.2 seconds between the next two. HRV is a measurement of the time variance between the heartbeats (see figure 11.3). When you have a high HRV, it means your body is responding to both parasympathetic and sympathetic inputs. This indicates that your nervous system is balanced and your body is capable of quickly adapting to its environment and performing at a high level relative to your physical capacity. In contrast, if you have a low HRV, it's because one branch (usually the sympathetic "fight-or-flight" branch) is sending stronger signals to your heart than the other. A low HRV score indicates that your body is working hard—often because you're stressed, injured, sick, or fatigued—and you need time to recover. This makes it a strong indicator of how well you're recovering between training and competition bouts and how ready you are to perform at a high level. If you log an extra-hard training day or push yourself for multiple days in a row, your HRV score will likely drop, indicating you are getting into an overloaded or overtrained state. Diet, travel, sleep quality, light exposure, hydration, and other lifestyle factors also have a dramatic impact on your HRV.

All of this begs the question: What is a good HRV target? And the answer, as with most things relating to biology, is . . . it depends. As Paul has emphasized in this chapter a few times, it really comes down to the individual. Age, genetics, gender, and physical conditioning all influence your HRV. The key to using it to manage recovery is to track your HRV over time and cross-reference it with other performance data. The trends are what matter. If you're seeing your HRV trending downward for several days in a row, it's a good indicator that you're training too hard, not sleeping well, eating poorly, or failing to hydrate enough between bouts.

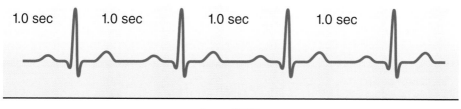

Low HRV

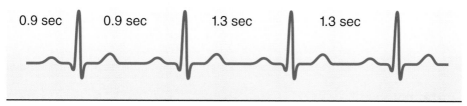

High HRV

FIGURE 11.3   HRV is a measurement of the variation of time between heartbeats that indicates how balanced your nervous system is.

"The important thing to remember about both resting heart rate and heart rate variability is that they are truly individualized," says Robbins. "They give you a reference for where you're at in time. But the real question is: What's good for you? The other key thing is that you need to look at both sides of the equation. With the NBA, we measure athlete loads using RFID technology and then determine what kind of recovery treatments and protocols are appropriate for them. Then we look at the sleep data results. We also do monthly assessment tests that help provide us with a quick snapshot that teams can use during the season to see if they're trending the right way so they can be peaking for the playoffs. That's how we manage the big picture."

Recovery Modalities

As the founder of an international speed school and owner of multiple training facilities, I can tell you firsthand that few markets are more crowded and profitable than the one catering to athletic recovery (see previous note about how much LeBron James spends on it every year). The promise of faster recovery with less pain, inflammation, and fatigue is almost as alluring as discovering the cure for cancer or reversing aging. That said, the combined research efforts and budgets of countless commercial enterprises and military organizations over the past 30 years have yielded some noteworthy advancements in our understanding of biological recovery and how to support it—including the use of compression sleeves and wraps, frequency-optimized vibration and percussion tools, contrast (hot to cold and vice versa) bathing, and cryotherapy. There are also a lot of scientifically unsupported claims around many of these new modalities and their ability to alter the basic physics of chemistry, biology, and time—because that's how marketing works. Let's take a New York minute to look at the physiological principles underlying some of these modalities in the interest of helping you understand how and when to use them as part of a well-engineered, speed-specific training program.

Compression

Compression sleeves, tights, jerseys, socks, and other garments have become ubiquitous in athletics over the past few years because they can provide a wide range of benefits. Graduated compression garments help counter the forces of gravity and vibration and improve fluid flow—including blood, lymph, and interstitial fluid—all of which enhances performance, reduces fatigue, accelerates recovery, and helps reduce injury. Think of compression as an added layer of fascia around your fascia. In fact, these garments function in very much the same way by helping to stabilize your joints, reduce the impact of vibration, and improve fluid flow. They also support the fascia itself by equalizing the pressure across the tissue structures, which encourages the areas of overly tight connective tissue to loosen up and the areas that are too loose to become more active. The added tension also stimulates your tissues to counter the extra external force, increasing muscle activation while improving motor control and shape stability. Arm and leg sleeves can also help reduce tension in tendons and reduce inflammation in joints over time. A wide array of products, styles, and tension levels are available on the market, with new products coming out every year and, again, there's no one size that fits all. Finding the optimal compression garments for your body type, sport, and movement needs is an extremely individual choice. Products such as NormaTec boots combine compression with percussion and vibration to amplify their combined effects. Some athletes even pay to have their limbs professionally wrapped by trained therapists. In sum, wearing compression garments both during and after bouts is one of the simplest ways to support the natural biological processes of recovery.

Vibration and Percussion

While there's a wealth of high-profile athletes and anecdotal evidence that all support the claim that the many vibration guns, plates, and percussion therapies flooding the market over the past few years work as advertised, it's worth noting that there just hasn't been a lot of evidence-based research done on these modalities. To be clear, it's not that vibration and percussion therapies don't work, it's that current studies indicate that they aren't significantly more effective than traditional manual therapies, such as deep tissue massage and active release technique (ART). The physiological benefits are essentially the same as getting a good deep tissue massage (Imtiyaz, Veqar, and Shareef 2014). Vibration, compression, and direct pressure increase fluid flow in the targeted structures, warm the tissues, and momentarily help muscles relax to restore mobility. One of the main advantages of using percussion and vibration tools—especially portable ones, such as guns—is that you can use them quickly for highly targeted self-myofascial release before and after training bouts to help warm tissues and improve fluid flow, without having to hire a massage practitioner to follow you around. Besides, massage therapy also takes longer. And let's be honest: It feels really good to use them. But, as Michol pointed out in chapter 3, this is because these tools stimulate tissues that are rich with nerve endings. While these percussive and vibration therapies can improve range of motion, research indicates these benefits are short-lived. When your body is already unstable because of injuries, inflammation, tissue adhesions, collagen buildup, or structural imbalances, your nervous system will not release the tightened muscles. Even though they still respond to a trigger point, loosening these tightened muscles would just result in more instability. Resolving these kinds of issues requires balancing the myofascial system and restoring tissue viscosity through whole-body movements, small motor unit recruitment, and other long-term approaches. Dense collagen adhesions in your fascia tissue are challenging to separate using a scalpel. You're not going to break them up with a vibration gun or foam roller. Percussive therapies are shown to improve fluid flow and temporarily reduce muscle tension and are certainly beneficial for recovery (and warm-up). Just remember to keep their benefits in perspective.

Cryotherapy and Contrast Bathing

Ice bath immersions and contrast bathing have become popular strategies for postexercise recovery—especially on Instagram. The problem is that the scientific research surrounding these modalities is either largely inconclusive or contradictory. In theory, submerging all or part of your body in cold water after an intense workout constricts the blood vessels to help flush waste products out of the tissues, reduce swelling, and decrease delayed onset muscle soreness (DOMS). Although results from a series of 17 studies, conducted mostly on runners, indicated that taking an ice bath after a bout of maximal exercise can reduce delayed onset muscle soreness when compared with simply resting, there was no significant evidence that it improved recovery times or reduced fatigue in any meaningful way (Bleakley et al. 2012). Also, if you're a fan of using cryotherapy or contrast bathing as part of your strength-training program, you probably want to sit down (somewhere warm) for this next part. An alternate study done by Llion Roberts and colleagues in 2015 comparing the effects of cold-water immersion with active-recovery techniques on changes in muscle mass and strength over 12 weeks of strength training actually found that postexercise cold-water immersion inhibited muscle hypertrophy signaling and satellite cell activity and resulted in smaller strength gains (Roberts et al. 2015). Basically, the study showed that cryotherapy can actually *impede* your body's natural healing process—which inevitably involves some degree of postexercise tissue inflammation. The same research team released a follow-up study in 2017 comparing cryotherapy with an active warm-down recovery routine. After a 45-minute session of doing lunges, squats, and other exercises, participants spent 10 minutes sitting in a tub of cold water.

Researchers took blood samples from the participants at various intervals before and after the exercise session and ice bath, and—while markers of inflammation and stress response increased after exercise—the ice bath made no difference in these levels. All of which suggests that an active warm-down spent doing things like slowly riding on a stationary bike for 10 minutes is more beneficial (and arguably more enjoyable) than sitting in a tub of ice or jumping from a warm one to a cold one. While, in theory, contrast bathing helps pump fluids through your body by alternating vasodilation and vasoconstriction, easier ways to accomplish the same goal include vibration therapy, massage, and active-recovery protocols (Bieuzen, Bleakley, and Costello 2013). In fact, simple cold-water baths (75 degrees Fahrenheit or 24 degrees Celsius) or even just a dip in the lake have been shown to be just as good or better than ice baths because the physiological benefit from water immersion doesn't come from the temperature. Rather, it comes from the hydrostatic pressure of simply floating in water, which allows your muscles to relax, improves circulation, helps flush out metabolic waste, and reduces the pressure on your joints.

There's no doubt that achieving a more complete postexercise recovery in less time can give you a significant advantage in field and court sports with intense training and competition schedules. Additionally, emerging technologies have yielded a number of beneficial modalities for helping the body recover from the stress of athletic output. But the reality is that the natural processes underlying human physiology are not something that can be easily hacked. Biological systems adapt to the demands of their environment, and shortcuts are hard to come by. Your body isn't a temple—or a machine. It's a self-regenerating biological organism similar to a plant. It grows in response to the stress of its environment and its access to food, light, water, and rest. As mundane as it sounds, at the end of the day, the best strategy for recovery is to listen to your mom: Eat your vegetables, get plenty of sleep and sunlight, drink lots of water, don't eat too many sweets, avoid excessive alcohol, and stay away from the kids smoking cigarettes behind the gym. And sure, while you're at it, remember to wear a jacket and bring a snack (body tissues like to be warm and snacks can always be bartered). Just don't tell her I told you it's okay to play video games. As I mentioned at the beginning of this book, speed is a battle against the most formidable force in the universe: gravity. The only way to get an edge in this battle is to respect the biological laws of nature. Master the fundamentals of speed, power, and agility like Bruce Lee—through constant practice with proper form. Work hard. Train smarter. Listen to your body. And when the time comes, punch gravity in the face with all the force you can muster.

That's how you outrun the bears and learn to fly.

12

PROGRAMMING MENUS

This chapter provides a set of menu templates you can use to create customized speed-training programs for your specific sport, athlete, or goal. The exercises highlighted in the speed chapters are just a select few of the exercises used at Parisi Speed School. The menus here include additional relatively common exercises you can choose from depending on need. They are by no means definitive, but once you understand how to mix the basic ingredients, you can use these menus to start improvising your own programs in ways that make your athletes faster, stronger, and less prone to injury. Speed coaching is both an art and a science. And, just like cooking, I can give you a book full of recipes but, ultimately, the magic comes from the chef. Keep in mind that while the exercises and drills listed here are categorized as basic, intermediate, and advanced, these designations are subjective. The relative difficulty of an exercise depends on the experience, conditioning, and injury history of the athlete; the speed and intensity of execution; and other variables like numbers of sets and reps. There are also progressions and regressions for most of them that can increase or decrease difficulty. This is where the art of coaching comes in.

For each training category of focus, a properly structured training session begins with a pre–warm-up, then moves into a general active dynamic warm-up and a speed-specific (or strength-specific) active dynamic warm-up, and finally anchor drills (loaded motor-learning drills) and application drills (full-intensity gamelike drills). The goal is to move from general to specific in order to warm the body's flight systems and progressively prime them for even higher levels of activity. Ideally, one phase flows seamlessly into the next. The key is to follow a logical sequence that allows the connective tissues, muscles, and joints to warm up by going through the ranges of motion required for the day's training goal—whether it's a linear-speed day, a multidirectional-speed day, or a strength-training day. The following is the basic sequence:

1. Pre–warm-up
2. General active dynamic warm-up (ADW)
3. Speed-specific ADW for
   » Linear-speed days
   » Multidirectional-speed days
   » Strength-training days
4. Anchor drills for the focus of the day (acceleration, max velocity, deceleration, change of direction, agility, or strength)
5. Application drills for the focus of the day (acceleration, max velocity, deceleration, change of direction, agility, or strength)

PRE–WARM-UP

Choose: 3 BASIC + 2 MODERATE

Exercise	Rep total or time	Number of sets	Page
BASIC			
Front plank	3-6 reps, hold each rep 6-10 sec	1	—
Curl-up	3-6 reps, hold each rep 6-10 sec	1	42
Side plank	3-6 reps per side, hold each rep 6-10 sec	1	43
Bird dog	3-6 reps per side, hold each rep 6-10 sec	1	44
Clamshell	15-20 reps per side	1	45
Resistance band clamshell	15 reps per side, hold 5 sec on reps 5, 10, and 15	1	46
MODERATE			
Power squat	8-12 reps	1	48
Resistance band overhead squat	8-12 reps	1	49
Lying prone hurdler	8-12 reps per side	1	50
Fire hydrant	8-12 reps per side	1	—
Supinated leg lift	8-12 reps per side	1	—
Iron cross	8-12 reps	1	—

GENERAL ADW

Choose: 3 BASIC + 1 MODERATE + 2 ADVANCED

Exercise	Time, rep total, or distance	Number of sets	Page
BASIC			
Half jack	10-15 reps	1-2	59
Full jack	10-15 reps	1-2	60
Seal jack	10-15 reps	1-2	62
Glute shift knee lift	4-6 reps per side	1-2	57
Pogo jump	20-45 sec	1-2	—
MODERATE			
Side lunge lift	10-12 reps per side	1-2	58
Squat jump	5 reps	1-2	—
Lateral jump	5 reps per side	1-2	214
Rudimentary jumps (double and single leg)	10-20 yd (9-18 m)	2-4	—
ADVANCED			
Forward overhead medicine ball throw	10-15 reps	1-2	64
Kneeling rotational medicine ball throw	10-15 reps per side	1-2	65
Overhead squat medicine ball throw	8-12 reps	1-2	66
Ice skater lunge	4-6 reps per side	1-2	63

SPEED-SPECIFIC ADW

Linear-Speed Day ADW

Choose: 1 BASIC + 1 MODERATE + 1 ADVANCED

Exercise	Distance or rep total	Number of sets	Page
BASIC			
Forward skip	10-20 yd (9-18 m)	1-2	68
Power skip	10-20 yd (9-18 m)	1-2	—
Hands-over-head skip	10-20 yd (9-18 m)	1-2	—
MODERATE			
Straight-leg shuffle bound	20-30 yd (18-27 m)	1-2	69
Focused tall build-up run	20-40 yd (18-37 m)	2	—
Resisted acceleration walk	5-15 yd (5-14 m)	2	—
ADVANCED			
A-walk triple extension	10-15 yd (9-14 m)	2	70
High-knee exchange balance	6 reps per side	2	—
Straight-leg-quick-leg	6 reps per side	2	—

Multidirectional-Speed Day ADW

Choose: 1 BASIC + 1 MODERATE + 1 ADVANCED

Exercise	Distance or rep total	Number of sets	Page
BASIC			
Gate swings	10-12 reps	2	—
Crossover lunge	6-8 reps per side	2	72
Wide out	8-12 reps	2	71
MODERATE			
Lateral wall slide hip lock	6 reps per side	2	—
Kneeling front-hip lock	6 reps per side	2	—
Side shuffle	15-20 yd (14-18 m) per side	2	194
ADVANCED			
High-knee carioca	15-20 yd (14-18 m)	2	73
Resisted lateral jump	6-8 reps per side	2	—
Resisted side run	15-20 yd (14-18 m) per side	2	—

Strength-Training Day ADW

Choose: 1 BASIC + 1 MODERATE + 1 ADVANCED

Exercise	Rep total	Number of sets	Page
BASIC			
Pull-apart	15	1-2	—
Resistance band overhead raise	15	1-2	74
MODERATE			
Resistance band overhead squat	15	1-2	49
Supinated pull-apart	15	1-2	75
ADVANCED			
Dumbbell high pull	10	1-2	—
Dumbbell hang clean	10	1-2	76
Dumbbell push press	10	1-2	110

LINEAR- AND MULTIDIRECTIONAL-SPEED DAYS: ANCHOR AND APPLICATION DRILLS

Acceleration Anchor Drills

Choose: 3

Progression or regression: BASIC / MODERATE / ADVANCED

Exercise	Time, rep total, or distance	Number of sets	Page
BASIC			
Wall drive plank	Hold for 20-30 sec	2-4	130
Feet-exchange wall drive	4-6 reps per side	2-4	132
MODERATE			
Sled drag or push	10-20 yd (9-18 m)	4-6	134
Medicine ball broad jump	5-10 yd (5-9 m)	4-6	137
ADVANCED			
Hill sprints or stadium stairs	20-30 yd (18-27 m)	4-6	—
10-20% incline treadmill sprints	4-8 sec	4-6	—

Acceleration Application Drills

Choose: 3

Progression or regression: BASIC / MODERATE / ADVANCED

Exercise	Distance	Number of sets	Page
BASIC			
Jump-back acceleration	10-15 yd (9-14 m)	4-6	142
Falling start	10-15 yd (9-14 m)	4-6	—
MODERATE			
Ball-drop acceleration	5 yd (5 m)	4-6	143
Push-up start	10-20 yd (9-18 m)	4-6	138
ADVANCED			
Acceleration ladder sprint	20 yd (18 m)	4-6	140
Acceleration sprint (2-point start)	10-20 yd (9-18 m)	4-6	—
Acceleration sprint (3-point start)	10-20 yd (9-18 m)	4-6	—

Max-Velocity Anchor Drills

Choose: 3

Progression or regression: BASIC / MODERATE / ADVANCED

Exercise	Time, rep total, or distance	Number of sets	Page
BASIC			
Arm action	Hold 1-2 sec per side	4-6	161
Lower-limb fast claw	6 reps per side	1-3	168
Lying leg recovery	Hold 1-2 sec per side	4-6	162
MODERATE			
A-march with force application	10-15 yd (9-14 m)	4	—
Straight-leg bound	20-40 yd (18-37 m)	4-6	165
Dribbles: low, medium, high	20-40 yd (18-37 m)	2-6	166
ADVANCED			
A-skip with force application	10-15 yd (9-14 m)	4	—
Power bound	20-40 yd (18-37 m)	4-6	163

Max-Velocity Application Drills

Choose: 3

Progression or regression: BASIC / MODERATE / ADVANCED

Exercise	Distance	Number of sets	Page
BASIC			
Overhead stick drill	20-40 yd (18-37 m)	2-6	171
A run	10-20 yd (9-18 m)	2-6	—
MODERATE			
In-and-out sprint	98 yd (90 m)	2-6	170
Wicket	20-100 yd (18-91 m)	2-6	172
ADVANCED			
Flying sprint	20-40 yd (18-37 m)	2-6	—
Max-velocity sprint	40-100 yd (37-91 m)	2-6	174
Assisted tow sprint	40-80 yd (37-73 m)	2-4	—

Deceleration and Multidirectional Anchor Drills

Choose: 3

Progression or regression: BASIC / MODERATE / ADVANCED

Exercise	Time, rep total, or distance	Number of sets	Page
BASIC			
Center-of-gravity management	2-4 sec per side	2-4	211
Snap down	6-8 reps	2-4	185
Stationary speed skater	4-6 reps per side	2-4	212
Vertical jump	6-8 reps	2-4	186
MODERATE			
Side-run hockey stop	2 reps of 5-10 yd (5-9 m) per side	2-4	220
Push lunge	4-6 reps per side	2-4	188
Rotational shovel	6-8 reps per side	2-4	190
ADVANCED			
Crow hop	6-8 reps per side	2-4	192
Resisted lateral shuffle	2 reps of 5-10 yd (5-9 m) per side	2-4	218
Speed skater bound	4-6 reps per side	2-4	216

Deceleration and Multidirectional Application Drills

Choose: 3

Progression or regression: BASIC / MODERATE / ADVANCED

Exercise	Time, rep total, or distance	Number of sets	Page
BASIC			
Loaded shuffle drill	10-20 yd (9-18 m) per side	2-4	—
Low–high pogo jump	10-20 sec	2-4	—
Front–back pogo jump	10-20 sec	2-4	—
MODERATE			
Side shuffle	15-20 yd (14-18 m) per side	2-4	194
Running speed skater	4-6 reps per side	2-4	—
Depth drop	4-6 reps	2-4	196
ADVANCED			
X or W run	5-10 yd (5-9 m)	2-4	224 or 225
Combination run (with aqua bag)	5-10 yd (5-9 m)	2-4	226
BlazePod reaction cone drills	5-10 yd (5-9 m)	2-4	—

STRENGTH-TRAINING DAY

Foundational Strength

Choose: 1 BASIC + 1 MODERATE + 1 ADVANCED

Exercise	Rep total	Number of sets	Page
BASIC			
Pull-up	2-12	3-8	88
Push-up	2-12	3-8	—
MODERATE			
Back squat	2-5	3-5	89
Front squat	2-5	3-5	—
ADVANCED			
Romanian deadlift	2-5	3-5	—
Trap bar deadlift	2-5	3-5	91

Core Strength

Choose: 1 BASIC + 1 MODERATE + 1 ADVANCED

Exercise	Time, distance, or rep total	Number of sets	Page
BASIC			
Pallof press	2-5 reps per side, hold each rep 6-10 sec	2-4	96
Kneeling Pallof press	2-5 reps per side, hold each rep 6-10 sec	2-4	—
Hanging leg raise	2-5 reps	2-4	—
MODERATE			
Farmer's carry	20-40 yd (18-37 m)	2-4	94
Suitcase carry	2-5 reps per side	2-4	—
Bear hug carry	2-5 reps	2-4	—
ADVANCED			
Ab rollout	8-15 reps	2-4	98
ViPR PRO lateral chop to balance	4-8 reps per side	2-4	—
Single-leg Romanian deadlift	2-5 reps per side	2-4	—

Lower-Body Strength

Choose: 1 BASIC + 1 MODERATE + 1 ADVANCED

Exercise	Rep total	Number of sets	Page
BASIC			
Step-up	5-8	3-5	—
Calf raise	6-12	3-5	102
MODERATE			
Reverse lunge	5-8 per side	3-5	—
Single-leg squat	5-8 per side	3-5	103
ADVANCED			
Piston lunge	5-8 per side	3-5	—
Nordic hamstring curl	4	1-3	101

Odd-Position and Dead Strength

Choose: 1 BASIC + 1 MODERATE + 1 ADVANCED

Exercise	Rep total	Number of sets	Page
BASIC			
Lateral block forced exhalation	4-8 per side	1-3	—
Lateral step shovel	4-8 per side	1-3	105
MODERATE			
Lateral lunge hold	4-8 per side	1-3	—
Transverse plane lunge with arc	4-8 per side	1-3	106
ADVANCED			
Lateral big arc dead shift	4-8 per side	1-3	107
360 lunge series	1-3	1-3	—

Power Day

Choose: 1 BASIC + 1 MODERATE + 1 ADVANCED

Exercise	Rep total	Number of sets	Page
BASIC			
Barbell snatch	2-5	3-5	—
Dumbbell snatch	2-5	3-5	—
MODERATE			
Barbell clean	2-5	3-5	111
Barbell clean pull	2-5	3-5	—
ADVANCED			
Dumbbell push press	2-5	3-5	110
Kettlebell snatch	2-5	3-5	113

SAMPLE FULL-TRAINING MENUS

Linear-Speed Day: Acceleration

	Exercise	Rep total, time, or distance	Number of sets	Page
Pre–warm-up activation	Curl-up	3-6 reps, hold each rep 6-10 sec	1	42
	Side plank	3-6 reps per side, hold each rep 6-10 sec	1	43
	Bird dog	3-6 reps per side, hold each rep 6-10 sec	1	44
	Lying prone hurdler	8-12 reps per side	1	50
	Resistance band overhead squat	8-12 reps	1	49
General ADW	Half jack	10-15 reps	2	59
	Full jack	10-15 reps	2	60
	Pogo jump (low)	20-45 sec	1	—
	Front or side lunge	10-12 reps per side	1	—
	Overhead squat medicine ball throw	10-15 reps	1-2	66
	Kneeling rotational medicine ball throw	10-15 reps per side	1-2	65
Linear-speed day ADW	Power skip	10-20 yd (9-18 m)	2	—
	Focused tall build-up run	20-40 yd (18-37 m)	2	—
	Mini-hurdle linear jump	5 reps	2	—
Acceleration anchor drills	Wall drive plank	Hold for 20-30 sec	2-4	130
	Feet-exchange wall drive	Hold for 2-4 sec per side	4-6	132
	Sled drag or push	10-20 yd (9-18 m)	4-6	134
Acceleration application drills	Acceleration ladder sprint	20 yd (18 m)	4-6	140
	Ball-drop acceleration	5-10 yd (5-10 m)	4-6	143
	Acceleration sprint (2-point start)	10-20 yd (9-18 m)	4-6	—

Linear-Speed Day: Max Velocity

	Exercise	Rep total, time, or distance	Number of sets	Page
Pre–warm-up activation	Front plank	3-6 reps, hold each rep 6-10 sec	1	—
	Side plank	3-6 reps per side, hold each rep 6-10 sec	1	43
	Bird dog	3-6 reps per side, hold each rep 6-10 sec	1	44
	Resistance band clamshell	15 reps per side, hold each rep 5 sec	2	46
	Iron cross	8-12 reps	1	—
General ADW	Half jack	10-15 reps	2	59
	Seal jack	10-15 reps	2	62
	Full jack	10-15 reps	2	60
	Front or side lunge	10-12 reps per side	1	—
	Forward overhead medicine ball throw	10-15 reps	3	64
	Kneeling rotational medicine ball throw	10-15 reps per side	3	65
Linear-speed day ADW	Hands-over-head skip	5-10 yd (5-9 m)	2	—
	Straight-leg shuffle bound	10-15 yd (9-14 m)	2	69
	Mini-hurdle linear jump	5 reps	2	—
Max-velocity anchor drills	Arm action	Hold 1-2 sec per side	4-6	161
	Lower-limb fast claw	6 reps per side	2	168
	Dribbles	20-40 yd (18-37 m)	2-4	166
Max-velocity application drills	In-and-out sprint	10-20 yd (9-18 m)	4-6	170
	Overhead stick drill	20-40 yd (18-37 m)	2-4	171
	Max-velocity sprint	20-60 yd (18-55 m)	4-6	174

Multidirectional-Speed Day: COD

	Exercise	Rep total, time, or distance	Number of sets	Page
Pre–warm-up activation	Front plank	3-6 reps, hold each rep 6-10 sec	1	—
	Side plank	3-6 reps per side, hold each rep 6-10 sec	1	43
	Bird dog	3-6 reps per side, hold each rep 6-10 sec	1	44
	Resistance band clamshell	15 reps per side	2	46
	Iron cross	8-12 reps	1	—
General ADW	Half jack	10-15 reps	2	59
	Seal jack	10-15 reps	2	62
	Full jack	10-15 reps	2	60
	Front or side lunge	10-12 reps per side	1	—
	Forward overhead medicine ball throw	10-15 reps	3	64
	Kneeling rotational medicine ball throw	10-15 reps per side	3	65
Multidirectional-speed day ADW	Wide out	8-12 reps	2	71
	High-knee carioca	15-20 yd (14-18 m)	2	73
	Side shuffle	15-20 yd (14-18 m) per side	2	194
COD anchor drills	Snap down	6-8 reps	2	185
	Rotational shovel	6-8 reps per side	2	190
	Stationary speed skater	6-10 reps per side	2	212
COD application drills	Loaded shuffle drill	10-20 yd (9-18 m) per side	2-4	—
	Side shuffle	15-20 yd (14-18 m) per side	2-4	194
	X or W run	5-10 yd (5-9 m)	2-4	224 or 225

Multidirectional-Speed Day: Agility

	Exercise	Rep total, time, or distance	Number of sets	Page
Pre–warm-up activation	Front plank	3-6 reps, hold each rep 6-10 sec	2	—
	Side plank	3-6 reps per side, hold each rep 6-10 sec	2	43
	Bird dog	3-6 reps per side, hold each rep 6-10 sec	2	44
	Resistance band clamshell	15 reps per side	2	46
	Iron cross	8-12 reps	1	—
General ADW	Half jack	10-15 reps	2	59
	Seal jack	10-15 reps	2	62
	Full jack	10-15 reps	2	60
	Front or side lunge	10-12 reps per side	1	—
	Forward overhead medicine ball throw	10-15 reps	3	64
	Kneeling rotational medicine ball throw	10-15 reps per side	3	65
Multidirectional-speed day ADW	Wide out	8-12 reps	2	71
	High-knee carioca	15-20 yd (14-18 m)	2	73
	Side shuffle	15-20 yd (14-18 m) per side	2	194
Agility anchor drills	Lateral jump	6-8 reps per side	2	214
	Speed skater bound	4-6 reps per side	2	216
	Command combination run	5-10 yd (5-9 m)	4-6	—
Agility application drills	BlazePod X or W run	5-10 yd (5-9 m)	4-6	224 or 225
	Command drop step	6-10 reps per side	2-3	—
	Tag games	—	—	241

Strength-Training Day: Foundational + Core

	Exercise	Rep total, time, or distance	Number of sets	Page
Pre–warm-up activation	Curl-up	3-6 reps, hold each rep 6-10 sec	2	42
	Side plank	3-6 reps per side, hold each rep 6-10 sec	2	43
	Bird dog	3-6 reps per side, hold each rep 6-10 sec	2	44
	Front plank	3-6 reps, hold each rep 6-10 sec	2	—
	Resistance band overhead squat	15 reps, hold 5 sec on reps 5, 10, and 15	2	49
General ADW	Seal jack	10-15 reps	2	62
	Full jack	10-15 reps	2	60
	Pogo jump (low)	20-45 sec	1	—
	Squat jump	5 reps	2	—
	Forward overhead medicine ball throw	10-15 reps	3	64
Strength-training day ADW	Supinated pull-apart	15 reps	1	75
	Resistance band overhead raise	15 reps	1	74
	Dumbbell push press	10 reps	2	110
Foundational strength	Push-up	2-12 reps	3-8	—
	Back squat	2-5 reps	3-5	89
	Romanian deadlift	2-5 reps	3-5	—
Core strength	Hanging leg raise	2-5 reps	3-5	—
	Farmer's carry	20-40 yd (18-37 m)	3-5	94
	Ab rollout	8-15 reps	3-5	98

Strength-Training Day: Lower Body + Odd Position

	Exercise	Rep total or time	Number of sets	Page
Pre–warm-up activation	Side plank	3-6 reps per side, hold each rep 6-10 sec	2	43
	Front plank	3-6 reps, hold each rep 6-10 sec	2	—
	Resistance band clamshell	4-6 reps per side	2	46
	Supinated leg lift	8-12 reps per side	1	—
General ADW	Seal jack	10-15 reps	2	62
	Full jack	10-15 reps	2	60
	Pogo jump (low)	20-45 sec	1	—
	Squat jump	5 reps	2	—
	Forward overhead medicine ball throw	10-15 reps	3	64
Strength-training day ADW	Resistance band overhead raise	15 reps	1	74
	Resistance band overhead squat	15 reps	1	49
	Dumbbell push press	10 reps	2	110
Lower-body strength	Calf raise	6-12 reps	3-5	102
	Reverse lunge	5-8 reps per side	3-5	—
	Piston lunge	5-8 reps per side	3-5	—
Odd-position strength	Lateral step shovel	4-8 reps per side	1-3	105
	Transverse plane lunge with arc	4-8 reps per side	1-3	106
	360 lunge series	1-3 reps	1-3	—

Strength-Training Day: Power + Speed

	Exercise	Rep total or time	Number of sets	Page
Pre–warm-up activation	Curl-up	3-6 reps, hold each rep 6-10 sec	2	42
	Bird dog	3-6 reps per side, hold each rep 6-10 sec	2	44
	Front plank	3-6 reps, hold each rep 6-10 sec	2	—
	Power squat	8-12 reps	2	48
General ADW	Half jack	10-15 reps	2	59
	Full jack	10-15 reps	2	60
	Pogo jump (low)	20-45 sec	1	—
	Front or side lunge	10-12 reps per side	1	—
	Forward overhead medicine ball throw	10-15 reps	3	64
Strength-training day ADW	Supinated pull-apart	15 reps	1	75
	Dumbbell complex	15 reps	2	—
	Dumbbell hang clean	10 reps	2	76
Power and speed strength	Dumbbell snatch	2-5 reps	3-5	—
	Barbell snatch	2-5 reps	3-5	—
	Barbell clean pull	2-5 reps	3-5	—
	Lateral big arc dead shift	4-8 reps per side	3-5	107

Chapter 1

Cheatham, S.W., Kolber, M.J., Cain, M., and M. Lee. 2015. "The Effects of Self Myofascial Release Using a Foam Roller Massager on Joint Range of Motion, Muscle Recovery, and Performance: A Systematic Review." *International Journal of Sports Therapy* 10:827-38.

Clark, K.P., Rieger, R.H., Bruno, R.F., and D.J. Stearne. 2019. "The NFL Combine 40-Yard Dash: How Important Is Maximum Velocity?" *Journal of Strength and Conditioning Research* 33:1542-50.

Delaney, J., Scott, T., Ballard, D., Duthie, G., Hickmans, J., Lockie, R., and B. Dascombe. 2015. "Contributing Factors to Change-of-Direction Ability in Professional Rugby League Players." *Journal of Strength and Conditioning Research* 29:2688-96.

Edouard, P., Mendiguchia, J., Guex, K., Lahti, J., Samozino, P., and J.B. Morin. 2019. "Sprinting: A Potential Vaccine for Hamstring Injury?" *Science Performance & Science Reports* 48 (1).

Weyand, P.G., Sandell, R.F., Prime, D.N., and M.W. Bundle. 2010. "The Biological Limits to Running Speed Are Imposed From the Ground Up." *Journal of Applied Physiology* 108:950-61.

Weyand, P.G., Sternlight, D.B., Bellizzi, M.J., and S. Wright. 2000. "Faster Top Running Speeds Are Achieved With Greater Ground Forces Not More Rapid Leg Movements." *Journal of Applied Physiology* 89:1991-9.

Chapter 2

Alexander, R.N. 2003. *Principles of Animal Locomotion*. Princeton, NJ: Princeton University Press.

Kubo, K., Kanehisa, H., Kawakami, Y., and T. Fukunaga. 2001. "Effects of Repeated Muscle Contractions on the Tendon Structures in Humans." *European Journal of Applied Physiology* 84:162-66. https://doi.org/10.1007/s004210000337.

McGill, S.M., Chaimberg, J., Frost, D., and C. Fenwick. 2010. "The Double Peak: How Elite MMA Fighters Develop Speed and Strike Force." *Journal of Strength and Conditioning Research* 24 (2): 348-57.

Nalbandian, M., and M. Takeda. 2016. "Lactate as a Signaling Molecule That Regulates Exercise-Induced Adaptations." *Biology (Basel)* 5 (34): 8. https://doi.org/10.3390/biology5040038.

Pearson, A.M. 1990. "Muscle Growth and Exercise." *Critical Reviews in Food and Science Nutrition* 29 (3): 167-96.

Schleip, S. 2017. "Fascia as a Sensory Organ: Clinical Applications." *Terra Rosa* 30:2-7. https://issuu.com/terrarosa/docs/emag_issue_20.

Chapter 3

Cheatham, S.W., Kolber, M.J., Cain, M., and M. Lee. 2015. "The Effects of Self-Myofascial Release Using a Foam Roller or Massager on Joint Range of Motion, Muscle Recovery, and Performance." *International Journal of Sports Therapy* 10 (6): 827-38.

Pearcey, G.E.P., Bradbury-Squires, D.J., Kawamoto, J.E., Drinkwater, E.J., Behm, D.G., and D.C. Button. 2015. "Foam Rolling for Delayed-Onset Muscle Soreness and Recovery of Dynamic Performance Measures." *Journal of Athletic Training* 50 (1): 5-13.

Selkowitz, D.M., Beneck, G.J., and C.M. Powers. 2013. "Which Exercises Target the Gluteal Muscles While Minimizing Activation of the Tensor Fascia Lata?" *Journal of Orthopedic Sports Physical Therapy* 43 (2): 54-64.

Chapter 4

Cheatham, S.W., Kolber, M.J., Cain, M., and M. Lee. 2015. "The Effects of Self-Myofascial Release Using a Foam Roller or Massager on Joint Range of Motion, Muscle Recovery, and Performance." *International Journal of Sports Therapy* 10 (6): 827-38.

Holt, B.W., and K. Lambourne. 2008. "The Impact of Different Warm-Up Protocols on Vertical Jump Performance in Male Collegiate Athletes." *Journal of Strength and Conditioning Research* 22 (1): 226-9. https://doi.org/10.1519/JSC.0b013e31815f9d6a.

Selkowitz, D.M., Beneck, G.J., and C.M. Powers. 2013. "Which Exercises Target the Gluteal Muscles While Minimizing Activation of the Tensor Fascia Lata?" *Journal of Orthopedic Sports Physical Therapy* 43 (2): 54-64.

Waryasz, G.R., Daniels, A.H., Gil, J.A., Suric, V., and C.P. Eberson. 2016. "Personal Trainer Demographics, Current Practice Trends and Common Trainee Injuries." *Orthopedic Reviews* 8 (3). https://doi.org/10.4081/or.2016.6600.

Winchester, J.B., Nelson, A.G., Landin, D., Young, M.A., and I.C. Schexnayder. 2008. "Static Stretching Impairs Sprint Performance in Collegiate Track and Field Athletes." *Journal of Strength and Conditioning Research* 22 (1): 13-9. https://doi.org/10.1519/JSC.0b013e31815ef202.

Chapter 5

Ayers, J.L., DeBeliso, M., Sevene, T.G., and K.J. Adams. 2016. "Hang Cleans and Hang Snatches Produce Similar Improvements in Female Collegiate Athletes." *Biology of Sport* 33:251-56. https://doi.org/10.5604/20831862.1201814.

Balshaw, T.G., Massey, G.J., Maden-Wilkinson, T.M., Tillin, N.A., and J.P. Folland. 2016. "Training-Specific Functional, Neural, and Hypertrophic Adaptations to Explosive- vs. Sustained-Contraction Strength Training." *Journal of Applied Physiology* 120:1364-73. https://doi.org/10.1152/japplphysiol.00091.2016.

Beardsley, C., and B. Contreras. 2014. "The Increasing Role of the Hip Extensor Musculature With Heavier Compound Lower-Body Movements and More Explosive Sport Actions." *Strength and Conditioning Journal* 36 (2): 49-55.

Chumanov, E.S., Heiderscheit, B.C., and D.G. Thelen. 2011. "Hamstring Musculotendon Dynamics During Stance and Swing Phases of High-Speed Running." *Medicine and Science in Sports and Exercise* 43 (3): 525-32.

de Hoyo, M., Pozzo, M., Sañudo, B., Carrasco, L., Gonzalo-Skok, O., Domínguez-Cobo, S., and E. Morán-Camacho. 2014. "Effects of a 10-Week In-Season Eccentric-Overload Training Program on Muscle-Injury Prevention and Performance in Junior Elite Soccer Players." *International Journal of Sports Physiology and Performance* 10 (1): 46-52.

Handsfield, G.G., Knaus, K.R., Fiorentino, N.M., Meyer, C.H., Hart, J.M., and S.S. Blemker. 2016. "Adding Muscle Where You Need It: Non-Uniform Hypertrophy Patterns in Elite Sprinters." *Scandinavian Journal of Medicine and Science in Sports* 27:1050-60. https://doi.org/10.1111/sms.12723.

Joy, J.M., Lowery, R.P., de Souza, E.O., and J.M. Wilson. 2016. "Elastic Bands As a Component of Periodized Resistance Training." *Journal of Strength and Conditioning Research* 30:2100-6. https://doi.org/10.1519/JSC.0b013e3182986bef.

Kelly, S.B., Brown, L.E., Swan, P.D., and S.P. Hooker. 2015. "Comparison of Concentric and Eccentric Bench Press Repetitions to Failure." *Journal of Strength and Conditioning Research* 29 (4): 1027-32.

Loturco, I., Nakamura, F.Y., Kobal, R., and S. Gil. 2015. "Training for Power and Speed: Effects of Increasing or Decreasing Jump-Squat Velocity in Elite Young Soccer Players." *Journal of Strength and Conditioning Research* 29 (10): 2771.

Mjølsnes, R., Arnason, A., Østhagen, T., Raastad, T., and R. Bahr. 2004. "A 10-Week Randomized Trial Comparing Eccentric vs. Concentric Hamstring Strength Training in Well-Trained Soccer Players." *Scandinavian Journal of Medicine and Science in Sports* 14:311-7.

Mora-Custodio, R., Rodríguez-Rosell, D., Pareja-Blanco, F., Yañez-García, J.M., and J.J. González-Badillo. 2016. "Effect of Low- vs. Moderate-Load Squat Training on Strength, Jump and Sprint Performance in Physically Active Women." *International Journal of Sports Medicine* 37:476-82. https://doi.org/10.1055/s-0042-100471.

Schache, A.G., Dorn, T.W., and M.G. Pandy. 2012. "Muscular Strategy Shift in Human Running: Dependence of Running Speed on Hip and Ankle Muscle Performance." *Journal of Experimental Biology* 215 (11): 1944-56.

Weyand, P.G., Sternlight, D.B., Bellizzi, M.J., and S. Wright. 2000. "Faster Top Running Speeds Are Achieved With Greater Ground Forces Not More Rapid Leg Movements." *Journal of Applied Physiology* 89 (5): 1991-9. https:/doi.org/10.1152/jappl.2000.89.5.1991.

Young, W.G. 2006. "Transfer of Strength and Power Training to Sports." *International Journal of Sports Physiology and Performance* 1:74-83. https:/doi.org/10.1123/ijspp.1.2.74.

Chapter 6

Clark, K., Rieger, R., Bruno, R., and D. Stearne. 2017. "The National Football League Combine 40 Yard Dash: How Important Is Max Velocity?" *Journal of Strength and Conditioning Research* 33:1542-55. https:/doi.org/10.1519/JSC.0000000000002081.

Morin, J.B., Gimenez, P., Edouard, P., Arnal, P., Jiménez-Reyes, P., Samozino, P., Brughelli, M., and J. Mendiguchia. 2015. "Sprint Acceleration Mechanics: The Major Role of Hamstrings in Horizontal Force Production." *Frontiers in Physiology* 6:404. https:/doi.org/10.3389/fphys.2015.00404.

Morin, J.B., Petrakos, G., Jiménez-Reyes, P., Brown, S.R., Samozino, P., and M.R. Cross. 2017. "Very-Heavy Sled Training for Improving Horizontal-Force Output in Soccer Players." *International Journal of Sports Physiology and Performance* 12:840-44. https:/doi.org/10.1123/ijspp.2016-0444.

Morin, J.B., Slawinski, J., Dorel, S., Saez de Villareal, E., Couturier, A., Samozino, P., Brughelli, M., and G. Rabita. 2015. "Acceleration Capability in Elite Sprinters and Ground Impulse: Push More, Brake Less?" *Journal of Biomechanics* 48:3149-54. https:/doi.org/10.1016/j.jbiomech.2015.07.009.

Nagahara, R., Matsubayashi, T., Matsuo, A., and K. Zushi. 2014. "Kinematics of Transition During Human Accelerated Sprinting." *Company of Biologists* 3:689-99. https:/doi.org/10.1242/bio.20148284.

Wiesinger, H.P., Rieder, F., Kösters, A., Müller, E., and O.R. Seynness. 2017. "Sport-Specific Capacity to Use Elastic Energy in the Patellar and Achilles Tendons of Elite Athletes." *Frontiers in Physiology* 8:132. https:/doi.org/10.3389/fphys.2017.00132.

Chapter 7

Clark, K.P., and P.G. Weyand. 2014. "Are Running Speeds Maximized With Simple–Spring Stance Mechanics?" *Journal of Applied Physiology* 117:604-17. https:/doi.org/0.1152/japplphysiol.00174.2014.

Edouard, P., Mendiguchia, J., Guex, K., Lahti, J., Samozino, P., and J.B. Morin. 2019. "Sprinting: A Potential Vaccine for Hamstring Injury?" *Science Performance & Science Reports* 48 (1).

Ekstrand, J., Hägglund, M., and M. Waldén. 2011. "Epidemiology of Muscle Injuries in Professional Football (Soccer)." *American Journal of Sports Medicine* 39:1226-32. https:/doi.org/10.1177/0363546510395879.

Weyand, P.G., Sandell, R.F., Prime, D.N., and M.W. Bundle. 2010. "The Biological Limits to Running Speed Are Imposed From the Ground Up." *Journal of Applied Physiology* 108:950-61.

Weyand, P.G., Sternlight, D.B., Bellizzi, M.J., and S. Wright. 2000. "Faster Top Running Speeds Are Achieved With Greater Ground Forces Not More Rapid Leg Movements." *Journal of Applied Physiology* 89:1991-9.

Chapter 8

Boden, B.P., Torg, J.S., Knowles, S.B., and T.E. Hewett. 2009. "Video Analysis of Anterior Cruciate Ligament Injury: Abnormalities in Hip and Ankle Kinematics." *American Journal of Sports Medicine* 37:252-9. https:/doi.org/0.1177/0363546508328107.

Musahl, V., and Karlsson, J. 2019. "Anterior Cruciate Ligament Tears." *New England Journal of Medicine* 380 (24): 2341.

Schleip, R. 2017. "Fascia As a Sensory Organ: Clinical Applications." *Terra Rosa*, June 18, 2017. https://issuu.com/terrarosa/docs/emag_issue_20.

Shimokochi, Y., and S.J. Shultz. 2008. "Mechanisms of Noncontact Anterior Cruciate Ligament Injury." *Journal of Athletic Training* 43:396-408. https://doi.org/10.4085/1062-6050-43.4.396.

Chapter 9

Fitzpatrick, J., Linsley, A., and C. Musham. 2019. "Running the Curve: A Preliminary Investigation Into Curved Sprinting During Football Match-Play." *Sports Performance & Science Reports*, March 2019. https://sportperfsci.com/running-the-curve-a-preliminary-investigation-into-curved-sprinting-during-football-match-play.

Franklyn-Miller, A., Richter, C., King, E., Gore, S., Moran, K., Strike, S., and E.C. Falvey. 2016. "Athletic Groin Pain (Part 2): A Prospective Cohort Study on The Biomechanical Evaluation of Change of Direction Identifies Three Clusters Of Movement Patterns." *British Journal of Sports Medicine.* Apr; 50 (7): 423-30. https:/doi.org/10.1136/bjsports-2015-094912.

Hirayama, K., Iwanuma, S., Ikeda, N., Yoshikawa, A., Ryochi, E., and Y. Kawakami. 2017. "Plyometric Training Favors Optimizing Muscle–Tendon Behavior During Depth Jumping." *Frontiers in Physiology* 8. https://doi.org/10.3389/fphys.2017.00016.

Olsen, O.E., Myklebust, G., Engebretsen, L., and R. Bahr. 2004. "Injury Mechanisms for Anterior Cruciate Ligament Injuries in Team Handball: A Systematic Video Analysis." *American Journal of Sports Medicine* 32:1002-12. https://doi.org/10.1177/0363546503261724.

Chapter 10

Nakamura, J., and M. Csikszentmihalyi. 2002. "The Concept of Flow." *Handbook of Positive Psychology* (p. 89-105). Oxford University Press. https://doi.org/10.1007/978-94-017-9088-8_16.

Potts, W. 1984. "The Chorus-Line Hypothesis of Maneuver Coordination in Avian Flocks." *Nature* 309:344–5. https://doi.org/10.1038/309344a0.

Schenk, S., Lech, R.K., and B. Suchan. 2017. "Games People Play: How Video Games Improve Probabilistic Learning." *Behavioural Brain Research* 335:208-14. https://doi.org/10.1016/j.bbr.2017.08.027.

Schleip, R. 2017. "Fascia As a Sensory Organ: Clinical Applications." *Terra Rosa*, June 18, 2017. https://issuu.com/terrarosa/docs/emag_issue_20.

Su, H., Chang, Y.K., Lin, Y.J., and I.H. Chu. 2015. "Effects of Training Using an Active Video Game on Agility and Balance." *Journal of Sports Medicine and Physical Fitness* 55:914-21.

Chapter 11

Bieuzen, F., Bleakley, C.M., and J.T. Costello. 2013. "Contrast Water Therapy and Exercise Induced Muscle Damage: A Systematic Review and Meta-Analysis." *PLoS One* 8:e62356.

Bleakley, C., McDonough, S., Gardner, E., Baxter, G.D., Hopkins, J.T., and G.W. Davison. 2012. "Cold-Water Immersion (Cryotherapy) for Preventing and Treating Muscle Soreness After Exercise." *Cochrane Database System Review* 2:CD008262.

Imtiyaz, S., Veqar, Z., and M.Y. Shareef. 2014. "To Compare the Effect of Vibration Therapy and Massage in Prevention of Delayed Onset Muscle Soreness (DOMS)." *Journal of Clinical and Diagnostic Research* 8:133-6.

Mah, C.D., Mah, K.E., Kezirian, E.J., and W.C. Dement. 2011. "The Effects of Sleep Extension on the Athletic Performance of Collegiate Basketball Players." *Sleep* 34:943-50.

Roberts, L.A., Raastad, T., Markworth, J.F., Figueiredo, V.C., Egner, I.M., Shield, A., Cameron-Smith, D., Coombes, J.S., and J.M. Peake. 2015. "Post-Exercise Cold Water Immersion Attenuates Acute Anabolic Signalling and Long-Term Adaptations in Muscle to Strength Training." *Journal of Physiology* 593:4285-301.

INDEX

Bill Parisi is the founder and CEO of the Parisi Speed School and developer of the Parisi Training System. He is a 1990 graduate of Iona College, located in New Rochelle, New York, where he was selected as a two-time Division I track-and-field All-American (in 1988 and 1989). Bill also qualified for and competed in the 1988 U.S. Olympic track-and-field trials in the javelin throw. He currently still holds the Iona College school record for the javelin throw and in 2003 was inducted into the school's hall of fame. In 1989, he traveled to Finland to train, learn from, and compete with some of the best athletes in the world. This international athletic training experience prompted Bill to start his own training business based on the strategies he learned.

In 1991, he earned the Certified Strength and Conditioning Specialist (CSCS) credential. In 1992, while $50,000 in debt, he founded the Parisi Speed School and, using a $500 van, traveled from school to school in New Jersey to deliver free speed clinics. In 1993, Bill opened his first speed-training location, a 2,500-square-foot facility in Wyckoff, New Jersey. In 2000, he opened his flagship speed school in Fair Lawn, New Jersey: a 32,000-square-foot facility specializing in youth speed training. This facility was recognized by *Men's Health* in 2009 as one of the top 10 gyms in the country. In 2015, *Active Times* named Parisi Speed School the number one training facility in America. Since then, the Parisi Speed Training System has certified over 2,500 speed coaches throughout the world. In addition, Parisi Speed School has over 90 licensed speed-training locations and a growing affiliate program of individually licensed coaches worldwide. The Parisi Training System has been used to train more than one million young athletes between the ages of 7 and 18, producing first-round draft picks in every professional sport—including more than 145 NFL draft picks—and a host of Olympic medalists and UFC fighters.

In addition to being a recognized expert in youth speed training, Parisi founded the Professional Football Strength and Conditioning Coaches Association (PFSCCA) in 2010, which is now partnered with the National Strength and Conditioning Association (NSCA). As executive director of the PFSCCA, he hosts annual summits for the strength and conditioning coaches of all 32 NFL teams, where he invites top experts in the field to present the latest evidence-based research on speed, power, and injury resilience. In 2019, Parisi also established the Fascia Training Academy, which provides cutting-edge educational resources for understanding how to better train the body's elastic connective tissue system.

Bill has coauthored and been a contributing author to numerous books, including *Success Patterns*, *Don't "Should" on Your Kids*, *Fascia Training*, *Fascia in Sport and Movement*, and *Fascial Fitness*. Bill has served as a consultant or featured lecturer for several sports-related organizations, including the NFL, USA Football, Nike, and Reebok, as well as numerous sports industry associations such as the National Strength and Conditioning Association (NSCA); National Academy of Sports Medicine (NASM); American College of Sports Medicine (ACSM); American Council on Exercise (ACE); and the International Health, Racquet & Sportsclub Association (IHRSA). He has also contributed content for USA Football's online coaches' library. In addition to speaking, writing, and consulting, Parisi has been featured on Fox Sports, ESPN, *The Today Show*, CNBC, *ESPN the Magazine*, *Sporting News*, *New York Times*, *USA Today*, *CBI* magazine, and *Running* magazine.

Bill lives in Wyckoff, New Jersey, with his wife and two sons.

You read the book—now complete the companion CE exam to earn continuing education credit!

Find and purchase the companion CE exam here:
US.HumanKinetics.com/collections/CE-Exam
Canada.HumanKinetics.com/collections/CE-Exam

50% off the companion CE exam with this code

AOS2022